ASSEMBLY OF RIVALS

ASSEMBLY OF RIVALS

Delhi, Lucknow and the Urdu Ghazal

CARLA PETIEVICH

MANOHAR
2020

First published 1992
POD reprint 2020

ISBN 978-93-88540-79-7

Published by
Ajay Kumar Jain
Manohar Publishers & Distributors
4753/23 Ansari Road, Daryaganj
New Delhi 110 002

Printed at
Replika Press Pvt. Ltd.

Contents

Acknowledgments

I would like to thank the many people and institutions without whose support this study could neither have been undertaken nor come to light. First and foremost, the American Institute of Indian Studies, whose generous Junior and Senior Fellowships have supported my research time in India; and the University of British Columbia, whose Graduate Fellowships saw me through most of my doctoral program.

In the company of Kenneth E. Bryant I learned much about how to read poetry, knowledge upon which I continue to draw, and for which I am extremely grateful.

David Gilmartin, Barbara and Thomas Metcalf, and Frances Pritchett all showed tremendous personal warmth and the generosity to read a succession of drafts, offering invaluable help and insight along the way.

I am indebted also to Professors C.M. Naim, G.C. Narang of Jamia Millia Islamia, and Nayyar Masud of Lucknow University for their aid and expertise. Professor M.A.R. Barker of the University of Minnesota shared the treasures of his personal library, and provided me with the only copies of Nasikh's collected poems that I have ever seen. To him, and to Shamsur Rahman Faruqi, whose time, care, inspiration and wealth of knowledge are at the heart of this work, there are no adequate words of thanks.

Despite the numerous people from whom I benefitted during the course of this project, whatever mistakes remain are my responsibility alone.

Finally, I wish to thank Kathryn Hansen, Zaida and George Petievich, Luba Ljepava and Constance Carlson; Marsha Ablowitz, Laura Chapman, Ina Dennekamp, Ruth Frankenberg, Lata Mani, Petra Liljestrand, Alice Philipson, A.L. Riley and Betsy Spaulding. Very special thanks to Jay Linder, Bitiya and Mehndi.

This book is dedicated to the memory of Rakesh Singhai, who struggled to live in multiple worlds.

Preface

The student of Urdu poetry cannot help but be exposed, very early on in her studies, to the magic of Mirza Asadullah Khan Ghalib (1797-1869). As Brian Silver observes, "No practitioner of the Urdu ghazal is more renowned" and "no other modern writer of the subcontinent--with the exceptions of Rabindranath Tagore and Muhammad Iqbal--has inspired such a range of critical and biographical literature in a variety of languages . . ."[1] and not all of them Indian languages.

All the more remarkable is the brevity of literary output which has inspired so much secondary literature. Ghalib's authorized Urdu *dīvān* consists of 1468 verses, while many major poets' collected works run to twenty or thirty times that volume.[2] Though tradition has it that Ghalib himself claimed to hold his Urdu poetry far inferior to his Persian verse—and this can be understood in view of the Persian cultural identification of Indian Muslims which will be discussed elsewhere in this study—his Urdu *dīvān* will continue to excite the critics and maintain for Ghalib widespread acclaim as classical Urdu's greatest poet.

The very fact of Ghalib's enormous popularity has led to a most unbalanced portrayal of the picture of Urdu poetry as a whole body of literature. Some scholars would even disclaim the merits of nearly any other Urdu poet. Only recently has a leading scholar been working on a commentary to the *Kulliyāt* (collected works) of Mir Taqi Mir,[3] who is said by some to have attained the Urdu ghazal's lyric heights. By contrast, commentaries on Ghalib abound,[4] while the remaining twenty or thirty-odd poets in the Urdu canon have been almost thoroughly neglected by commentators.[5]

Given the paucity of critical attention it has received, an entire period of Urdu literature (the early 19th century) might as well never have occurred, yet it is this very period which represents the heyday of Urdu's efflorescence. To the lover of the Urdu ghazal it seems unfortunate to dismiss the greater bulk of classical poetry just because it was not composed by Ghalib, for the other poets by whom it was composed were products and artistic exponents of the same cultural tradition. These other poets; and their poetry were received in their own time with delight, appreciation and great reverence. Yet today it is almost impossible to locate the collected works of many nineteenth century Urdu poets, either in manuscript or published form. Furthermore, the focus of attention in the existing body of scholarship has been almost entirely devoted to poets of Delhi--at the expense of poets assocated with the court cultures of Lucknow, Rampur, Hyderabad and others.

In the past several decades some redress has been sought for the neglect of Urdu's other important poets, and much of this new attention has been focused upon poets associated with the court at Lucknow (1775-1856). This choice of focus is logical, even necessary, since Lucknow was Delhi's rival centre of Urdu culture (*markaz*) from its inception in 1774 until 1856.[6] Important work has been done, for instance, on Lucknow's two masters of the *marṡiya* (elegy), Anis and Dabir.[7] And Lucknow's two masters of the ghazal, Nasikh and Atish, are also being gently rehabilitated, with two full-length works now published on Nasikh and several others on Atish.[8] Although several editions of Atish's poetry are available,[9] a single article[10] and no book at all has yet been published in English on any poet of Lucknow, despite a burgeoning interest in the West in Urdu literature.[11] This study is undertaken with the need firmly in mind to address these unfortunate circumstances.

My own introduction to Lakhnavi poetry's reputation came in reading the following anecdote:

One evening toward the close of the eighteenth century, the popular poet of Lucknow, Qalandar Bakhsh Jur'at, was entertaining a *mushā'ira* (poetic assembly) with his recitation of a ghazal. Also present was Mir Taqi Mir, the most venerated living master of Urdu poetry, who had, in the preceding few years, migrated to Lucknow from the Mughal capital of Delhi. Jur'at was among the leading poets of Lucknow, and his poetry met with an enthusiastic response, the praise increasing with each verse. But when Jur'at sought the approval of Mir for his recitation, the Dihlavi *ustād* (poetic master) is said to have disgustedly pronounced Jur'at's work to be not poetry, but *chūmāchāṭī*-descriptions of kissing and cuddling.[12]

This story is often retold, for its denunciation of a Lakhnavi's poetry by a Dihlavi poet reflects a stereotype in Urdu poetry which developed in literary criticism much later than the incident just reported —a criticism which is known to nearly every modern reader of Urdu.

As a student of Urdu literature, I had heard the names of Nasikh and Atish, the two Lakhnavi poets featured in this study, but had never read them. The few surveys of Urdu poetry available in English reported that Atish and Nasikh had created a decadent style, and had founded a Lucknow School of poetry. I wanted to learn more about this decadent style, and what constituted the Lucknow school.

Lucknow bears a fascinating, fairy-tale reputation as a centre of Indo-Muslim culture. The paradox of its place in history is quite intriguing: it is acclaimed as the quintessential symbol of what Muslim culture in India achieved, yet is simultaneously denounced today for the societal immorality, waste and decadence of its past. To explore this paradox, and to study the culture of Lucknow, as a complement to recent work done on its political history. was a motivating force behind this study.[13]

Reading what I could find of the poetry of Nasikh and Atish did not satisfy my curiosity. From the brief selections available, both seemed to be very much like most of the other Urdu poets I had read in similarly limited volume. True, Nasikh's language seemed heavily Persianized, and therefore difficultly ornate, while Atish often read more easily and provided fewer lexical difficulties. But they reminded me, respectively, of what I had seen in Ghalib and Sauda, or in Mir and Dard, who were considered to be the founders and standard bearers of the Delhi School of poetry. Where, exactly, lay the distinction between the two so-called schools *(dabistāns)*?

Nasikh and Atish both fulfilled my expectations of the ghazal genre, and reading them was a pleasure. What was it that caused so much consternation in the critics? What was so objectionable about this poetry, how was it different from Dihlavi poetry, and what was I missing in not being more offended by it?

It seemed a strong possibility that the criteria brought to bear in the judgements I read of Lakhnavi poetry (which were so different from my own) were grounded more in cultural rivalry between Delhi and Lucknow than on strictly defined literary principles. Names widely hailed in one generation as creators of a new poetic language are rarely dropped flat in the next without significant reasons. What were those reasons?

Delving into literary criticism, where the terms "Lucknow and Delhi Schools" had been coined, I read much about the sensuousness and degeneracy of the Lakhnavi populace. Far less prominently featured were the actual literary traits which distinguished Lucknow's poetry from that of Delhi. It also seemed that the poets favoured by critics tended to be labelled "Dihlavi," even when their domicile was Lucknow;[14] while the poets whose work was less favoured tended to be grouped with the Lakhnavis.[15] It also emerged, rather quickly, that the two most important Urdu critics whom everyone else cited repeatedly,[16] and whose opinions understandably carry tremendous weight, were both Dihlavis. Furthermore, they were both students of the two most prominent *ustāds* who had adorned the last culturally active Mughal court at Delhi, that of Bahadur Shah Zafar.[17]

The following *sher's* (couplet, verse) by Shaikh Imam Bakhsh Nasikh (1771-1838), also known as the "Imam of *Lakhnavīyat*,"[18] fulfills the "worst" expectations of the "Two Schools" stereotype, to the extent that it is physically explicit and sensual in nature:[19]

شاخ آہو ہے بھنویں آنکھیں ہیں چشم آہو
مشک نافہ تھا کوئی ناف میں گر تل ہوتا

{N:I.70.4} Shākh āhu hai bhaveñ ānkheñ haiñ chashm-i āhū
Mashk nāfa thā koī nāf meñ gar til hotā.[20]

Your eyebrows are soft, fuzzy antlers
Your eyes those of the gazelle:
Were there a mole on your navel
It would be a gland of musk.

Dihlavīyat (literally, "Delhi-ness"), of whom one of the acknowledged masters is Mir Taqi Mir, might be exemplified by a *she'r* like the following:

عشق ہمارے خیال پڑا ہے خواب گئی آرام گیا
جی کا جانا ٹھہر رہا ہے صبح گیا یا شام گیا

{Mir:V.11.11} 'Ishq hamāre khyāl paṛā hai khvāb gaī ārām gayā
Jī kā jānā ṭhahr rahā hai subḥ gayā yā shām gayā.[21]

Since my thoughts have fixed upon love
repose eludes me, dreams have fled--
Imminent death is now quite certain,
will it come by dusk or dawn?

In the world of the ghazal, an entire spectrum separates the two *she'rs*, although they both fit within that spectrum by virtue of being inspired by the experience of love, or *'ishq*. Descriptions of the beloved's beauty form a central, stock theme in the ghazal, but Nasikh's graphic metaphors--except for the gazelle-eyes--represent a shocking departure from the standard images evoked upon this theme. For example, the *'āshiq* (lover) might refer, in any given *she'r*, to the down on the beloved's cheeks, to the lovely arch of his/her eyebrow; or to his/her tall, slim, willowy stature; but to draw attention to limbs or navel would be thought of as rather off-colour. An Urdu critic noted, "there is an element of (disagreeable) eroticism in talking about the navel and the mole on it."[22]

Mir's verse, on the other hand, conforms to the notion of the ghazal as the ideal expression of that loftiest human experience, *'ishq*. The image of this *she'r* is that of the *'āshiq's* tormented state as he meditates on the idea (*taṣavvur*) of the unattainable beloved. He anticipates death, the inevitable end for any true *'āshiq*. The beloved's identity remains ambiguous in Mir's verse, and this ambiguity provides much of the ghazal's special appeal: it is not apparent whether the *maḥbūb* (beloved) is male or female, human or divine. The distraction which the *'āshiq* describes is appropriate to all of those possibilities. Unlike the explicitly profane love referred to in Nasikh's verse,[23] the emotion described by the lover in Mir's verse is life-forsaking. This *'āshiq* does not even hope for, let alone refer to, the physical union with his beloved implied by Nasikh's reference to her navel. Mir's *she'r* therefore affirms the ideal nature of the ghazal so important to its audience.

If the above two couplets were an adequate representation of the essence of Dihlavi and Lakhnavi poetry, then there would be little problem with the critical theory which divides the two bodies of poetry into separate schools. The characterisation of Lakhnavi poetry as a "vehicle for coquetry, blandishments, coarse language and enumerations of feminine beauty"[24] which "glorifies the erotic pleasures of the flesh"[25] and the notion that Dihlavi poetry was "rife with the pain of existence and the sorrow of love. . . founded upon the Dihlavi legacy of Sufism"[26] might also then be more persuasive. But the two verses just cited are not necessarily representative. From the same two poets, each considered the exemplar of his particular *dabistān*, one can as readily encounter *she'rs* which would reverse the above characterisations:

ہم زبانِ شمع سے سنتے ہیں ہجرِ یار میں
چاہیئے گھل گھل کے مرنا عشق کے آزار میں

Ham zabān-i shama' se sunte haiñ hijr-i yār meñ
Chāhiye ghul ghul ke marnā 'ishq ke āzār meñ.

From the candle's tongue
I hear what to do
separated from the beloved:
In love's inferno I, too,
should melt and waste away.

and

گوندھ کے گویا پتی گل کی وہ ترکیب بنائی ہے
رنگ بدن کا تب دیکھو جب چولی بھیگے پسینے میں

Gūndh ke goyā pattī gul kī voh tarkīb banāī hai
Rang badan kā tab dekho jab cholī bhīge pasīne meñ.

Look how her body takes on the look
of a mound of kneaded rose-petals
When the sweat soaks through
her bright red blouse.

The former of these two *she'rs* is by Nasikh[27] and the latter by Mir.[28] Here it is Nasikh who evokes the poignant plight of the suffering *'āshiq*, employing the popular image of the candle-flame. Mir's *she'r* evokes a vivid image, too, but its effect is erotic and not plaintive. Nor does it exude the "loftiness of thought" which critics allege characterizes *Dihlavīyat*.

How representative are these examples of the poetry of Mir and Nasikh; and of Dihlavi and Lakhnavi ghazal in general? According to the Two School theory's characterisations, the first pair of couplets is quite representative, while the second is an anomalous exception. But short of conducting a protracted survey of all classical poetry, one is left to consult literary criticism in order to discern what characterises each body of poetry. The problem there is that so widespread has been the impact of the Two School theory that Dihlavi and Lakhnavi poetry are almost always discussed with constant reference and comparison to one another.[29] Poetry is seen essentially as an expression of culture, and much of that cross-referencing has focused upon Delhi and Lucknow as cultural centres (*marākiz*), or upon how the two cities and their societies are understood to have differed. In the case of Lakhnavi poetry, most critics have described the society of Lucknow as leisured, pleasure-loving and courtesan-pursuing, and said: "That was Lakhnavi society, and its poetry is a vivid reflection of that culture."[30]

Entrapped in the Two School theory, Lakhnavi poetry has been treated as the literature of a particularly anomalous, and somehow unworthy, time and place in Indo-Muslim history rather than as literature composed in an Urdu *markaz* during a time when Urdu poetry as a whole became firmly established as the literature of Indian Islam. In order to assess its literary value in the broader terms of classical Urdu literature, Lakhnavi and Dihlavi poetry both must be removed from the context of the Two School theory and placed in the greater context of the classical Urdu ghazal—a literary genre which developed and flourished over a period of nearly four centuries.

One Urdu critic, Ali Javad Zaidi, has indeed come forth to challenge the Two School theory,[31] and his work is discussed in Chapter IX. Despite the considerable merits and strength of his arguments, Zaidi does not seem to have dissuaded the Urdu audience away from the Two School theory: a number of important works have been published since 1970 which freely refer to the Delhi and Lucknow "schools" and they are noted further on in this study.

The present study complements Zaidi's rejection of the Two School theory, reiterating that the school-designating critics can be challenged readily on their own terms, but its two-fold method differs from that of Zaidi. First, the major steps in the theory's development in literary criticism over time will be traced for the English audience, and much of the critical literature which has dealt with Lakhnavi poets and poetry will be examined and reinterpreted. Facts of the Two School theory's genesis provide one basis for refutation, for this literary distinction appears to have developed to a great degree on extra-literary criteria.

Secondly, in contrast to the method of poetic analysis employed by others, this study compares a controlled sample of Dihlavi and Lakhnavi ghazal poetry based on examination of structural variables inherent in the genre, and discusses their influence on poets' thematic choices. One purpose of this method is to demonstrate that, whether the comparison is based on theme (*maẓmūn*) or on formal structure (*zamīn*), differences between Lakhnavi and Dihlavi poetry do not occur in characteristic enough or observable enough patterns of frequency to warrant "school" designations for the respective poets of Delhi and Lucknow. This both bolsters, and provides one possible corroboration for, Zaidi's argument. It may also be seen as an attempt to address the need which Zaidi announces for less "unscientific" (*nā-sāyinsī*) approaches to the Two School question.

As far as I know, this is the first attempt to analyse Dihlavi and Lakhnavi poetry using this method. The ghazal's inherent structure is posited here as the essential and most important force to determine all Urdu poets' compositional choices, be the poets Dihlavi or Lakhnavi: previous studies, including Zaidi's, have all selected verses for comparison on the basis of thematic content, examining poets' specific social environments as determinants.

A final aspect of the present refutation is based on contradictions in the Two School theory's characterisation of Lucknow's two primary ghazal poets. Although Nasikh and Atish were contemporaries and, reputedly, co-founders of the so-called Lucknow School, critics emphasize that "the style of these two masters is completely different."[32] In fact, some recent scholarship goes so far as to designate separate schools (*dabistāns*) for the pupils of Nasikh and Atish, creating not only the *dabistān-i Lakhna'u* and the *dabistān-i Dillī* but also the *dabistān-i Ātish* and the *dabistān-i Nāsikh*.[33] The question will be raised as to how two poets could have simultaneously founded a Lucknow school of poetry distinct from Dihlavi poetry and yet write in "completely different styles," one of which is the style that characterises the rival "Delhi School."

In light of these points of refutation, the underlying cause for the Two School distinction will be argued as, essentially, the result of a cultural rivalry between Delhi and Lucknow, particularly the reaction of India's Mughal- and Delhi-identified cultural élite against Lucknow as Delhi's cultural successor.[34] It will be argued that the historical polarisation between Nasikh and Atish parallels the polarisations between Lakhnavi and Dihlavi poetry; that both polarisations follow an established pattern which is perhaps more convenient as a discursive device than it is reflective of literary facts; and, finally, that these two polarisations ultimately contradict one another and weaken the premises of the Two School theory.

The best justification for a study featuring the poetry of Nasikh, Atish and lesser-known nineteenth century poets is to acknowledge their historical importance and contribution. This is especially true for

Nasikh, the "Imam of the Lucknow School," since his work has suffered greater suppression than that of Atish. It is also true for Dihlavi poets like Shah Nasir, whose style has been compared to that of the Lakhnavis, and whose work also seems to have been largely suppressed.[35] The work of all but the best-known—and, therefore, best-studied—poets calls for greater attention, and can shed light on the development of Urdu literature as a whole. Examples of both Lakhnavi and Dihlavi poetry—including Nasikh, Atish and Shah Nasir as well as Ghalib, Momin, Zafar and Zauq—will be drawn upon to substantiate the arguments put forth. All translations, unless otherwise noted, are original.

A note on reference to *she'rs* in Chapters X and XI: notations appearing in { } brackets at the side of individual verses refer to the name of the poet; the collection from which the verse was culled; the ghazal; and the verse number within the ghazal. Thus, {N: I. 140.5} refers to Nasikh : 1st *dīvān*, ghazal number 140, verse number 5.

Atish is represented by "A"; Nasikh by "N"; Momin by "M"; Ghalib by "G"; Zafar by "Zf"; Zauq by "Zq"; and Shah Nasir by "ShN".

NOTES

1. Brian Q. Silver, *Nuclear Structure and Poetic Connotation in the Urdu Dīvān of Mirza Ghalib (1797-1869)*, Ph.D. Dissertation, University of Chicago, 1980, p.3.
2. Mir's *Kulliyāt* runs to six *dīvāns* of some 1818 full ghazals alone, perhaps ten to fifteen times as many verses as are contained in Ghalib's *dīvān*, *Dīvān-i Ghālib*, Arshi edition, New Delhi: Anjuman-i Taraqqi-i Urdu [Hindi], 1982; Jur'at's *Kulliyāt* contains nearly twenty thousand *she'rs*. See Dr. Iqtida Hasan, ed. *Kulliyāt-i Jur'at*, Naples: Istituto Universitario Orientale, 1970-1975. The only notable exception to this pattern is Dard, whose *dīvān* contains only about half as many *she'rs* as does that of Ghalib.
3. The scholar is Shamsur Rahman Faruqi, Winner of the 1987 Sahitya Akademi Award for Urdu, Editor of the literary journal *Shab Khūn*, published in Allahabad since 1969, and author of numerous critical and creative writings on Urdu poetry.
4. Silver, *op. cit.*, p. 5, note 1.
5. A few studies exist in English of the other "Pillars of Urdu"--Sauda and Dard--though they are by no means as comprehensive as those dedicated to Ghalib. Cf. Ralph Russell and Khurshidul Islam, *Three Mughal*

Poets: Mir, Sauda and Mir Hasan, London: George Allen and Unwin, Ltd., 1969; and Annemarie Schimmel's study of Khvaja Mir Dard.

6. Delhi's cultural revival in the Red Fort during the 1840s, while symbolically important for the Mughal Empire's swan song, did not create enough momentum to completely shift the focus—and thus the *markaz*--away from Lucknow.
7. Cf. S.R. Faruqi, "The Problem of Interpretation in Mir Anis," in *The Secret Mirror: Essays on Urdu Poetry*, Delhi: Academic Literature, 1981, pp. 107-118; Dr. Akbar Haidari, *Intikhāb-i Mirāsī-i Mirzā Dabīr*, Lucknow: Uttar Pradesh Urdu Akademi, 1979; and Prof. G.C. Narang, *Anīs Shanāsī*, Delhi: Educational Publishing House, 1981.
8. Cf. Dr. Shabihul Hasan, *Nāsikh: Tajzīya-o Taqdīr*, Lucknow: Uttar Pradesh Urdu Akademi. 1974; Rashid Hasan Khan, *Intikhāb -i Nāsikh*, Delhi: Maktaba Jami'a Ltd., 1972; and Khalilur Rahman Azimi, *Muqaddma-i Kalām-i Ātish*, Aligarh, 1959; Dr. Aijaz Husain, *Intikhāb-i Kalām-i Ātish*, Allahabad: Hindustani Akademi, Uttar Pradesh, 1972; Shah Abdus Salam, *Dabistān-i Ātish*, Delhi: Maktaba Jami'a Ltd., 1977.
9. Sayyid Martaza Husain Fazil Lakhnavi, *Kulliyāt-i Ātish*, Lahore: Majlis-i Taraqqi-i Adab, 1973, Volumes I and II; Dr. Zahir Ahmed Siddiqi, *Kulliyāt-i Ātish*, Allahabad: Ram Narayan Lal Beni Madhav, 1972; *Dīvān-i Ātish*, Pocket Book edition, Delhi: 1972; *Kulliyāt-i Ātish: Ḥālāt-i Zindagī*, Lahore: Urdu Akedmi-i Sindh, n.d.
10. See note 7 above.
11. Although Iqtida Hasan has given us a welcome three-volume edition of Jur'at's collected works, which includes a substantial critical introduction in English. Iqtida Hasan observes that although Jur'at is generally considered to be a Lakhnavi poet, he is really one generation too old to have been part of what became known as the Lucknow School. See *Kulliyāt-i Jur'at*, Vol. III, pp. 34-38.
12. Cf. Shamsul Ulama Muhammad Husain Azad, *Āb-i Ḥayāt*, Allahabad: Ram Narayan Lal Beni Madhav, 1970, p. 241; also cited in M. Sadiq, *A History of Urdu Literature*, London: Oxford University Press, 1964, p. 130; in Annemarie Schimmel, *Classical Urdu Poetry from the Beginning to Iqbal*, Wiesbaden: Otto Harrassowitz, 1975, p. 195; and in nearly every extant history of Urdu literature.
13. Cf. Richard B. Barnett, *North India Between Empires: Awadh, the Mughals, and the British, 1720-1801*, Berkeley: University of California Press, 1980; Michael H. Fisher, *A Clash of Cultures; The Awadh of British and the Mughals*; Manohar Publications, 1987. Thomas R. Metcalf, *Land, Landlords, and the British Raj: Northern India in the Nineteenth Century*, Berkeley: University of California Press, 1979; Veena Talwar Oldenburg, *The Making of Colonial Lucknow, 1856-1877*, Princeton: Princeton University Press, 1984.
14. Mir, Mushafi, and Atish, for example.

15. In Ahmed Ali's *Golden Tradition,* for example, Zauq's poetry is characterised "by polish of language and didacticism" [p.58 fn. 6.]; by "the perfections of labor, didacticism, embellishment and polish of phrase and style;" [p.218] and "even Zauq . . . displayed the decay of thought [that] had become apparent in the fleshly school [ie. in Lakhnavi poetry]." [p.274] Polished language and embellishment are oft-cited characteristics attributed to Lakhnavi poetry, as will be seen.
16. Maulana Azad and Khvaja Altaf Husain Hali.
17. The *ustāds* were Zauq and Ghalib, respectively.
18. Dr. Sayyid Abdullah refers to Nasikh as the "Imam of the Lucknow School" in his essay "*Nāsikh kī Mansūkh Shā'irī*," from *Valī se Iqbāl Tak,* 3rd ed. Lahore: Maktaba Khayaban-i Adab, 1966, p.224. *Lakhnaviyat* translates roughly as "Lucknow-ness."
19. Although it does not allude specifically to kissing and cuddling.
20. *Kulliyāt-i Nāsikh,* Lucknow: Naval Kishore, 1891, *Dīvān-i Avval,* p.28.
21. *Kulliyāt-i Mīr,* Allahabad: Ram Narayan Lal Beni Madhav, 1972, volume I, p. 596.
22. S.R. Faruqi, personal correspondence, 25 May 1984.
23. While Nasikh's verse also maintains ambiguity with reference to the beloved's gender, there is no doubt that the physical attributes described are those of a human.
24. A.L. Siddiqi in *Lakhna'u kā Dabistān-i Shā'irī,* Lahore: Urdu Markaz, 1955, p. 47.
25. Ahmed Ali, *The Golden Tradition,* New York: Columbia University Press, 1973, p. 212.
26. Nurul Hasan Hashmi, *Dillī kā Dabistān-i Shā'irī,* Lucknow: Uttar Pradesh Urdu Akedmi, 1971, 1980, p. 13.
27. Nasikh, *Kulliyāt, Dīvān-i Avval,* p.55.
28. *Kulliyāt, Dīvān-i Chahārum,* volume I, p. 596.
29. Examples are given in Chapter III's discussion of *Lakhnavīyat* and *Dihlavīyat* below.
30. M. Sadiq, *A History of Urdu Literature,* p. 121.
31. In *Do Adabī Iskūl,* Lucknow: U.P. Urdu Akedmi, 1970.
32. Maulana Azad, *Āb-i Ḥayāt,* Allahabad: Ram Narayan Lal Beni Madhav, 1980, p. 355.
33. See especially Shah Abdus Salam, *Dabistān-i Ātish,* Delhi: Maktaba-i Jami'a Limited, 1977.
34. While Lakhnavis may also be assumed to have participated in the rivalry, the early literary critics whose work appears to have provided the foundation for the Two School theory were, significantly, Dihlavis.
35. However, larger-scale studies of these poets will have to come from others than myself.

CHAPTER I

Introduction to Conventions of the Urdu Ghazal

The ghazal is by far the most popular of the four major poetic genres in classical Urdu.[1] It is a love-lyric form, consisting of varying numbers of two-line verses called *she'rs* (pronounced much like the English word "share").[2] Cohesion within a ghazal is considered, conventionally, to be provided by the uniform structural pattern of all its *she'rs* rather than by a narrative sequence such as that which exists in a ballad. Thus, in a manner of speaking, individual *she'rs* rely on the greater context of the ghazal genre rather than on a context provided by verses in sequence, as would be the case in a ballad or other narrative verse form.

Each *she'r* is composed in a particular structural framework called a *zamīn*.[3] That *zamīn* is defined by its metre (*baḥr*) and rhyme-scheme. *Baḥr* (literally, "sea, bay, flow, rhythm")[4] consists of a fixed sequence of short and long syllables. End-rhyme has two components, *qāfiyah* and *radīf*. The *radīf* of a ghazal is the repeated portion which concludes each verse, while the *qāfiyah* is a single syllable leading into the *radīf*, which rhymes in the same way that rhyme is experienced in Western literatures. Thus, in the *she'r* below the *radīf* is "*kā*"[5] while the *qāfiyah* is the long syllable "*-āñ*," giving this *she'r* (and the entire ghazal in which it appears) the end-rhyme "*-āñ kā*:"
{N:I.11.1}

مرا سینہ ہے مشرق آفتابِ داغِ ہجراں کا
طلوعِ صبحِ محشر چاک ہے میرے گریباں کا

Mirā sīna hai mashriq āftāb-i dāgh-i hijrāñ kā
ṭulū-i ṣubḥ-i maḥshar chāk hai mere girībāñ kā

My breast is the eastern horizon
whence the wounded sun of separation rises:
The dawn of doomsday breaks
through the rend in my collar.

The *qāfiyah*-word in the second line (called a *miṣra'*) is *girībāñ*—the *qāfiyah* itself being "*-āñ*"— and the *radīf*, as we have said, is "*kā*."

The reader may have noticed that this *she'r* has end-rhyme in both lines. While the rhyme-scheme of a ghazal typically appears only in the second *miṣra'* of each *she'r*, the ghazal's opening verse (called *maṭ̤la'*) reveals the poem's *zamīn* by including the end-rhyme in both *miṣras'*. Thus, the rhyming pattern of every ghazal is AA, BA, CA, DA, etc. with the end-rhyme contained in every A line. The second *she'r* in the ghazal from which the above *maṭ̤la'* was taken shows the rhyming pattern (BA):

ازل سے دشمنی طاؤس و مار آپس میں رکھتے ہیں
دلِ پُر داغ کو کیونکر ہے عشق اس زلف پیچاں کا

Azal se dushmanī ṭ̤ā'us-o mār āpas meñ rakhte haiñ
Dil-i pur dāg͟h ko kyonkar hai 'ishq us zulf-i pechāñ kā

The peacock and snake maintained
and will always
maintain deep enmity:
Why then does this scar of a heart
so love those coiling tresses?[6]

The pattern of Western-style rhyme can be seen in the final long syllable of the words *hijrāñ*, *giribāñ* and *pechāñ*.

In the following pages we will present selected *she'rs*, along with notes, in order to introduce the reader to the poetry under consideration in this study. The purpose of the notes is to provide some of the background necessary to render the Urdu ghazal more accessible to those readers with limited exposure to the genre. This study's ensuing literary arguments will rely, to some extent, on a familiarity with this background.

All ghazal poets address themselves to the subject of love (*'ishq*) and write in the persona of an *'āshiq*, or lover. He is, by definition, hopelessly in love with an indifferent, even cruel, beloved (*maḥbūb*, *ma'shūq*) and is therefore generally miserable. He is obsessed by his condition (*ḥāl*), and it is mostly in the form of ruminations upon this condition that *she'rs* are composed. The expressions of his oppression follow certain conventional exaggerations: an *'āshiq* suffers almost unto death, but is denied death's final relief; his heart is literally wounded by suffering—innumerable *she'rs* create graphic images of the heart's scars and wounds (*dāgh*, *zakhm*), comparing them to the fiery sun, for example, or to the markings on a peacock's tail; he is driven insane by his untenable position—like the legendary Persian *'āshiq*, Majnun (whose name means "the crazy one")—and so tears his hair and clothing, and wanders through the wilderness or desert, barren places like his heart. All these conventions are evoked in the *maṭla'* we now recall by Nasikh, the great poet of Lucknow:

میرا سینہ ہے مشرق آفتابِ داغِ ہجراں کا
طلوعِ صبحِ محشر چاک ہے میرے گریباں کا

Mirā sīna hai mashriq āftāb-i dāgh-i hijrāñ kā
Ṭulū-i ṣubḥ-i maḥshar chāk hai mere girībāñ kā

My breast is the eastern horizon
whence the wounded sun of separation rises:
The dawn of doomsday breaks
through the rend in my collar.[7]

Here the *'āshiq*-narrator gives eloquent voice to the extent of his suffering and affliction. The sense of his first *miṣra'* is: "My heart is so wounded by separation (*hijr*, *hijrāñ*) from the beloved that it feels like a burning sun within my bosom." The second *miṣra'* follows through this thought with an almost parallel statement: "The tear in my collar (*chāk-i girībāñ*)—which I have made in the anguish of my suffering, as I struggle for relief—serves as the horizon over which the sun rises, ushering in the dawn of the final day (*maḥshar*), the day of judgement.[8]

Brian Silver has aptly observed that "The words, motifs, and images of the ghazal are important not in isolation, but rather in their relationships to each other . . ." and that "the experience of [many] ghazals . . . is more than the sum of its parts."[8] Such is certainly the case in this verse of Nasikh's. The amount of allusion and imagery packed into this *she'r* is greater than in the average verse but is by no means unheard of; nor would it be considered inappropriate or undesirable by the ghazal audience. In fact, it is quite desirable, and this verse represents something of a triumph in its construction of layers of meaning.

In the first place, by mentioning his torn collar, the *'āshiq* is testifying to the fact that he is in a frenzied state, and that he has been driven there by the affliction of love. That his collar is torn attests to the *'āshiq*'s implicit claim that he is a paragon of *'āshiqī* (the state of being a lover); and that dawn is about to break confirms that the *'āshiq* has withstood his anticipatory suffering throughout the long night. In other words, he has been true to his beloved by carrying on his vigil as long as the night has lasted. Such self-aggrandising claims of *'āshiqī* constitute another common convention in the ghazal.

An *'āshiq* generally tears his collar at some point during the long (seemingly endless) night of separation, signifying that he has reached the final point of his endurance. He is usually driven beyond endurance by the sight of the moon, which reminds him of his beloved's beautiful, lustrous face. Comparison of the moon with her face is among the most primary images in the ghazal's stock. Mention of the *chāk-i girībāñ*, evoking the night of separation, offers a contrast with the breaking dawn which the *she'r* explicitly evokes. That dawn moves the suffering heart (implicitly present in the verse's opening *miṣra'*) out into the open, where it bursts forth as the red, fiery sun. Although the sun is not explicitly described as red and fiery, the reader knows that it is so because the heart (or the heart's wound) is red and fiery, burning with the *'āshiq's* affliction.

Finally, exaggeration is also embodied in this verse by the fact that the dawn which breaks is that of the final day. The night of separation which has wreaked such havoc on this *'āshiq* must, therefore, have been the final night of separation. By relating his own suffering to the termination of time past and present (which *maḥshar* brings about), the *'āshiq* raises himself and his personal condition to epic proportion.

A final statement which is subtly implied by Nasikh's verse is that those who would torment this particular *'āshiq* had better beware the consequences—the advent of the dawn of the final day!

A contrasting perspective on the same futile wait for union with the beloved is offered in the following famous *maṭla'* by Ghalib:

یہ نہ تھی ہماری قسمت کہ وصالِ یار ہوتا
اگر اور جیتے رہتے یہی انتظار ہوتا

Yih na thī hamārī qismat kih viṣāl-i yār hotā
Agar aur jīte rahte yahī intiẓār hotā

It was not my fate
to unite with the beloved:
had I gone on living
there would still have been
this same waiting.[9]

Here Ghalib's *'āshiq* reaffirms his commitment to the beloved. His life is already over. Death is usually sought by the *'āshiq*, since it is his only hope for respite from his suffering, and since union (*viṣāl-i yār*) cannot be attained during his lifetime (especially if he is referring to a divine beloved). That the beloved might be either human or divine is another essential convention of the ghazal. His/her identity was similarly ambiguous in Nasikh's *she'r* above.

In this particular *she'r* the *'āshiq* implies that the futile waiting (*intiẓār*), while inevitable for a mortal lover, is perhaps an end in itself: "Had I gone on living I would have kept on waiting" is certainly a bald statement of fact, but it also implies that "Had I my life to live over again I would follow the very same path again, despite its futility, because I am so committed to my beloved (*yār*)."

Ghalib's *she'r*, at a more immediate level than Nasikh's, highlights the role of *taṣavvuf* (Sufism, mysticism) in the ghazal. According to Sufis, the mystic's desire to know God is the manifestation of true love (*'ishq-i ḥaqīqī*). It is paralleled on the profane level in human beings' desire for union with human beloveds. That profane level of love is called *'ishq-i majāzī*, or metaphorical love, because the human experience is merely a metaphor for essential experience, that of the Divine.

Enumerations and declarations of the beloved's beauty, playfulness and indifference bordering on cruelty provide tremendous grist for the ghazal's mill. The likening of her beauty to the moon has already been noted. To liken her face to other radiant objects like the sun and the candle-flame is also standard:

آمد آمد اس سراپا نور کی ہے بزم میں
شمع اڑ جاوے جو ہاتھ آویں پر پروانہ آج

Āmad āmad us sarāpā nūr kī hai bazm meñ
Shama' uṛ jāve jo hāth āveñ par-i parvāna āj

She approaches the assembly
radiant from head to foot:
If the moth's wings were on hand today
the candle itself would take flight.[10]

Aside from the beloved's radiant countenance, her entire form is beautiful. Her stature is tall and elegant like the cypress tree (*sarv*). Cypress stature is not specifically mentioned in this *she'r* by Atish, but it is alluded to by the description of her graceful approach into the assembly of admirers, radiant from head to foot (*sarāpā nūr kī āmad*). Head-to-foot radiance connotes the tall graceful candle, and, with another conventional device, the poet suggests that her beauty is even more radiant than that of the candle (an exemplar of radiance). His proof: the candle would fly away in shame at being outdone.

Whenever the candle-flame is mentioned in the ghazal, a moth is not far to be found. Their relationship parallels that of the *'āshiq* and beloved, with the moth helplessly drawn to the beauty of the candle, even though union with it means self-immolation. This theme, although not explicitly stated in Atish's *she'r*, is certainly alluded to; and it is given a little twist to keep it fresh by placing the candle-flame—normally representing the beloved—in opposition to the real beloved whose approach is described in the verse's first *miṣra'*. Unable to bear the fact that its radiance is wanting in comparison with that of the approaching beloved, the candle wants to "borrow" its *'āshiq's* wings and flee.

Perhaps the most conventional metaphor for the beloved's beauty is the rose (*gul*). Thousands of Urdu *she'rs* use this device. Generally, the rose's *'āshiq* is the *bulbul*, or nightingale, who is caged and can only admire the object of his desire from afar. The rose, like the beloved, is quite indifferent to its admirer's attentions and affliction.

A final convention to be introduced is the theme of wine-drinking. Since to imbibe alcohol (*sharāb, mai*) is forbidden to Muslims, wine imagery serves two purposes: first, on the *majāzī* or metaphorical level, it signifies that an *'āshiq* is so enamoured of the beloved that he will commit grievous sins to prove his love. This theme is reinforced by the *sāqī*, or cup-bearer—who pours wine for the drinkers who go to the tavern (*mai-khāna*)—coming to represent the beloved. Since he provides the wine, the source of their intoxication, the *sāqī* becomes the *'āshiq*-drinkers' object of desire. The tavern scene is evoked in the following *maṭla'* by Atish:

فصلِ گل ہے لوٹیے کیفیتِ میخانہ آج
دولتِ ساقی سے مالا مال ہے پیمانہ آج

Faṣl-i gul hai lūṭiye kaifiyat-i maikhāna āj
Daulat-i sāqī se mālāmāl hai paimāna āj

Press from the spring the tavern's essence!
Let the wine-cup spill over today
with the Saqi's abundance.[11]

Wine imagery also lends itself to *ḥaqīqī* or mystical themes in the ghazal. To interpret the above verse on a *ḥaqīqī* level, the *sāqī* would represent the *'āshiq*-seeker's *pīr*, or spiritual preceptor. The wine he serves the drinkers represents mystical wisdom and guidance along the path leading to ultimate intoxication, i.e. union with the Divine. Again, this theme is so general to the ghazal that it would be less appropriate to elaborate upon it here than to discuss it in terms of the specified *she'rs* which contain it elsewhere in this study.

Other principal characters besides the *'āshiq* and his beloved are his rivals for her attention (*ghair* or *raqīb*) and the messenger (*qāṣid*) who ostensibly carries messages back and forth between the *'āshiq* and the *ma'shūq* (but who often uses the opportunity to plead his own case or to otherwise foil the plans of his employer, the *'āshiq*). Similarly, there is the *nāṣiḥ* (confidant, moral teacher, and busybody), who tries to talk sense into the *'āshiq*'s head and save him from the calumny and disgrace into which *'ishq* leads his friend. He becomes a suspect, however, since the *'āshiq* sees anyone who tries to dissuade him from his obsession as a person with his own intentions toward the beloved—after all, who could not be drawn into her snare, once he had set eyes upon her, or even heard about her second-hand? Such is the case evoked in the following verse by Ghalib:

ذکر اس پری وش کا اور پھر بیاں اپنا
بن گیا رقیب آخر تھا جو رازداں اپنا

Ẓikr us parīvash kā aur phir bayāñ apnā
Ban gayā raqīb ākhir thā jo rāzdāñ apnā

Mention,
in the end,
of her fairy-like beauty—
and my elaborations on that theme—
have made a rival of my closest friend.[12]

The commonly mentioned places where the '*āshiq* finds himself are the garden (*chaman*, *gulistāñ*); the lane outside the beloved's house (*kū-i yār*) where he sits along with her other admirers, waiting in vain for a glimpse of her;[13] the desert or barren place (*vaḥshat, vīrān, biyābān*) which epitomises the desolation of his condition;[14] and the assembly of the beloved's admirers (*majlis* or *bazm*).

These motifs form the core of the ghazal's stock. Below are listed a few more examples of poetry by Nasikh and Atish in which the reader will recognise a number of the motifs just introduced:

تیرے کوچے کا ہے اے خانہ خراب افسانہ آج
شیخ کعبہ چھوڑتا ہے برہمن بت خانہ آج

Tere kūche kā hai ai khāna-kharāb afsāna āj
Shaikh kā'aba chhoṛtā hai barhaman but-khāna āj

What stories they tell, home-wrecker,
of the lure of your lane:
the shaikh abandons the Ka'ba today
the Brahmin his idol-house.[15]

کوئے قاتل میں پہونچکر سر ہوا مجھ کو وبال
بوجھ اترنے کی جگہ دم چڑھ گیا مزدور کا

Kū-i qātil meñ pahuñch kar sar hu'ā mujh ko vabāl
Bojh utarne kī jagah dam chaṛh gayā mazdūr kā

I arrived in the executioner's lane
staggering under the burden of my head—
instead of laying down my load
I panted even harder.[16]

میرے مرنے کی دعا مانگے وہ بت پڑھ کر نماز
کس طرف جا کر کروں میں سجدۂ شکرانہ آج

Mere marne kī dū'ā mānge voh but paṛh kar namāz
Kis t̤araf jā kar karūñ maiñ sajda-i shukrāna āj

If in her prayers
she begs the blessing of my death
should my grateful prostration be
toward Mecca
or to her?[17]

Around the subject of supplication, prayer and prostration, Atish gives playful twists to the standard themes of death and the beloved-as-idol, or *but*. A common phrase used to refer to *'ishq-i majāzī* is "idol-worship" because love for an earthly beloved interferes with the *'āshiq's* absolute supplication to Allah. The poet has combined this idol-characterisation with that of the beloved's perennial cruelty toward the *'āshiq*. It is written into the script of the ghazal genre that the beloved deny the *'āshiq* his heart's desire, while keeping him hanging on with the merest glimmer of hope that she might, just this once, actually keep her glib promises to meet him or acknowledge him in some form or another.

To a Muslim, a *but* connotes graven images and paganism. In his view, one submits to Allah; while to a *but* (say, for example, to a Hindu deity) people pray for the bestowal of a favour or boon. In this *she'r* the beloved performs Islamic worship, *namāz paṛhnā*, but also pleads for a boon—in this case the death of the *'āshiq*. Thus the Islamic tone is partially mixed with one of idolatry. The verse's success lies in its open-ended, or non-resolved, resolution: "If she should pray for my death, that cruel idol; and if the boon should be granted and then I die; her power, as well as that of God, will be proven. Her power over me will be confirmed, showing once again that she can do with me as she will. And if Allah, too, lets her have way with me, then is the act of killing me a demonstration of her ultimate power, or of His? I must determine this in order to give my prayerful thanks."

In the second line the query about whom to supplicate in thanksgiving (*sajda-i shukrāna*) arises because, even though it is out of cruelty that the beloved wishes the '*āshiq*'s death, it is in death that he, too, finds his own wishes (at least partially) fulfilled. Not only is it miserable to live with a hopeless love for a cruel idol, it is only through death that ultimate union with the true beloved (i.e. God) will be achieved.[18] Therefore death is quite welcome to the '*āshiq* and he is thankful for its prospect. But his dilemma lies in trying to decide whether to thank the true God for his death, or to thank the beloved *but* who has put in a word for him, so to speak. He asks, "In which direction should I prostrate myself?" As a Muslim he should face Mecca, but as an idol-worshipper he should bow in the direction of the *but* whom he worships.

کب ہمارے فکر سے ہوتا ہے سودا کا جواب
یاں تتبع کرتے ہیں ناسخ ہم اس مغفور کا

Kab hamāre fikr se hotā hai Saudā kā javāb
Hāñ tatabbu' karte haiñ Nāsikh ham us maghfūr kā

When could our thoughts ever
keep pace with those of Sauda?
Nasikh, we but follow in the footsteps
of that departed one.[19]

In the nineteenth century the great poets (*ustāds*) often made reference to earlier masters of their literary tradition. One finds this especially in the poetry of Nasikh and Ghalib, who were themselves both noted innovators in the Urdu ghazal. In spite of a desire to carve out a special place for themselves, it was very important for them to be acknowledged as part of their own tradition; they were wholly identified with the tradition of Perso-Urdu literature, and from it they gained cultural legitimacy.

This *she'r* is one of a number of those in collected works of Nasikh which honour a great master (usually Sauda, but often Mir or Dard as well), sending the poet's own name along in the wake of the earlier bard. The effect of this is to claim legitimacy by association, often to compete with the venerated *ustāds* for a paramount position in the culture, but always to keep company with them. Here, Nasikh does not challenge Sauda's authority; rather, he restricts himself to paying homage. When he says, however, "We follow that departed one" ([ham] *tatabbu' karte haiñ*), he implies a carrying on of Sauda's noble tradition, a firm entrenchment within it. Since Sauda was unquestionably the most revered poet of the eighteenth century, deferred to even by the talented and arrogant Mir Taqi Mir, Nasikh chooses august company for himself in this verse, perhaps even suggesting that just as Sauda was the great bard of the eighteenth century so is he, Nasikh, the greatest in the nineteenth.

The previous discussion was intended to outline some of the Urdu ghazal's conventions and literary aesthetic and provide a context for this study's literary analyses. Chapters II and III offer a general description of the Two School theory and its genesis in the literary criticism of Urdu; and Chapter IV fills in some of the historical facts pertaining to the Delhi-Lucknow rivalry from which it evolved. Chapters V-IX trace the development of the Two School theory in Urdu critical literature, while Chapters X and XI present close readings of Dihlavi and Lakhnavi poetry, and challenge the notions of literary *Dihlavīyat* and *Lakhnavīyat*. Finally, Chapter XII attempts to grapple with how the Two School theory fits into the socio-political milieu of the post-1857 Urdu-speaking, Indo-Muslim élite.

NOTES

1. The others are the narrative form, *masnavī*; the panegyric *qaṣīda*; and the elegiac *marṣiya*. For fuller discussion of these other forms, see M.A.R. Barker, *A Reader of Modern Urdu Poetry*, Montreal: McGill University, 1968, Introductory chapter on Poetics, p. xvii.
2. Though the plural of *she'r* is technically *ash'ār* we will refer to the plural as *she'rs* for the sake of reading fluency in English.
3. Literally, *zamīn* is defined as "the earth, soil, land, ground, region," etc. John T. Platts, *A Dictionary of Urdu, Classical Hindi and English*, London: Oxford University Press, fifth imprint, 1974, p. 617.
4. Platts, p. 137.

5. *Kā* is the masculine singular possessive postposition, roughly equivalent to "'s" in English orthography.
6. *Kulliyāt-i Nāsikh*, Lucknow: Naval Kishore, n.d., p. 7.
7. Ibid.
8. Brian Quayle Silver, *Nuclear Structure and Poetic Connotation in the Urdu Dīvān of Mirza Ghalib*, Ph.D. Dissertation, University of Chicago, 1980, p. 51. In fact, for an interesting introduction to the major topoi of the ghazal, emphasizing Ghalib's poetry, see Silver's Chapter II, pp. 50-85, passim.
9. *Dīvān-i Ghālib*, Arshi edition, New Delhi: Anjuman-i Taraqqi-i Adab, 1982, p. 186.
10. *Kulliyāt-i Ātish*, ed. Z. A Siddiqui, Allahabad: Ram Narayan Lal Beni Madhav, 1972, p. 122.
11. Ibid.
12. *Dīvān-i Ghālib*, Arshi edition, p. 186.
13. See Chapter XI for further discussion of how Nasikh and Atish employ the *kū-i yār* theme in their poetry.
14. From these places the *'āshiq* compares his lot to that of the legendary Persian *'āshiq*, Majnun, who wandered insanely over the desert in separation from his beloved Laila.
15. Atish, *op. cit.*, p. 122.
16. *Kulliyāt-i Nāsikh*, p. 11.
17. *Kulliyāt-i Ātish*, p. 122.
18. It is understood that the *'āshiq's* love for a cruel idol is merely a metaphor for his devotion to the true beloved.
19. *Kulliyāt-i Nāsikh*, p. 11.

CHAPTER II

Literary Tenets of the Two School Theory

The Two School theory serves as an organising principle for surveying Urdu poetry. Its first tenet, implicitly, is that nearly every major Urdu poet can be considered either a Dihlavi or a Lakhnavi because the overwhelming bulk of classical poetry was composed in Delhi and Lucknow, Muslim India's two major cultural centres (*marākiz*). Though there is universal agreement that the Delhi School was anteceded by Dakani poetry from Muslim courts in southern India and that the classical ghazal tradition ended with the death of Dr. Muhammad Iqbal (d. 1938), classical poetry (specifically the ghazal) is understood by the critics to be primarily that which was composed from about the middle of the eighteenth century to the late-middle nineteenth century in the two great seats of culture: Delhi and Lucknow.

The second tenet, as has been indicated, is that Lakhnavi and Dihlavi poets wrote in characteristically different styles. The terms by which these characteristic styles are known are *Dihlavīyat* and *Lakhnavīyat*. The literature of the Two School theory is essentially comprised of various critics' assays at defining *Dihlavīyat* and *Lakhnavīyat*. Nurul Hasan Hashmi, the author of *Dillī kā Dabistān-i Shā'irī*, a leading reference work on Dihlavi poetry in the context of the Two School theory, offers the following description:

> *Dihlavīyat* is the name of a point of view, an outlook, an intellectual simplicity, a poetic temperament, in order to comprehend which a step-by-step comparison with *Lakhnavīyat* will be made . . .[1]

Abul Lais Siddiqi's primary definition of *Lakhnavīyat* is:

> What is meant by *Lakhnavīyat* in poetry and literature is that special quality which the early poets of Lucknow adopted and established, and whose special characteristics distinguish it from traditional[2] poetry . . .[3]

Perhaps the most common attributes of Lakhnavi poetry in the eyes of the critics are sensuality and effeminacy:

> A general effeminacy (*zanānapan*) was born in Lucknow's populace and society and its influence is manifest in the poetry as well . . . . From a survey of Lucknow *dīvāns* a detailed index of women's jewels, dress, and adornments can be compiled. Furthermore its (Lakhnavi poetry's) idiom and expression is often that of the *zanāna*. The poets of Delhi do not speak in women's idiom (*bolī*).[4]

Besides effeminacy, other non-traditional features of *Lakhnavīyat* are said to be (1) new conventions in describing the beloved's beauty which pay special attention to her particular items of apparel (as suggested above by Nadvi's initial distinguishing characteristic) and (2) a tendency toward *mu'āmla bandī*, or repartee between the '*āshiq* and the *maḥbūb*.[5]

Both of these tendencies are thought to weaken the conventional ambiguity of the beloved's identity and gender. The first point not only suggests very strongly that the beloved is female,[6] but also that she is unequivocally mortal. Not only gender ambiguity, but also the divine/human ambiguity are important parts of the traditional ghazal. Based largely on the Lakhnavi convention of elaborately enumerating the (female) beloved's dress and adornments, critics have argued that the Lakhnavi ghazal is almost devoid of spiritual or mystical thought or emotion.[7] This particular charge is perhaps the most devastating condemnation that could be made, since it alters the entire nature of ghazal expression, robbing it of its essential truth (*ḥaqīqat*).

Mu'āmla bandī (amorous banter, repartee)[8] is also consistently listed as a feature of *Lakhnavīyat*:

> The general style of Lakhnavi poets is *mu'āmla bandī* which, spreading over all, created the tenor of the marketplace, and one does not, therefore, find the vigorous and genuine style that is found in the writings of the poets of Delhi . . .[9]

Mu'āmla bandī is felt to debase the beloved's traditionally superior position with regard to the '*āshiq* insofar as repartee implies greater equality than would be expected between a supplicant and his omnipotent bestower — or non-bestower — of favours. One reason for this is that a previous union (*viṣāl*) is often implied in verses of *mu'āmla bandī*. While physical union with a courtesan is not uncommon, the traditional ghazal has been a poetry of love in separation.[10] The courtesan may not always bestow her physical favours on all the men who frequent her salon and exchange clever and lively witticisms with her[11] but she certainly does make herself available to the select few who are willing to pay a high enough fee. To equate the beloved with such a woman is heretical to the idealized discourse on the ghazal's character.

Language usage is another area where the Two School critics distinguish between the "more traditional" poetry of Delhi and that of Lucknow. They argue that Lakhnavi poets employ too much word-play,[12] and that it is employed in a base fashion; similarly, that they affect excessive delicacy of expression which results in abstruseness of thought rather than "charming and delightful constructions which resulted from the Persian and Dihlavi poets' usage of language."[13]

Critics overall find Lakhnavi poetry to exhibit "a certain vulgarity,"[14] and they tie it to language use in several ways. Firstly, the desired diction of the ghazal is elegant and plaintive, employing words and phrases which allude to greater layers of meaning than are obvious from their surface definitions.[15] To be too specific is to overstate oneself, and that is considered vulgar in noble (*sharīf*) society, which has been the ghazal's preferred venue.[16]

Secondly, the excessive wordiness of Lakhnavi poets is considered to render their poetic output frivolous. One critic claims that this frivolous love of word-play contributed to a trend of much-lengthened ghazals in Lucknow which resulted in "ridiculous resolution of *qāfiyas* and, therefore, degraded themes," while "the poets of Delhi, in accordance with tradition, generally wrote short ghazals and thereby avoided superfluity and degraded themes."[17]

This general outline of the Two School critics' literary differentiation between the poetry of Lucknow and that of Delhi, although necessarily abbreviated, includes all the major distinctions articulated in relevant literary criticism. The theory's articulated elements of differentiation rest largely in the realms of thematic content, or subject matter, and in language usage. Distinctions of special note are the Lakhnavi poets' attention to the details of female dress and adornment and the Lakhnavis' elaborate diction, as opposed to the spirituality and *Fārsī tarākīb* (Persian manner of verbal construction) of Dihlavi poetry. Critics think that these two key elements—elaborate diction and details of female apparel—produce an overall aesthetic in Lakhnavi poetry that is more sensual and frivolous than in the "traditional" ghazal, which is better preserved in Dihlavi poetry. The next chapter begins to reconstruct the genesis and evolution of the Two School theory in Urdu literary criticism.

NOTES

1. "*Dihlavīyat Kyā Hai?*" in Nurul Hasan Hashmi, *Dillī kā Dabistān-i Shā'irī*, pp. 257-327.
2. This notion of Dihlavi poetry as "traditional" and of Lakhnavi poetry as a departure from tradition carries profound implications, which are explored in the final chapter's cultural interpretation of the Two School theory.
3. Abul Lais Siddiqi, *Lakhna'u kā Dabistān-i Shā'irī*, Lahore: Urdu Markaz, third edition, 1967, p. 39.
4. Abdus Salam Nadvi, *She'rul Hind*, vol. I, pp. 204-5.
5. Both features are apparently attributed to the influence of courtesans in Lakhnavi society. See Nadvi, *She'rul Hind*, vol. I, p. 204.
6. See Andalib Shadani's first point of differentiation in "*Lakhnavī Shā'irī kī Chand Khuṣūṣiyāt*" from *Taḥqīq kī Roshnī meṅ*, Lahore: Shaikh Ghulam Ali and Sons, 1963, p. 249: "Lakhnavi poets focused on a female beloved while . . . the beloveds of the Dihlavi poets were foppish young boys. . . ."
7. Nadvi, *She'rul Hind*, p. 209: "*Sho'rā-i Lakhna'u ke kalām meṅ rūḥānī jazbāt bahut kam pā'e jāte haiṅ.*"
8. This term is discussed further in later chapters.
9. Nadvi, p. 211.
10. Recall the quintessential *she'r* by Ghalib which was cited in the background discussion of ghazal conventions: "*yih na thī hamārī qismat kih viṣāl-i yār hotā/ agar aur jīte rahte yahī intiẓār hotā.*"
11. Cf. Mirza Ruswa, *The Courtesan of Lucknow*, Khushwant Singh and M.A. Husaini, trans., Delhi: Hind Pocket Books, n.d., pp. 55-56.
12. "*ri'āyat-i lafẓī*"—Nadvi's fifth point of distinction, *She'rul Hind*, p. 210.
13. Nadvi, pp. 212-13. The expression used to indicate the charming and delightful Persian constructions is *Fārsī tarākīb* or *Fārsī tarkībeṅ.* This point of Nadvi's is also a primary complaint of Maulana Azad's in *Āb-i Ḥayāt*. He discusses differences in idiom between the two cities on p. 341; he also objects to the general diction of Lucknow during

Nasikh's and Atish's time [p. 348]; and observes that there are internal, if not external, faults in Nasikh's poetic writing, pp. 355-6.

14. Nadvi's sixth point, *She'rul Hind*, I, p. 210.
15. That was the great strength of Nasikh's and Ghalib's *maṯla's* that were featured in the prefatory discussion of ghazal conventions: "*Mir ā sīna hai mashriq āftāb-i dāgh-i hijrāñ kā* ..." and "*Yih na thī hamārī qismat*. ..."
16. For a discussion of *sharāfat* and its relation to Urdu poetry, see Chapter XII of this study.
17. This is Nadvi's third point of distinction between the two schools, *She'rul Hind*, p. 208. Azad, too, on p. 81 of *Āb-i Ḥayāt*, mentions the degraded themes which predominate in the Urdu ghazal of the nineteenth century, especially in those of Lakhnavi poets, as does Khvaja Altaf Husain Hali on p. 130 of his *Muqaddma-i She'r-o Shāirī*.

CHAPTER III

Tracing the Genesis of the Two Schools

Dihlavīyat and *Lakhnavīyat*

Because the concepts of *Lakhnavīyat* and *Dihlavīyat* are fundamental to the Two School theory, it is important to come to an understanding of the values and assumptions which these terms connote for the modern reader of Urdu poetry. Some of the Two School critics' specific statements on *Lakhnavīyat* and *Dihlavīyat* are examined below.

Two books have served as standard references for the past several decades on the subject of Lakhnavi and Dihlavi poetry. Written as doctoral theses in 1942 and 1943 for Aligarh Muslim University, and entitled *Lakhna'u kā Dabistān-i Shā'irī* by Abul Lais Siddiqi, and *Dillī kā Dabistān-i Shā'irī* by Nurul Hasan Hashmi, they have been published and reprinted under the same titles several times each. Both books are primarily concerned with presenting biographical and historical information about the varied and numerous poets of Lucknow and Delhi, respectively. Both are modelled on the *tazkira* form of secondary literature.[1] Where they differ from the *tazkira* model is that they both start from the premise that Dihlavi and Lakhnavi poetry constitute two separate schools, and both authors attempt to define which characteristics distinguish one *dabistān* (school) from the other. Recall their definitions of *Dihlavīyat* ("Delhi-ness") and *Lakhnavīyat* ("Lucknow-ness"):

> *Dihlavīyat* is the name of a point of view, an outlook, an intellectual simplicity, a poetic temperament, in order to comprehend which a step-by-step comparison with *Lakhnavīyat* will be made. . .[2]

and

> What is meant by *Lakhnavīyat* in poetry and literature is that special quality which the early poets of Lucknow adopted and established, and whose special characteristics distinguish it from traditional poetry. . .[3]

And what were the traditional literary principles and values? Neither are they anywhere articulated by Hashmi or Siddiqi, nor does the "traditional" vs. "non-traditional" polarity between Dihlavi and Lakhnavi poetry originate with these two critics.[4] Both were building on earlier critics' work, the most important of whom, for the purposes of this study, were Maulana Azad, Altaf Husain Hali and Abdus Salam Nadvi.

Nadvi had been Hashmi's and Siddiqi's most recent predecessor. His *tazkira*, *She'rul Hind* (1926), marks the point at which the Two School theory was formally articulated and its authority cemented in the Urdu critical tradition. Nadvi refers to an "Intermediate Era" of Urdu literature, the time following Mir and Sauda, as the time when

> Lakhnavi poetry became established and Delhi's and Lucknow's two separate schools were founded . . . the period's various masters were Momin, Zauq, Shah Nasir, Ghalib, Nasikh, Atish, and their disciples. . .[5]

Here Nadvi is building on earlier work. In *Āb-i Ḥayāt* (1880) Maulana Azad treats all Lakhnavi poetry as an entity separate from the rest of Urdu poetry. Dihlavi poetry he considers to comprise the remainder, while Lakhnavi poetry developed later than, as well as at variance with, earlier, more "traditional" poetry. This distinction is clearly implicit in many of Azad's remarks in *Āb-i Ḥayāt*, although it is nowhere articulated. The second work of Urdu criticism, Hali's *Muqaddma*, builds heavily upon it.

Without being explicit, Azad gave voice to the Delhi-Lucknow cultural rivalry in his strongly-conveyed preference for traditional (i.e. Dihlavi) practices. The concept of tradition, both in language and in culture, threads its way through the pages of *Āb-i Ḥāyat*, which is its author's reverent offering to a noble, dying tradition embodied in the Mughal culture of Delhi. Its death knell seems to have begun to toll, for Maulana Azad, with the advent of culture and poetry in Lucknow. Later critics, too, accepted and developed Azad's point of view. His immediate successor in literary criticism, though a chronological contemporary, was Khvaja Altaf Husain Hali, author of the *Muqaddma-i She'r-o Shā'irī* (1893).[6] Ostensibly an introduction to Hali's own *dīvān*, the *Muqaddma* is, in fact, a protracted treatise on the state of Urdu poetry in general. Hali's position is that all Urdu poetry had suffered a deplorable decline during the nineteenth century, and he sets out a sort of agenda for the reform and revival of the Urdu ghazal. Of particular relevance to this inquiry is his citation of Lakhnavi poetry as a primary example of Urdu poetry's general decline.

Lakhnavi poets, and discussion of Lucknow in general, figure far less in the *Muqaddma* than in *Āb-i Ḥāyat*, appearing almost incidentally to its focal discussion of Urdu literature's fate. Yet this second work of Urdu criticism was extremely important in shaping analytical criteria for assessing Urdu poetry. Some criteria—especially Hali's notion of what constitutes "natural poetry"— later became integrated into the full-blown Two School theory. As such, "these criteria" have had an impact on most subsequent analysis of Lakhnavi poetry.[7]

The *Muqaddma* complements *Āb-i Ḥāyat* in certain ways, elaborating upon a number of issues given briefer mention in the earlier work. For example, Hali echoes Azad's decrying of "worn-out themes" in the ghazal, and the need to have poetry "fully express our every goal and every kind of desire in our hearts."[8] This latter point is not argued prominently in the *Muqaddma*, although it contributes significantly to the major thrust of Hali's treatise. "Worn-out themes" run contrary to the concept of Reality (*aṣlīyat or kā'ināt kā muṭāl'a*), and interfere with the achievement of a poetry which is "natural."[9] Another quality in Urdu poetry which Hali decries is over-elaborated, or artificial, language. Both qualities, in his eyes, contribute to an emotional shallowness, and thus to the moral decline of literature.

Both Azad and Hali were reformers, but Azad's work is not primarily a piece of reformist literature, while Hali's unabashedly is, as later discussion will demonstrate. Whatever need there was for ghazal reform, as perceived by Azad, seems to have lain mainly in the realm of aesthetics — in other words, a "getting back to the basics" of the existing Perso-Arabic literary tradition. Hali, by contrast, called for literary reform as part and parcel of a widespread moral reform in Indian Islam. What they have in common is a belief that the qualities most in need of reform in Urdu poetry were to be found in the verse of Lucknow's poets.

Nadvi does not call for reform but he does build on Azad's historical framework, directly reiterating the major events and poets of the *pānchvāñ daur* (Fifth Epoch) delineated in *Āb-i Ḥayāt*. It had been in the context of the Fifth Epoch that Azad discussed Dihlavi and Lakhnavi poetry as two diverging streams, writing that the new age ushered in two kinds of poets: those who honoured their ancestors and those who forged new paths of their own.[10] Along the new paths, according to Azad, lay flights of fancy and linguistic creations of great delicacy. Such an advent is explained as natural in the course of any language's evolution, and the point is illustrated by the observation that Delhi's linguistic authority had begun to be less strictly observed within a generation after its artistic élite's migration to Lucknow. Examples of difference in idiom were drawn from Nasikh's *dīvān*.

In *She'rul Hind* Nadvi offered an even more formal statement of what Azad's writings had implied:

> Although the delineation of a [distinct] Lakhnavi style of poetry had already begun in the time of Mushafi and Insha, even so a distinction of schools had not yet been formalized. But Nasikh and Atish further developed this [special] style, and as a result of this, from their time onward two separate schools of Delhi and Lucknow were established, whose special characteristics can be distinguished from one another . . .[11]

Conceptions of *Dihlavīyat* and *Lakhnavīyat* are typically approached against the backdrop of Lucknow and Delhi as centres of culture (*marākiz*). The conventionally held picture of Delhi and Lucknow as *marākiz* depicts rivers of wealth flowing in Lucknow in contrast to a desperation in Delhi that gave rise to melancholic spirituality:

> The political conditions created great despair. Delhi's poetry is thus rife with the pain of existence and the sorrow of love. The legacy of Sufism had given birth to a climate of spirituality, upon which Dihlavi poetry was founded . . .[12]

while in Lucknow

> Rivers of wealth flowed, riches rained down from the sky...there was a proliferation of pleasure-seeking, an excess of material wealth. This state of affairs brought about licentiousness and imbalanced thoughts and actions . . . The result was that poetry

> became a vehicle for coquetry, blandishments, coarse language and enumerations of feminine beauty . . .[13]

Hashmi also writes:

> In comparison with *Dihlavīyat 's* spirituality and attachment to sorrow Lucknow's superficial gaiety seems thin and cheap. Lakhnavi poets concentrated on enumerations of feminine beauty but omitted loftiness of thought. There is not that flame, that profound lamentation, that tone of longing which there is in the poetry of Delhi . . . [14]

The prejudice against Lucknow apparent in the remarks above has permeated nearly every critical work since the earliest publications in Urdu literary criticism. This is true even of those critical works which pay homage to the *markaz* of Lucknow, in affirmation of its importance as a major Urdu centre.[15]

For example, in his introduction to the chapter entitled "Urdu Poetry's Two Different Schools: Delhi and Lucknow,"[16] Nadvi features a *she'r* by Nasikh which serves well to illustrate the characteristic depiction of Lucknow and *Lakhnavīyat* in literary criticism overall:

راستی کا نام بھی اس شہر میں سنتے نہیں
کیوں نہ ہوں سب لکھنؤ کے کوچے و بازار کج

Rāstī kā nām bhī is shahr meñ sunte nahīñ
Kyoñ na hoñ sab Lakhna'u ke kūche-o bāzār kaj

Straightforwardness in this city
is unknown even by name:
Why then should not Lucknow's
every lane and bazaar
be crooked?[17]

The effect of this introduction on the audience is to associate Lucknow at once with crookedness and deceit—leaving rectitude and forthrightness to the domain of the Dihlavis. Indirectly, the reader has already been forewarned to expect deviant poetry from Lakhnavi poets.[18]

It is little surprise, then, that Urdu readers find crookedness, deceit and "untraditional" poetic values in the poetry of Nasikh and Atish Lakhnavi; or that, by the same token, readers approach Momin or Zauq or Ghalib as Dihlavis, expecting to see characteristic *Dihlavīyat* : lofty thought, spirituality, the "pain of existence and the sorrow of love."

All the more unfortunate, in this light, is the omission of illustrative *she'rs* in Hashmi's and Siddiqi's definitions of *Dihlavīyat* and *Lakhnavīyat* . The critics thereby miss what would have been a welcome opportunity to make explicit what they mean by *Dihlavīyat 's* "spirituality," "rifeness with the pain of existence and sorrow of love;" and *Lakhnavīyat 's* "licentiousness, coquetry and blandishments, etc."[19]

Furthermore, Hashmi's discussion of *Dihlavīyat* draws heavily on Siddiqi's remarks about *Lakhnavīyat* . This implies mutual understanding between the two critics which requires no explicit definition of terms from either. Such internal cross-referencing leaves the outside reader with little sense of what the critics' evaluative criteria are.

Although the ghazal is known to exist in a realm independent of the temporal and political worlds (at least as far as subject matter is concerned), it is precisely this temporal, political world which Urdu critics often evoke in their literary analysis. Their discussions of the two so-called *dabistāns* become descriptions instead of the actual cities of Delhi and Lucknow — as perceived in retrospect by their cultural successors. Recall that the reason Hashmi and Siddiqi posited for their characterisations of Lakhnavi poetry (as flirtatious and sensual) and Dihlavi poetry (as spiritually oriented and expressive of lofty thought) was that in the late eighteenth century Delhi had been plundered and impoverished while Lucknow enjoyed wealth and leisure. In this regard Hashmi and Siddiqi were merely reiterating conventional wisdom.

In other words, the critics seem to have confused the concept of *dabistān* with that of *markaz*. While *markaz* signifies a locus of activity, *dabistān* signifies a group of poets who subscribe to certain shared literary principles that distinguish them from other poets in their own tradition.

Dillī kā Dabistān-i Shā'irī and *Lakhna'u kā Dabistān-i Shā'irī* serve very well as compendia of information and conventional wisdom regarding Lucknow and Delhi as *marākiz* though they contribute little analysis that enhances understanding of the elusive question, "What comprises literary *Dihlavīyat* and *Lakhnavīyat* ?" In their assumption that readers already know what is implied by the terms *Lakhnavīyat* and "traditional poetry" Hashmi and Siddiqi indicate that Nadvi's formal declaration of the existence of two schools for Dihlavi and Lakhnavi poetry was already firmly entrenched by the time their own books were being written.

Nadvi's formal delineation of two schools, in turn, had met with no apparent opposition in the world of Urdu letters, most probably because it merely made formal what had already been established as conventional wisdom by Maulana Azad and Altaf Husain Hali. We will examine in detail the discussions of Lakhnavi poetry in *Āb-i-Ḥayāt* and the *Muqaddma-i She'r-o Shā'irī*, tracing the impressionistic foundation of the Two School theory in these two works.

In summary, then, the publication of *She'rul Hind* in 1926 represented a culmination of the Two School theory's transition from a prototypical idea in Azad's discussion of what kind of poetry honoured tradition (Dihlavi) and what did not (Lakhnavi), through Hali's employment of Dihlavi and Lakhnavi poetic examples to highlight the reforms required to insure Urdu's "naturalness," into a fully articulated distinction based on specific literary criteria. Among those who took up and discussed these criteria were Abul Lais Siddiqi and Nurul Hasan Hashmi in their studies of the two *dabistāns*. Critics in the middle decades of this century, in turn, drew heavily on work such as Hashmi's and Siddiqi's, contributing to the propagation of the Two School theory. One of its final reiterations has been Andalib Shadani's essay "A Few Special Characteristics of Lakhnavi Poetry."[20] This essay — which is almost an exact restatement of Nadvi's argument in *Sher'rul Hind* — and Ali Javad Zaidi's challenge to the Two School theory based on refutation of Shadani's arguments, will be taken up in later chapters.[21] The following chapter will continue to lay out a cultural and historical context into which the Two School theory can be placed.

NOTES

1. *Taẕkiras* were biographical memoirs of poets, usually including selected samples (*intikhāb*) of their poetry.
2. Hashmi, *Dillī kā Dabistān-i Shā'irī*, p. 257. [hereafter referred to as *D.D.S.*]
3. Siddiqi, *Lakhna'u kā Dabistān-i Shā'irī*, p.39. [hereafter referred to as *L.D.S.*]
4. Ali Javad Zaidi, for example, writing in 1980, considers the Delhi-Lucknow distinction to have been in currency for seventy or eighty years; see *Do Adabī Iskūl*, Lucknow: Nasim Book Depot, 1980, Preface to the Second Edition.
5. Nadvi, *She'rul Hind*, vol. 1, p. 10.

6. Altaf Husain Hali, *Muqaddma-i She'r-o Shā'irī*, Delhi: Maktaba Jami'a Limited, 1981.
7. Later discussion will include, where appropriate, Hali's ideas about "natural poetry" since he came to represent an authority for later critics drawing distinctions between *Lakhnavīyat* and *Dihlavīyat* .
8. Azad, *Āb-i Ḥayāt*, p. 51.
9. *Aṣlīyat* and "*kā'ināt kā muṭāla'a*—the examination of real things" — are two expressions used by Hali to describe the quality of Reality, which was one of three essential features in *necharal* ("natural") poetry. Natural poetry was the end sought by Hali's proposed reforms.
10. Azad, *Āb-i Ḥayāt*, p. 339: "Do qism ke bā-kamāl naẕar ā'enge. Ek voh kih jinhoñ ne apne buzurgoñ kī pairvī ko dīn ā'eñ samjhā . . . dūsre voh 'ālī dimāgh jo fikr ke dukhan se ījād kī havā'eñ uṛā'enge."
11. Nadvi, vol. I, p. 204. The Mushafi and Insha referred to in this statement were Shaikh Ghulam Hamdani Mushafi [1750-1824] and Insha Allah Khan Insha [1756-1818], who were of the first generation of poets in Lucknow, the generation which preceded Nasikh and Atish.
12. Hashmi, *D.D.S*. p. 13.
13. Siddiqi, *L.D.S*., p. 47.
14. Hashmi, *D.D.S*, p. 13.
15. Cf. such works as Siddiqi's *L.D.S*., Nadvi's *She'rul Hind*, and Abdul Halim Sharar's *Guẕishta Lakhna'u*, Lucknow: Nasim Book Depot, 1974.
16. Nadvi, pp. 204-215.
17. Shaikh Imam Bakhsh Nasikh, *Dīvān-i Duvvam*, Lucknow: Naval Kishore, A.H. 1324, p. 49.
18. We also see this notion of Lakhnavi poetry as a conscious departure from tradition reflected in Abul Lais Siddiqi's definition of *Lakhnavīyat* cited above.
19. This missed opportunity is significant because it exemplifies why understanding, analysis, and even refutation of the Two School theory are so elusive and difficult.
20. In *Tahqīq kī Roshnī meñ*, Lahore: Shaikh Ghulam Ali and Sons Publishers, 1963, pp. 247-272.
21. See Ali Javad Zaidi, *Do Adabī Iskūl*, Lucknow, 1970.

CHAPTER IV

Cultural and Historical Background to the Two School Theory

The *marākiz* of Delhi and Lucknow flourished, broadly speaking, at different times. Lucknow emerged as a centre toward the end of the eighteenth century just as Delhi's cultural efflorescence began to decline. Lucknow's establishment as a centre of culture was, in fact, the direct result of political events. Repeated invasions of the Mughal centre at Delhi—by Persians, Afghans and Marathas—had rendered the capital weak, impoverished, and generally destitute. The *Navābs* of Avadh, though also nominally serving as *Vazīrs* (Prime Ministers) of the Mughal empire, began to establish themselves as virtually independent rulers to the east of the imperial centre.[1] They were able to achieve this independence by virtue of Avadh's wealth and relative security, off the beaten track of the marauders. Additionally, the *navābs* were able to offer asylum and cultural patronage on a grand scale, attracting the destitute intellectual and artistic élite from Delhi.

Initially, patronage had come from Navab Shuja' ud-Daula (r. 1754-1775),[2] whose capital was at Faizabad:

> In Shuja's time various classes of people . . . especially from Delhi, began pouring in [to Faizabad]. Architects, engineers, physicians, artisans and poets flocked to the city . . .[3]

Shuja's son and successor, Asif ud-Daula, is perhaps the most important *navābī* patron of the arts. Upon his ascension to the throne, he moved the capital and court from Faizabad to Lucknow and began to pour enormous wealth into beautifying the city and developing it as a seat of culture. During Asif's reign (1775-1797) the greatest names in Urdu literature migrated from Delhi and Faizabad to Lucknow, attracted by the *navāb's* generous patronage. Among them were Sauda, Mir Taqi Mir, Mir Hasan, Soz, Insha, Jur'at, and Mushafi. Lakhnavi culture—particularly its poetry—became a legend within a single generation; the *markaz* established by Asif ud-Daula flourished for more than a century, and lasted for nearly two hundred years in all:

> The high culture of Lucknow was in full flower from the last quarter of the eighteenth century until the collapse of the Lucknow monarchy in 1856. It actually survived, however, as long as the feudal system survived in U.P.—that is, until the British left India in 1947.[4]

A significant byproduct of Lucknow's new role as the Urdu *markaz* was the intense cultural rivalry between Delhi and Lucknow which lies at the heart of the Two School theory. This rivalry persisted for generations, and is manifest in the words of nineteenth century writers as well as those of the twentieth. Though the stubbornness of venerated Dihlavis like Mir[5] wavered little despite his nearly thirty-year tenure as Lucknow's leading resident *ustād*, there was, necessarily, some softening on the part of poets of the following generation. Insha Allah Khan Insha (1756-1818), an émigré poet, who became famous in Lucknow during the final quarter of the eighteenth century, indicates in the following remarks a grudging acknowledgement of Lucknow's achievements (though he is adamant in attributing their cause to the efforts of émigré Dihlavis):

> Is there anyone in this place of asylum [Lucknow] whose family house was built even a hundred years ago? Among men of letters there is not a single house which could be even fifty years old . . . the reason Lucknow stands above other cities is that poets who were born and beloved of Delhi have come to this city. Thus, Lucknow was moulded in Delhi's image, according to its rule, and is its spirit, its life, its *jān* . . .[6]

What lay at the heart of this rivalry between the two cities? I suggest that it was the issue of cultural authority, wherein the role of patronage was a crucial element. Cultural patronage is a valuable political resource. The *navābs* of Avadh, in extending patronage to Delhi's leading lights after the demise of Delhi's court culture, began to compete with the Mughal emperor for political and cultural pre-eminence. Ostensibly, the patronage extended to Delhi's greatest exponents showed the *navābs* to be loyal supporters of the empire, interested in bolstering its artistic endeavours and helping to perpetuate its cultural achievements. In fact, by drawing the great names to their own court the *navābs* were also enhancing their own stature as rulers. An understanding of this phenomenon is implicit in the following remarks of historian K.S. Santha. They are a continuation of the passage cited earlier, referring to the growth of Faizabad as the capital of Avadh:

> [These] artisans and poets flocked to the city *to diminish the glory of Delhi and to enhance the richness of Faizabad.* The very seat of Muslim culture and civilization was thus eclipsed by the emergence and rise of a new centre of culture at Faizabad.[7]

The Lakhnavi writer Abdul Halim Sharar suggests that the *navābs* were well aware of the implications of their patronage:

> [Asif ud-Daula] collected to himself all the pomp and splendour that could be found in the world, and his ambition was that the magnificence and grandeur of no court should equal that of his own . . .[8]

Other scholars write that Lakhnavis were very keen to create a rival culture to that of Delhi. In his *History of Urdu Literature* M. Sadiq says:

> Lucknow is not content with just being the continuator of the traditions of Delhi in life and civilization. It wishes to evolve a civilization of its own . . . to mould a new idiom of its own and to mark it off from that of Delhi . . .[9]

Rashid Hasan Khan also states that in the new kingdom a need was felt for styles and manners of speech, dress and artistic endeavour which would distinguish Lakhnavi culture from that of Delhi.[10]

And Abul Lais Siddiqi writes in *Lakhna'u kā Dabistān-i Shā'irī*:

> Just as the Navab Vazīr obtained freedom from the Delhi court, Lakhnavis freed themselves in every respect; new standards arose in culture and society, including new fashions in dress, apparel and adornments. There arose differences in polite discourse. In

> keeping with all this, writers and poets also began to rebel against the literary conventions which had been in vogue [in Delhi]. There, if it had been expressive of natural, straightforward ideas, then here the standard was toward fanciful fabrication; there simplicity and propriety had prevailed, while here it was excessive formality and making a display of art . . .[11]

It is significant that where new styles arose in Lucknow modern critics see them as manifestations of rebellion against the traditional status quo. Even Siddiqi, a critic who sincerely attempts to present a Lakhnavi perspective, sees the standards and norms of Delhi as ultimately authoritative.

The infallibility of the Delhi *markaz* may be seen as a manifestation of the widespread (and well-recognised) political phenomenon of Mughal legitimacy. By the 1760s Mughal power was no longer the strongest politically or militarily, and numerous other powers (the Afghans, Marathas and British, to name a few) were competing to fill the vacuum. Under these circumstances this special legitimacy was manifest in various ways. Percival Spear observes that

> The emperor's was the ultimate legal authority in India and there was for his authority a spirit of reverence and acceptance . . . [this] intangible but not negligible authority of the imperial name explains the constant efforts of rival politicians to get the imperial sanction for their acts, and if possible, to keep the imperial person in their camps.[12]

Just as the politically ambitious sought the rubber stamp of Mughal approval to justify their claims over rivals and those whom they aspired to control, so may Lucknow be understood to have sought legitimacy as the new standard-bearer of Mughal culture. Delhi, too, sought to retain control over the symbols of legitimacy. While unable to maintain control over patronage of the arts because of the reversal in circumstances which it suffered at the time, Delhi could still withhold sanction of Lakhnavi artistic efforts by refusing to recognise them as successful, and so could wield the modicum of power it held by virtue of historical precedent.[13] As we examine how this exercise of power ties in with the attitudes propagated in the Urdu critical literature of a century later, we will see that the "modicum" of power held a significance not to be underestimated.[14]

In light of these consequences of Lakhnavi patronage, one can appreciate why some of the émigré poets and artists reacted to Lucknow with ambivalence. Dihlavis often resisted any identification with their new home, vociferously disdaining Lakhnavi ways. Sadiq writes that "despite the manifold attractions of Lucknow and Faizabad, and the magnificent patronage he enjoyed there, Sauda keenly yearned for Delhi and its associations" and that "this nostalgic reversion … is a characteristic he shares with Mir and, in fact, with practically all other poets, who had sought refuge in Lucknow."[15] This nostalgia for Delhi, combined with disdain for Lucknow, is reflected in the verses of Mushafi and Mir below:

یارب شہر اپنا یوں چھڑایا تو نے
ویرانے میں مجھکو لا بٹھایا تو نے
میں اور کہاں یہ لکھنؤ کی خلقت
اے وائے کیا کیا خدایا تو نے

Yārab shahar apnā yūñ chhuṛāyā tū ne
Vīrāne meñ mujh ko lā biṭhāyā tū ne
Maiñ aur kahāñ yih Lakhna'u kī khilqat
A'e vāe kyā kiyā khudāyā tū ne

You've robbed me of my own city
and led me into this wilderness:
What can there be between me and these Lakhnavis?
Dear God, what have you done to me?

(Mushafi)

and

خرابہ دلّی کا دہ چند بہتر لکھنؤ سے تھا
وہیں اے کاش مر جاتا سراسیمہ نہ آتا یاں

Kharāba Dillī kā dah-chand bahtar Lakhna'u se thā
Vahīñ ae kāsh mar jātā sarāsīma na ātā yāñ

Far better than Lucknow
were the ruins of Delhi:

Would that I had died back there
than let my madness lead me here! (Mir)[16]

The nobles of Delhi could not help but perceive Lucknow and its citizenry as provincial upstarts. To pretend that this new city could replace their beloved and once-magnificent Delhi as the centre of Mughal culture was to add insult to the injury of having been forced to flee. Dihlavi émigrés therefore set themselves apart from Lakhnavi manners and customs in every conceivable way, and their distinctions naturally extended to the realm of poetry as well. All this lay at the heart of Mir's famous *chūmāchāṭī* remark about Jur'at's poetry.

The Indo-Muslim culture felt to be unquestionably "legitimate," then, was Mughal culture. The city which could claim to be the Mughal *markaz* held ultimate cultural legitimacy. It is in conjunction with this idea of cultural legitimacy, I would argue, that the term "traditional" (and references to departures from tradition) arose in Urdu critics' characterisations of Lakhnavi culture. Because poetry was to them, after the Urdu language, the single most important identifier of Indo-Muslim culture, to characterise Lakhnavi culture as departing from the "traditional" was, by extension, to negate its legitimacy.

In the middle decades of the nineteenth century Delhi's court culture began to reemerge within the walls of the Red Fort, under the auspices of the Mughal heir-apparent,[17] who was also the popular poet Bahadur Shah Zafar (1775-1862). Surrounded by the very gifted poets Momin Khan Momin (1800-1851), Shaikh Ibrahim Zauq (1789-1854), and Mirza Asadullah Khan Ghalib (1797-1869), Bahadur Shah was able to sponsor the Mughal empire's—and Delhi's—cultural swan song. Later generations of Dihlavis, bolstered by this final flurry of literary achievement, began to seek ways to reclaim for themselves the paramount place in Urdu culture. This reclamation required a diminishing of the position which Lucknow had built up over the preceding half-century, and was brought about by something of a campaign to discredit Lucknow in the annals of Urdu literary criticism.

Whether consciously or not, this campaign was engineered and set in motion by the pioneers of literary criticism, Maulana Shamsul Ulama Muhammad Husain Azad (1830-1910) and Khvaja Altaf Husain Hali (1837-1914). It will be argued here that it was not coincidence that both pioneers were Dihlavis[18] and students of the great masters Zauq and Ghalib, respectively.

The purpose here has been to outline the historical circumstances which nourished the Delhi-Lucknow rivalry on a political as well as cultural level. Knowledge of this inter-city rivalry helps to elucidate the distinctions drawn by critics between the poetry of the two *marākiz* which eventually became expressed formally in the Two School theory. Those distinctions, though sporadically hinted at in various *she'rs* of numerous poets, and in works like Insha's *Daryā-i Laṭāfat*, begin to be developed consistently over the years from 1880 to 1926, beginning with Azad's *Āb-i Hayāt* and culminating in Nadvi's *She'rul Hind.*

NOTES

1. For an excellent, full study of this process see Richard B. Barnett, *North India Between Empires: Awadh, the Mughals, and the British, 1720-1801*, Berkeley: University of California Press, 1980.
2. It is the opinion of K.S. Santha in *Begams of Avadh*, Varanasi: Bharati Prakashan, 1980; and Iqtida Hasan, in *Kulliyāt-i Jur'at*, Naples: Instituto Universitario Orientalis, 1970-75, p. 21, that Shuja's wife, Sadr un-Nisa "Navab Begam" was an even greater patron than her husband.
3. K.S. Santha, *Begams of Avadh*, p. 9.
4. Fakhir Husain, Introduction to Abdul Halim Sharar's *Lucknow: The Last Phase of an Oriental Culture*, Boulder: Westview Press, 1976, p.13.
5. Recall that Mir called the Lakhnavi poet Jur'at's poetry "*chūmāchāṭī*."
6. *Daryā-i Laṭāfat* [1807], Urdu translation by Brij Mohan Datatariya Kaifi, Aurangabad: Anjuman-i Taraqqi-i Adab [Deccan], 1935, p.117. Ali Javad Zaidi also points to the time of Navab Sa'dat Ali Khan [r. 1801-1814] as the time when this rivalry was expressed first on a literary plane: "*Lakhna'u aur Dillī kī bahs ghāliban Sa'dat Alī ke zamāne meñ 'ilmī-o adabī saṭh par pahlī bār uṭhī . . .*" *Do Adabī Iskūl*, p. 73.
7. K.S. Santha, *Begams of Avadh*, p. 9. Emphasis mine.
8. *Lucknow: The Last Phase*, p. 48.
9. Sadiq, *A History of Urdu Literature*, London: Oxford University Press, 2nd Edition, 1984, p. 171.
10. *Intikhāb-i Nāsikh*, New Delhi: Maktaba Jami'a Limited, 1972, pp. 10-13. This is the context in which he explains Nasikh's development of a "new style" which he wanted to set up "in opposition to *Dihlavīyat*."
11. Siddiqi, *L.D.S.*, p. 55.
12. Percival Spear, *Twilight of the Mughals*, p. 9.
13. Whether the Dihlavis were absolutely deliberate in their denial of Lakhnavi achievements, or whether they were merely manifesting a

parochial attitude is difficult to determine. It does not change the force of their behaviour, however.

14. An interesting aspect of this legitimacy is that Lakhnavis did little to challenge the Dihlavis' sense of superiority, or their exercise of power and cultural authority.
15. Sadiq, *op. cit.*, p. 108.
16. Fourth Divan, *Kulliyāt-i Mīr*, Allahabad: Ram Narayan Lal Beni Madhav, 1972, volume I, p. 597.
17. Zafar later became the last Mughal emperor, Muhammad Bahadur Shah, r. 1847-1857.
18. In Hali's case Delhi was his adopted home. He was born in Panipat.

CHAPTER V

Origins of the Delhi-Lucknow Differentiation in Azad's *Āb-i-Ḥayāt*

Azad's *Āb-i Ḥayāt* was, according to at least one modern critic, "the first attempt to pull things together"[1] into a comprehensive history of Urdu literature. In his study of Maulana Azad, Muhammad Sadiq writes that, in addition to being

> an up-to-date account of the Urdu poets, embodying the maximum amount of information, critical and biographical, along Western lines,

Āb-i Ḥayāt was also

> . . . much more than a history of Urdu poetry; it [was] a human document, intense, vital, vibrating with life, and is, without doubt, one of the most brilliant reconstructions of the past that we possess.[2]

There are few opinions found anywhere in the entire corpus of Urdu literary criticism that cannot be traced back to *Āb-i Ḥayāt*.[3] So impressive is the range of material presented in *Āb-i Ḥayāt* that in the last hundred years critics have been able to add little new critical analysis or biographical information about Urdu's great writers to that which was collected and reported by Azad. It is in *Āb-i Ḥayāt* that we read of such widely-repeated anecdotes as Mir's famous "*chūmāchāṭī* remark" about Jur'at's poetry and of the legendary rivalries between Sauda and Mir, Mushafi and Insha, Nasikh and Atish, and Zauq and Ghalib.

While it is certainly not the work's primary focus, *Āb-i Ḥayāt* does represent perhaps the earliest example in Urdu criticism of Lakhnavi poetry being differentiated from Dihlavi poetry. Here begins the first glimmer of the notion, which later grew and strengthened, that Lakhnavi poetry developed later than—and at variance with—the standard set by earlier, more "traditional" poetry. It will also be suggested here that a polarisation between Nasikh and Atish parallels that drawn between Delhi and Lucknow; and although this polarisation is really elaborated upon by later critics, it can be traced back to *Āb-i Ḥayāt*. Particular attention will be paid to specific passages in *Āb-i Ḥayāt* which provide a basis for this dual point of view.

The section on Urdu literature's Fifth Epoch opens with a short essay on how the new era brought in a kind of poet who ceased to honour his venerated predecessors in traditional fashion, striking out on his own path; and how, being timely, this new style brought acclaim to the newer poets. But Azad also goes on to say that "those first excellent masters of Lucknow were the destroyers of Delhi;" and that they began to flout the authority of Delhi, especially in the realm of language usage.[4] The offender he specifically cites in this context is Nasikh; and the first section on poets of the Fifth Epoch is devoted to the life and work of Nasikh. Azad thus moves from general comments on the era into a very specific discussion of Nasikh—the poet who would seem to characterise the undesirable departure from tradition which can be seen in the Fifth Epoch. That that poet is the "*Imām* of *Lakhnavīyat*" is neither insignificant nor, very likely, coincidental.

Atish and Nasikh are the only two Lakhnavi ghazal poets whom Azad mentions in detail, in contrast to Abul Lais Siddiqi's discussion of twenty-five to thirty major Lakhnavi poets' work in *Lakhna'u kā Dabistān-i Shā'irī*.[5] Whether this was his intention or not, with his discussion of Lakhnavi ghazal poetry in the Fifth Epoch limited to the work of just two poets, Azad diminishes the scope and importance of the Lucknow *markaz* in the history of Urdu literature.[6]

Also in *Āb-i Ḥayāt* is a depiction of Lucknow's culture and customs as discrete from the social and linguistic or artistic customs of Delhi. Again, it is significant that where Azad addresses himself to such differences he often uses Nasikh as his Lakhnavi example. From Azad's time onward, just as Lucknow became the cultural *enfant terrible* of Indian Islam, so did Nasikh become Lucknow's exemplar. The two stigmas reinforced one another, and left room for Atish—a poet upon whom Azad and the rest of the tradition have looked with greater favour—to be appreciated as a desirable exception to the Lakhnavi stereotype.[7]

It is relevant in this context to observe that Azad himself was not only a proud and loyal Dihlavi; he was also the pupil of Shaikh Ibrahim Zauq (d. 1854), a "Poet Laureate" of the Mughal Empire. When Azad speaks of the Delhi-Lucknow split, he is speaking of "us" and "them."

Another example of such differentiation can be seen when Azad relates how Insha's friend, the Persian poet Qatil, toyed with the traditional manner of identifying metre: where it had been customary to communicate metre by reciting patterns using Arabic words *fa'ilūn, fa'ilūn*, etc. he amused himself by choosing words which evoked dalliance with beautiful nymphs.[8] Again, the effect of citing such examples was to suggest that Lakhnavi tastes and customs were not only different, but also rather vulgar as compared with those of Delhi. Most sensible critics would agree that the recitation of *parī k͟hānum* instead of *mafā'ilūn* was a playful gesture which might just as well have been practiced in Delhi as anywhere, including Lucknow. Nonetheless, this anecdote bolsters the impression that Lakhnavi poets were vulgar and frivolous.

Within the framework of the Fifth Epoch, Azad presents the two Lakhnavis in very different fashions and thereby establishes a polarisation within the polarisation between Lucknow and Delhi.[9] When he exempts Atish from Lakhnavi traits, as will be illustrated shortly, he appears to attribute to Atish the status of someone who is "more like one of us." By extension then, Atish's polar opposite must be Nasikh, the Lakhnavi par excellence: "one of them."

Language usage appears to form Azad's primary criterion for Delhi-Lucknow and Nasikh-Atish distinctions. In this matter, he conveys critical judgements in two basic ways: first, through anecdotes wherein revered Dihlavis, such as Mir Taqi Mir, freely express contempt for Lakhnavi language and poetry.[10] Although Azad does not explicitly corroborate Mir's suggestion that Lakhnavi language is faulty and so, in all probability, is its poetry, he does not challenge it, thereby allowing the audience to infer that "if Mir himself thought thus and so about Lakhnavi language, it must be true." Secondly, Azad's own assessment of the work of Lakhnavi poets often begins with a discussion of their employment of language, where the primary criterion is how appropriate their use of language is (as in the following remarks on Nasikh's poetry):

> Generally, Nasikh's poetry is quite free of apparent defects and verbal or grammatical faults . . . although there is a difference between adroit cleverness of composition and creative passion he makes a great effort not to let [the proper] principles get out of hand . . . In his ghazals there is much grandeur of language, lofty diction and delicate imagery but little *tāṣīr* . . .[11]

Although Azad acknowledges that inappropriate language usage is not a deficiency in Nasikh's poetry, he contrasts the grandeur of language (*shaukat-i alfāẓ*), lofty diction (*buland parvāzī*) and delicate imagery (*nāzuk khayālī*) with the ability of a verse to touch the heart (*tāṣīr*) of its audience. He draws a distinction between mere verbal accomplishment and creative passion (*kalām kī garmī*) in poetry. His phrasing suggests that Nasikh must work hard to keep the "proper principles in hand." Furthermore, although there is no specific verbal defect in Nasikh's poetry, there is also little emotional effect. Few would disagree with the opinion that there is more to poetry than just verbal pyrotechnics. What the reader is likely to infer from these comments, then, is that Lakhnavi poetry, in general, is verbal accomplishment masquerading as poetry, like the work of its foremost exponent, Nasikh; and that Lucknow's poets speak and write a different kind of Urdu than do Dihlavis. While Nasikh's language is not faulty grammatically, his diction is too "grand and lofty" to touch the heart and therefore merit acceptance.[12]

Compare Azad's remarks on Nasikh's diction with what he has to say about Atish's style of composition:

> His writing is virtually a handbook of colloquial Urdu and a first-rate example of the elegant expression of India. It presents the idiom and manner of speech of the nobility of Lucknow. Just as the nobility of Lucknow spoke, so did Atish compose his poetry. His writing both pleased the gentry and engendered admiration in the common folk . . . [13]

The point Azad is making here is that it is desirable to write poetry that reflects the spoken idiom of the people (in this case, the noble, or *sharīf*, people). This point is one of the tenets of the call for reform in the ghazal, and is a prominent theme in Hali's *Muqaddma-i She'r-o Shā'irī*. It was inspired by the Romantic movement in English poetry, launched nearly a century earlier by Wordsworth and Coleridge.[14]

A contradiction arises here. It is brought to the attention of the reader because Azad, though perhaps the first, is by no means the sole critic to fall victim to certain contradictions which strike us as inherent in the Delhi-Lucknow school distinction. A great fault perceived in Nasikh as a poet (indicated by the previous quotation from *Āb-i Ḥayāt*) was that his language was too fancy to be colloquial. On the other hand, as was suggested by the anecdote involving Mir's journey with a Lakhnavi, colloquial Lakhnavi Urdu was considered to be so vulgar as to pose a threat of corruption to a well-spoken Dihlavi. Yet a number of critics cite the great virtue of Atish's poetry as its colloquial felicity. And Atish is the second greatest exemplar of the so-called Lucknow School.

It can be seen from the above contradiction that the criteria cited for Delhi-Lucknow distinctions have not been consistent or concrete; and also that—even when stated in a concrete fashion—their inherent contradictions often render the Two School critics' arguments unconvincing. Nonetheless, Azad's implication—that just as idiom differed from one city to the other, so did each city's approach to literature—comes through loud and clear.

The prose style of Azad's section on Nasikh is extremely complicated, florid, and difficult to decipher. The messages it contains are mixed, and his critical comments are offered in an indirect manner. Laudatory exclamations about the marvellous style Nasikh achieved are followed by statements which, under scrutiny, prove to contradict the thrust of their complimentary neighbours (as in the passage cited earlier). Azad's biographical information concerning Nasikh's life consists largely in several anecdotes featuring "Shaikh Sahib" [Nasikh], through which the picture emerges of an arrogant glutton of formidable physique with a gregarious—even garrulous—personality, who eventually found himself at odds with many of Lucknow's famous men (not the least of whom were the King himself and his Prime Minister).[15] Azad then moves on to a discussion of the great rivalry which existed between Nasikh and Atish, and between their respective students and followers.

It is in the context of the Atish-Nasikh rivalry that Azad compares the poetic styles of the two Lakhnavi masters. Discussion of their difference in poetic diction has already been illustrated. In *Āb-i Ḥayāt*'s section devoted to each poet there is a sub-section which compares either poet's work with that of the other. Azad writes that the styles of the two masters are "absolutely different from one another" and that scores of Lucknow's litterateurs took the side of one *ustād* or the other. Augmenting this picture of polarity, the Maulana then moves on to cite certain "objections which the followers of Atish made to Nasikh's style of poetry,"[16] and vice versa. For example:

> The followers of Khvaja Sahib [Atish] make several kinds of objections to Shaikh Sahib's [Nasikh's] style . . . and since there is some force to some of their arguments, one is obliged to report them . . .[17]

It must be said that Maulana Azad does not agree with the followers of Atish on all these points. He does offer the following defense:

> Khvaja Sahib's followers say that those people who have truly understood the principles of the ghazal—for example Khvaja Hafiz and Shaikh Sa'di in Persian; and, in Urdu such authorities as Soz, Mir and Jur'at—will not call [these verses of Nasikh's] "ghazal". But the matter is not as simple as that, because in Persian, too, such revered poets as Jalal, Asir, Qasim Mashhadi, Bedil and Nasir Ali made names for themselves with the help of their *nāzuk khayālī* and *khayāl bandī*. If Shaikh Sahib also followed their style, what's wrong with that?[18]

The role of personality is paramount in much Urdu criticism.[19] It has just been shown how Azad introduces Nasikh through reports of his habits and personality. He goes even further with a short discourse on the personality of the kind of poet who tends toward the literary tastes to which "the followers of Atish" object. Just as *Lakhnavīyat* in literature is "defined" by means of painting a picture of Lucknow's character as a city, so also is Nasikh's poetic style implied to be a manifestation of his character and personality.

Azad's depiction of Atish strikes the reader as quite a contrast to his treatment of Nasikh. Biographical comments on Atish report in sympathetic terms Atish's tall, frail bearing; his unworldly disregard of comforts, as exemplified by the penury in which he lived; his Dihlavi and Sufi heritage, and his simple personality.[20]

The one bone of contention which Azad does pick with Atish's poetry lies in the realm of language use. He feels obliged to point out certain faults in Atish's employment of Persian, Arabic and Turkish words or expressions, at least, according to others: just as Nasikh's poetry is criticised in the words of Atish's followers, so too does Azad now present criticisms of Atish's faulty language use as objections voiced by the followers of Nasikh. For example:

دختر رز مری مونس ہے مری ہمدم ہے
میں جہانگیر ہوں وہ نور جہاں بیگم ہے

Du<u>kh</u>tar-i raz mirī mu'nis hai mirī hamdam hai
Maiñ jahāngīr hūñ voh nūr jahāñ begam hai

The daughter of the vine is my solace and my intimate:
I am Jahangir and she my Nur Jahan.[21]

Azad reports that when Atish recited the above *she'r*, Nasikh's champions objected to his pronunciation of *begam*, saying that since it was Turkish word, and was pronounced *begum* in Turkish—with a short "u" sound instead of a short "a" sound—Atish's *qāfiyah* was faulty. Azad reports that Atish retorted with the observation that he was speaking Urdu and would pronounce the word as it was pronounced in Urdu—when speaking Turkish he would alter his pronunciation accordingly. The effect of the above anecdote is twofold: it points up the fact that Nasikh's followers faulted Atish—whose education was not as extensive as that of certain of his contemporaries, notably their own *ustād*—for lacking sufficient erudition to know the difference between Urdu pronunciation and that of the languages from which its vocabulary is borrowed.[22] In this way the anecdote reinforces the polar opposition between the two *ustāds*. Secondly, it depicts Atish as a straightforward, no-nonsense person who was content to operate within the realm of his personal experience. In other words, it sets him up against the pretensions of Nasikh's followers who cited technical rules of a language that they did not even speak, and presents his simplicity of personal habit as a complementary virtue to his simplicity of language and poetic style.

Azad's prose style when discussing Atish is very straightforward, clear and easily comprehended, complementing its characterisation of Atish's poetic style as pure, simple and colloquial—in short, as unpretentious as the man himself. After thus characterising Atish's style (*ṭarz-i kalām*) Azad reiterates the contrast it represents to Nasikh's "complicated, convoluted, hair-splitting style of composition."[23]

Finally, we would suggest that comments directed in simple, clear language are almost guaranteed to make the desired impression on the readers they are intended to instruct. Azad's choice of diction in his discussions of both Atish and Nasikh has, no doubt, contributed to the conventional wisdom about, and constancy of, both poets' reputations within the critical tradition, that of Atish as being simple and mellifluous of diction and Nasikh as being convoluted, even obscure. By pointing out—with elaborate courtesy, of course—Atish's imperfect understanding of Persian and by depicting Nasikh as a brash, almost comically obtuse buffoon, Azad dissuades his readers from judging the poetry of these two Lakhnavi *ustāds* with the same seriousness and consideration which the Urdu audience could normally be expected to extend toward great masters. And, as we have said, although he defends Nasikh in places Azad definitely promotes the polarisation between Nasikh and Atish by presenting qualities—which Nasikh might be inferred to display—in terms of the kinds of objections which Atish and his followers expressed. This effect is achieved without any statements direct enough to leave Azad at risk of being accused of chauvinism or partisanship.

It is not this study's purpose to disagree with Azad's construction of a polar opposition between Atish and Nasikh. There are, indeed, certain valid grounds for contrast. Rather, the intention is to point out that this particular polarisation is framed in the context of individual personalities, personal habits, family background, etc. instead of according to more concrete, and thus more credible, literary criteria. Similarly, it is fruitless and possibly inaccurate to argue here that the qualitative differences between Lakhnavi and Dihlavi poetry claimed by Urdu critics and scholars are not genuinely felt. The point is that this alleged "differentness" has thus far proved impossible to articulate in such a way as to convince those who do not acknowledge it; and it cannot, therefore, be accepted that these felt "differences" are crucial enough to warrant a formal division of Dihlavi and Lakhnavi poetry into separate schools. The "differences" which have been articulated in the major works of Urdu critical literature simply do not bear up under close scrutiny, as will be shown in later chapters. We will continue to assert that the major characteristics of Atish and Nasikh as poets, and of Lakhnavi and Dihlavi poetry as bodies of literature, reproduce the wide variety of elements and features found in classical Urdu poetry as a whole.

Āb-i Ḥayāt serves as an illustration of how myths can be born and legends sustained. Though a document of great interest and value to social and cultural historians, it cannot always be relied upon for factual accuracy. Rather, as Muhammad Sadiq has said, the abiding value of

Āb-i Ḥayāt lies in its vivid picture of the cultural milieu of the waning Mughal empire's literary and social élite. There is unquestionably much that this work has contributed to the world of Urdu letters. The time and circumstances of its publication, together with the position Azad enjoyed in Indo-Muslim culture, have ensured for *Āb-i Ḥayāt* a subtle authority which leaves little room for challenge. Its invulnerability stands, preventing even its own literary descendants—were they so inclined—from questoning a number of deeply-held beliefs Azad puts forth as fact. The most important of these, for the purposes of this study, are his convictions that Muslim culture in India was in distressing decline, inferior to that of the Mughals' glorious past, and that the expression of culture in Lucknow was a chief example of the present age's unworthiness. Recall Sadiq's assessment of *Āb-i Ḥayāt* as a cultural chronicle:

> It is really a living book, in the sense that it is not the picture of a world dead and embalmed; but a living page torn out of the past, which was, perhaps, never present, but which, as presented to us, throbs with life, and is, therefore, real.[24]

In other words Sadiq astutely observes that the veracity of cultural images and stereotypes is not as important as the affirmation which they provide to members of the culture concerning who they are and where they came from.

Nowhere in *Āb-i Ḥayāt* does Azad expressly state that Lakhnavi poetry constitutes a separate school of Urdu poetry. Nor does he ever come right out and say that either Nasikh or Atish is not a major poet of the nineteenth century. He devotes about fifty pages—a substantial portion of his book—to discussing their lives and work. In fact, the thirty-five pages devoted to Nasikh equal the amount of space given to Ghalib, and are slightly more than Azad devotes to either Sauda or Mir.[25] Yet one must ask what sort of information is contained in those pages on Nasikh and Atish. What tone does Azad choose for his treatment of the Lakhnavi masters? Anecdotes about Nasikh range from reports of his gluttony[26] as we have seen, to accounts of his feisty temperament and the quarrels he had with everyone from his rival, Atish, through the Prime Minister of Avadh, to the ruler himself.[27] Such accounts do create a rather subjective impression. Of the thirty-five pages on Nasikh, fully half involve this sort of anecdotal material about his habits and lifestyle.

Still, interpreting *Āb-i Ḥayāt* is a complicated business. Intermingled with these anecdotes are genuine comments in the realm of literary criticism. And Azad does defend Nasikh's right to follow a style which, even if unpopular or not to the Maulana's personal taste, has its precedent in the Persian and Urdu literary tradition.[28] A little less than a third of the Nasikh section is comprised of such comments. Azad mentions that Nasikh has a tendency toward such stylistic elements as *nāzuk khayālī; sakht-o sangīn alfāẓ* (unnecessarily difficult lexical items which obscure the verse's meaning); *khayāl bandī* and *dushvār pasandī* (love of difficult and complicated images); *phasīnḍe alfāẓ;*[29] *taṣavvuf* (mystical themes); and *namak-i zarāfat* in language (spicy witticisms).[30] Later critics have clearly incorporated Azad's insights into their own terms of analysis. For example, most of the above characteristics seem to be implied by the terms *ri'āyat-i lafẓī* and *maẓmūn āfirīnī*, perhaps the two most common characterizations of Lucknow's poetic style in twentieth century criticism.

Azad is indeed a masterful rhetorician and diplomat. While drawing a great deal of attention to linguistic usage as a primary deficiency of Lakhnavi poetry in his section of critical comments on Nasikh's poetry, he strongly suggests that Atish, on the other hand, is not too difficult or abstruse, but rather that he is refreshingly simple.[31] Yet Azad will not commit himself to forthright statements of his own preference. He ends by saying that

> In my own opinion there is no reason to fault either of the two rivals or their followers, since there is no lack of accomplishment on either side. Rather, they were of two different dispositions, therefore their tastes were different. People can say whatever they will . . .[32]

Once again, Azad's discussion of Atish reiterates a polarisation between the two Lakhnavi *ustāds*.

Nasikh, the exemplar of the Lakhnavi style, which Azad suggests is not quite up to standard, is given about three times as much space as Atish, to whom literary criticism has been consistently more sympathetic. The section on him is only fourteen pages long. Of this, three-and-a-half pages comprise the *intikhāb* of his ghazals; about five contain specific examples of poetry with critical commentary; and five contain biographical information on Atish, including a brief list of his most famous pupils. There is only one anecdote about Atish which does not specifically relate to his poetry, it relates to his fondness for the company of his pupils and his regard for his great rival, Nasikh.[33]

In short, Azad seems to view Atish quite sympathetically. Even when he discusses questionable language use in Atish's poetry, he is inclined to consider these as "words which reflect the difference between the eastern and western idioms."[34] By contrast, the selection on Nasikh and language reform—for which Lucknow is famous to this day—is limited to a few expressions. Even these refinements he scrupulously credits to Nasikh's pupil Rashk (who presented his own work merely as an edited version of his late *ustād's* work)[35] rather than to Nasikh himself. Once again, Nasikh's contribution to Urdu literature is effectively diminished.

Despite his apparent prejudice against poets like Nasikh, and his strong partisanship in favour of his own *ustād* Zauq, Azad, in *Āb-i Ḥayāt*, contributes much invaluable information about major poets that might otherwise be lost to modern Urdu readers. He also conveys a deeply felt critical sense about Urdu literature. His observations on Lakhnavi language reflect a genuine concern about the directions in which Urdu was moving as it continued to develop as a literary language. This concern is not superficial by any means. The significance of Azad's specific comments regarding Lakhnavis' command of language, such as that which related Atish's "mispronunciation" of the word *begam* (or *begum* as the case may be), may not be fully apprehended by the outsider. Yet they certainly convey a crucial connection between how a language is spoken and what that speech tells about its speaker. Language—like the literature for which it is a vehicle—is a reflection of a speaker's identity, of what his or her values are. Since the ebb of Mughal culture and its values is Azad's primary inspiration for writing *Āb-i-Ḥayāt*, the reflection of that ebb in Lakhnavi language spoke worlds to the Maulana. Although such differences in dialect or idiom alone would not justify a designation of separate poetic schools—and indeed we reiterate that Azad did not in fact make such a formal designation—their weight in a culture which defines itself a great deal by language must not go unrecognised. That Azad conveyed this aspect of cultural identification so strongly leaves little wonder that his writing has proved to be the cornerstone of Urdu literary criticism, and perhaps the single most important monument of self-identification to many Indian Muslims.

NOTES

1. M. Sadiq, *Azad: His Life and Works*, Lahore: West-Pak Publishing Co. Ltd., 1965, p. 47.
2. Ibid.
3. Azad does not necessarily claim to be the original source for much of the information he presents. *Āb-i Ḥayāt* is a compilation of vast amounts of material gleaned from numerous sources. For example, M. Sadiq credits the source of much of Azad's biographical and anecdotal information to an earlier work, the *Majmū'a-i Naghz, or Tazkira-i Shu'arā-i Urdū* by Hakim Abul Qasim Mir Qudrat-Ullah Qasim, (Sadiq, *M.H. Azad*, p. 140).
4. Azad, *Āb-i-Ḥayāt*, p. 339.
5. Three other Lakhnavi poets were included in *Āb-i-Ḥayāt*, namely Mir Khaliq, Mir Anis, and Mirza Dabir, but they were not ghazal poets, and it is the ghazal with which critical literature has generally been concerned. Khaliq was likely included out of respect for his father, Mir Hasan; while Anis and Dabir, as Urdu's greatest *marṣiya* writers, could hardly be ignored altogether. He also mentions Jur'at and Insha, but these two poets are not considered to be part of the Fifth Epoch, the time when the Delhi-Lucknow distinction is alleged to have first been manifest; and both migrated to Lucknow as mature artists, so it is questionable as to which *markaz* to associate them with.
6. This is mildly counteracted by the assiduous lip service he pays Lucknow, along with Delhi, as a *sanad*, or established centre of cultural authority, from whose example all Indian Muslims took inspiration. Cf. *Āb-i-Ḥayāt*, pp. 66-67.
7. Not only is Atish established as Nasikh's polar opposite, he is even called a Dihlavi type poet by one critic, Z.A. Siddiqi, in *Kulliyāt-i Ātish*, Allahabad: Ram Narayan Lal Beni Madhav, 1972, Introduction. The implications of this claim will be discussed later on. For now, suffice it to say that Z.A. Siddiqi is not alone in labelling Atish more a "Dihlavi style" poet than a Lakhnavi.
8. *Āb-i-Ḥayāt*, p. 66.
9. It will later be discussed how the modern critic Shah Abdus Salam, in *Dabistān-i Ātish* (Delhi: Maktaba Jami'ah Limited, 1977) extends this polarization to positing two separate *dabistāns* for the pupils of Nasikh and Atish.
10. Cf. *Āb-i-Ḥayāt*, p. 205 in which Azad tells of Mir's refusal to pass the time with a Lakhnavi travelling companion en route from Delhi to Lucknow by conversing, lest his own diction be compromised by the exchange—"*Āp kā shughal hai merī zabān kharāb ho jātī hai.*"
11. *Op. cit.*, p. 354. *Tāṣīr* refers to the heart of the audience being touched by the idea-content of a *she'r*.

12. For further discussion of where "grand and lofty" diction is—and is not—considered appropriate see Chapter XII's discussion of *sharāfat*.
13. *Āb-i-Ḥayāt*, p. 389.
14. Later in the present work it will be discussed in the context of Hali, Azad and other early Urdu reformist critics. See especially Chapters VI and XII below.
15. In subsequent editions Azad explains that the first edition of *Āb-i-Ḥayāt* could contain very little biographical information on Nasikh because the author had been unable to find any. However, he was later supplied with a good deal of anecdotal information from a family friend, and these are the anecdotes referred to above.
16. *Āb-i-Ḥayāt*, p. 356.
17. Ibid.
18. Ibid: "*Khvāja Sāhib ke mo'taqid kahte haiñ kih jin logoñ ne ghazal ke 'uṣūl ko samjhā hai ya'nī Fārsī meñ Khvāja Ḥāfiẓ aur Shaikh Sa'dī se aur Urdū meñ Soz, Mīr aur Jur'at se sanad pā'ī voh use ghazal na kahenge. Magar yih bāt aisī girift ke qābil nahīñ kyonkih Fārsī meñ bhī Jalāl, Asīr, Qāsim Mashhadī, Bedil aur Naṣīr 'Alī vaghairah ustād ho guẓre haiñ jinhoñ ne apne nāzuk khayāliyoñ kī badaulat "khayāl bandī" aur ma'nī yāb laqab hāsil kiyā hai. Shaikh Ṣāḥib ne un kī ṭarz ikhtiyār kī to kyā burā kiyā?*"
19. Cf. titles of literary studies such as *Ghālib kī Shakhsiyat aur Shā'irī* — "Ghalib's Personality and Poetry"—by Rashid Ahmad Siddiqi, Delhi: Department of Urdu, Delhi University, 1969.
20. *Āb-i-Ḥayāt*, pp. 387-89.
21. The reference is to Emperor Jahangir [r. 1605-1627] and his consort, Nur Jahan. See *Āb-i-Ḥayāt*, p. 356.
22. The Mughals' mother-tongue was originally Turkish even though their court language was Persian.
23. *Āb-i-Ḥayāt*, pp. 390-91.
24. Sadiq, *Azad: His Life and Works*, p. 53.
25. The section on Mir consists of twenty-eight pages of text, and that on Sauda is thirty-two pages long. Cf. *Āb-i-Ḥayāt*, pp. 203-231; and 148-180, respectively.
26. Azad, *op. cit.*, p. 347.
27. *Op. cit.*, pp. 352-56, passim.
28. As in the excerpts from *Āb-i-Ḥayāt*, p. 356 cited above.
29. It is unclear what is meant by this phrase.
30. Azad, *op. cit.*, pp. 347; 356-62.
31. *Āb-i-Ḥayāt*, p. 356.
32. *Op. cit.*, p. 361.
33. *Āb-i-Ḥayāt*, p. 397.
34. *Āb-i-Ḥayāt*, p. 394.

35. I have never seen a copy of this work, but various scholars in India agree to its existence, e.g. Professor Naiyar Masud of Lucknow University and Shamsur Rahman Faruqi.

CHAPTER VI

Lakhnavi Poetry in Hali's *Muqaddma-i She'r-o Shā'irī*

The *Muqaddma-i She'r-o Shā'irī* (1893)[1] is the second pioneering work of Urdu literary criticism, and is of rather a different nature than Azad's *Āb-i Ḥayāt*. Originally written and published as the introduction to Hali's *dīvān*, the *Muqaddma* is a treatise on how to reform Urdu poetry, especially the ghazal. Though different in its main thrust from *Āb-i Ḥayāt*, Hali's work has had an influence no less significant on the development of a critical framework in Urdu literary theory. A devout Muslim, Hali was dedicated to using his own literary efforts to advance the cause of Indian Islam. Because of his piety, his conversance with Western literature, and his well-known association with the great *ustād* Mirza Ghalib, Hali commands a tremendous respect in the world of Urdu letters. His word is considered no less authoritative than that of Maulana Azad.

As was mentioned in the earlier outline of the Two School theory's genesis in literary criticism, Lakhnavi poets—and discussion of Lucknow in general—figure much less prominently in the *Muqaddma* than in *Āb-i-Ḥayāt*. Nowhere are they singled out—either individually or as a group—for specific scrutiny by Hali. A very few examples of verse by Nasikh and Atish are presented in illustration of Hali's enumerations of where change is needed, and only one *she'r*, by Atish, is cited for poetic virtue. In fact Lakhnavi poetry is mentioned almost incidentally to the *Muqaddma's* focal discussion of the fate of Urdu literature.

Yet this second work of literary analysis has been instrumental in forming a critical framework for assessing Urdu poetry in the modern era, and Hali's notions of what constitute "natural poetry"[2] later became integrated into criticism's full-blown Two School theory. As such, they have had a crucial impact on Urdu critics' analysis of Lakhnavi poetry.

Also mentioned earlier was the association of both Azad and Hali with groups of literary reformers.[3] Both men were concerned about, and motivated by, the alarming decline of Muslim culture in late-nineteenth century India. But while *Āb-i-Ḥayāt* was a monument to Indo-Muslim culture's former glory—to traditions which were dear to Azad's heart and which he regretted to see die—the primary emphasis of the *Muqaddma* is to impress upon its audience the importance of incorporating the reforms outlined by its author into a fresh, revitalised literature for Indian Muslims. The difference may be expressed as follows: Azad's point of view was inclined toward a glorification of the old aesthetics, rather than the discovery of new solutions for Indo-Muslim culture.[4] One infers that Azad sought reforms which would involve a re-establishment or revitalisation of traditional standards and practices. The internal standards would be drawn from the example set by the great Dihlavi poets, who, in opposition to the Lakhnavis, are presented as adherents to the traditional aesthetic of Persian poetry. This is Azad's frame of reference. It renders quite comprehensible his stress on perceived cultural and literary differences between Delhi and Lucknow as deliberate. Also understandable is Azad's reader's inference that these differences may have been perversely instigated by the Lakhnavis and causal in the decline of Mughal culture.[5]

Hali, on the other hand, blames Mughal decline on a sort of pervasive moral lassitude in Muslim society, tying it to the military and political decline of the Mughals in the face of British territorial expansion. He seeks salvation in adoption of Western modes: since Westerners were the new conquerors of India their culture must, therefore, be more vital than that of Indian Islam.[6] This contrast in outlook is reminiscent of that which existed between the Western-looking "Aligarh School" and Deoband's Islamic revivalists.[7] They will be discussed, briefly, in the concluding chapter of this study.

The reforms Hali calls for are based on his understanding of Western literary principles. He had been introduced to the writing of Milton, Macaulay and a few other English writers[8] during the course of his employment by the British government, in which capacity he corrected translations of English works into Urdu. The primary conditions for good poetry are cited in the *Muqaddma* as *takhaiyyul* (imagination), *kā'ināt kā muṭāla'a* (consideration of existing things), and *tafaḥḥuṣ-i alfāẓ* (scrutiny of word choice);[9] and later on, essentially referring to the same desired conditions, the qualities are listed as *sādagī* (simplicity), *josh* (passion, emotion) and *aṣlīyat* (reality).[10] These principles are openly borrowed from Milton's exhortation that poetry should "have simplicity, should spring from emotion, and should be based on truth."[11]

It is not within the scope of this particular study to address the full scale of Hali's literary vision. That has been done by other scholars.[12] The purpose here is to examine the extent to which Hali's *Muqaddma*, in contributing to the development of literary criticism in Urdu, helped to establish the literary reputation of Lucknow and so to pave the way for the articulation of a Two School theory, based on *markazī* distinction.

Consistent with the difference in thrust from Azad's work, the *Muqaddma* differs structurally from its predecessor. *Āb-i Ḥayāt* had vaguely followed the *taẕkira* format—while also providing a narrative describing the historical evolution of Urdu literature—and thereby reiterated the established method for presentation of secondary literature in the Perso-Arabic tradition.

The *Muqaddma*, however, is the first book of criticism in Urdu not based on the *taẕkira* model. Hali's *Muqaddma* employs a new rhetorical technique for writing in Urdu. Having the form of an essay, it is a didactic call for reforms in poetry and society through their interdependence upon one another. Along the way, it traces the history of Islamic literary antecedents to Urdu. Hali assesses the state of Urdu during his own time (the assessment is not favourable) and then outlines what changes would be required for the sort of reform he envisions. He does not focus upon the work of specific poets, presenting brief *intik͟hābs* of their verse, as a *taẕkira* writer would do. He however draws heavily upon a few poets of his own choosing in corroborating arguments about what is good and bad in poetry in general. Hali's approach—in both the *Muqaddma's* formal and analytical scope—constitutes a significant turning point for Urdu letters.

In further contrast to the structure of *Āb-i Ḥayāt*, the *Muqaddma* manifests less concern with the Delhi-Lucknow rivalry. Hali believes that Urdu poetry *as a whole* requires serious reform, and he does little to bolster the idea that two separate schools exist, or that different standards pertain in the two seats of Urdu culture.[13] To the extent that he offers polar opposites of "what is good and what is bad," the two poles would be Indian (Urdu) literature and Western (English) literature rather than Dihlavi and Lakhnavi. In the matter of language, Hali writes:

> Those people who consider themselves masters of language, that is, the people of Delhi or the people of Lucknow, should not take too much pride in this matter, thinking that the authority of their particular idiom should be observed. They must remember that if they do not take care to improve and protect their language . . . it will neither progress nor develop in poetry or prose.[14]

In other words, rather than place one *markaz* in a position of higher authority than other, Hali designates both places as the bastions of cultural authority in the Urdu world. In fact he asserts that differences between the two centres are minimal anyway. Hali's emphasis is on the imminent danger facing both Delhi and Lucknow as sustainers of Indo-Muslim culture; and on the urgent need for practitioners of language in both places to pay heed to the changing needs of language and literature in a changing society, lest they completely lose their artistic vitality.[15]

Given that for Hali both *marākiz* together represent a dual authority to Indian Muslims, there would seem to be little point in promoting an identification of oneself as Lakhnavi or Dihlavi: both are Urdu speakers, and must address themselves to the requirements of Muslim society in a changing India. One of the greatest changes of his times is the loss of a "ruler vs. ruled" relationship between Muslims and Hindus—they are now all ruled by the British. Implicitly acknowledging this change, Hali remarks upon the need for Urdu's leadership to look thoroughly at its own environment, not just at the Islamic antecedents of Urdu, to Indian influences as well:

> It is not enough to simply follow in the footsteps of Dihlavi and Lakhnavi languages if [we are] to achieve high standards in Urdu. . . rather it is also necessary to pay attention to Arabic and Hindi. . ..[16]

This prescription runs counter to the general nineteenth century trend to make Urdu more esoteric, more elegant and elaborate, by discarding Indian words and replacing them with vocabulary borrowed from Persian and Arabic. Examples of this Persianate language are to be found in most of the Urdu poets of the century.[17] In this way Hali advocates a new sort of identification for Indian Muslims, one which emphasises the "Indian" as well as the "Muslim." Within such an "umbrella" identification the importance of individual city-identification is diminished; thus comparisons of Lucknow and Delhi in cultural terms are not at all emphasised in the *Muqaddma*.

The *Muqaddma* elaborates upon a number of issues given briefer mention in *Āb-i Ḥayāt*. For example, Hali echoes Azad's decrying of "worn-out themes" in the ghazal, the need to have poetry "fully express our every goal and every kind of desire in our hearts."[18] Azad did not argue this point prominently, but it contributes significantly to the major thrust of Hali's treatise. "Worn-out themes" run contrary to the concepts of *aṣlīyat*, or *kā'ināt kā muṭāla'a*, and interfere with the achievement of a poetry which is "natural." As did Azad, Hali decries over-elaborated, or artificial language. In his eyes, such language contributes to an emotional shallowness, and thus to the moral decline of literature.

And yet it must be realized that the *Muqaddma* contains a number of contradictions. Hali makes the general statement that "artifice in words (*san'at-i alfāẓ*) has caused infinite damage to our poetry, in fact to our entire literature,"[19] for example, but then contradicts himself on the very next page by laying that crime at the feet of Lakhnavi poets only:"

> In general, artificial and ingenious constructions and rhetorical flourishes are rarely—in fact, it must be said, never—found in the poets of Delhi; while a number of the Lakhnavi poets made its strict application compulsory. And in comparison with the people of Delhi, even the most ordinary Lakhnavi poets were overly concerned with *ri'āyat-lafẓī* (word-play).[20]

This particular statement is not corroborated by examples of Lakhnavi poetry to illustrate its concern with *ri'āyat-i lafẓī*, nor, indeed, to illustrate what Hali means by the term. Furthermore, the claim runs contrary to the impression given by corroborative examples presented elsewhere throughout the *Muqaddma*. Those corroborative examples are drawn almost exclusively from Dihlavi poets (when they are not drawn from Persian), and would appear to serve as instances of *san'at-i alfāẓ* (artifice in words), improper treatment of themes (*maẓāmīn*), and other poetic defects in addition to excellences achieved by the same poets.[21]

There are eight *she'rs* by Atish in the *Muqaddma* and two by Nasikh. Though these numbers seem almost too few to extrapolate any particular point of view at all on Hali's part, they do appear to reinforce the Delhi-Lucknow and Atish-Nasikh polarisations that were suggested in *Āb-i-Ḥayāt*, and which have been since reiterated in succeeding criticism. Both *she'rs* by Nasikh are presented as examples of "unnatural" poetry, as are six of those by Atish, while two of Atish's verses are presented for their literary merit. On pages 85 and 86 two sets of three *she'rs* each are presented as illustrations of failed "naturalness:"

فرصت اک دم عہدِ طفلی میں نہ رونے سے ملی
پرورش پایا ہوا ہوں دامانِ سیلاب کا

Furṣat ik dam 'ahd-i ṯiflī meñ na rone se milī
Parvarish pāyā hu'ā hūñ dāmān-i sailāb kā

In my childhood not for a moment
Did I gain respite from crying:
I've been brought up in the skirts of the flood.

جمعِ تن ہو گیا راہِ عدم میں نذرِ گور
بوجھ اٹھایا تھا مگر ٹھگ کیلئے اسباب کا

Jama'-i tan ho gayā rāh-i 'adam meñ naẕr-i gor
Bojh uṭhāyā thā magar ṭhag ke līye asbāb kā

Along the road to non-being
the effects of my body
became an offering for the grave:
It was as if I'd borne this burden
for the sole sake of the robber.

ساحلِ مقصود دیکھا میں نے جا کر گور میں
ڈوبنا کشتیٔ تن کو مژدہ تھا پایاب کا

Sāḥil-i maqṣūd dekhā maiñ ne jā kar gor meñ
Ḍūbnā kashtī-i tan ko muzhda thā pāyāb kā

I went to the grave
and saw the desired shore:
The drowning of the ship of my body
brought the glad tidings
of feet touching the ground.[22]

Hali's criticism of these first three verses is that "while one might, with great difficulty, extract some sense of reality (*aṣlīyat*) from them, there is neither, as is apparent, *sādagī* in their expression, nor *josh*."[23]

Unfortunately, the truth of Hali's assessment—while very likely unimpeachable—is not necessarily apparent, and is not elaborated upon as are other such claims elsewhere.[24]

Of the second set Hali says, "although these three *she'rs* are unblemished, apart from simplicity of expression—as is apparent—there is neither *aṣlīyat* nor *josh*:"[25]

تری تقلید سے کبکِ دری نے ٹھوکریں کھائیں
چلا جب جانور انساں کی چال اس کا چلن بگڑا

Tirī taqlīd se kabk-i darī ne ṭhokareñ khāyīñ
Chalā jab jānvar insān kī chāl us kā chalan bigṛā

Imitating you
the mountain partridge stumbled.
When an animal walks like a human being
its gait is compromised.

نہیں بے وجہ ہنسنا اس قدر زخمِ شہیداں کا
تری تلوار کا منہ کچھ نہ کچھ اے تیغ زن بگڑا

Nahīñ be-vajh hansnā is qadar zakhm-i shahīdān kā
Tirī talvār kā munh kuchh na kucch ae tegh-i zan bigṛā

The wounds of the martyrs
do not laugh for no reason:
Swordswoman, your weapon
seems to have lost face.

امانت کی طرح رکھا زمیں نے روزِ محشر تک
نہ اک مو کم ہوا اپنا نہ اک تارِ کفن بگڑا

Amānat kī ṭaraḥ rakhā zamīñ ne roz-i maḥshar tak
Na ik mū kam hu'ā apnā na ik tār-i kafan bigṛā

The ground provided safekeeping
till the Day of Judgement:
Not a hair was out of place
not a strip of my shroud decayed.

Again, Hali does not elaborate upon these *she'rs*' manifest lack of *aṣlīyat* and *josh*.

The *she'r* below is cited in the context of a generation-by-generation sampler of classic treatment of *'ishq* in the Urdu ghazal. The implied honour to Atish is considerable, since he is the representative of the Fifth Epoch[26] here, following Mir, Sauda, and Shah Abru:

تختۂ نردِ عشق دل کھیلا جو حسنِ یار سے
چھٹ گئے ایسے مرے چھکے کہ ششدر ہو گیا

Ta<u>kh</u>ta nard-i 'ishq dil khelā jo ḥusn-i yār se
Chhuṭ gaye aise mire chhakke kih shashdar ho gayā

On the chess-board of love
where the heart
squares off against the Beloved
I'm bewildered into checkmate.

In the final appearance of Atish's poetry in the *Muqaddma*, the following *she'r* is cited for how true its expression is to idiomatic speech:

چال ہے مجھ ناتواں کی مرغِ بسمل کی تڑپ
ہر قدم پر ہے یقیں یاں رہ گیا واں رہ گیا

Chāl hai mujh nātavāñ kī murg<u>h</u>-i bismil kī taṛap
Har qadam par hai yaqīñ yāñ rah gayā vāñ rah gayā

My exhausted gait
is the flapping of a wounded bird:
Every step I'm certain is my last
—or maybe the last-but-one.[27]

The fact that a satisfactory translation yet eludes this writer corroborates Hali's assessment that this *she'r* is completely idiomatic.

The *Muqaddma's* only two examples of Nasikh's verse appear in the introductory discussion of "natural poetry." Directly following a list of eight *she'rs* which manifest "naturalness"[28] Hali begins his examples of failed "naturalness" with this verse by Nasikh:

کبھی ہے دھیان عارض کا کبھی یادِ مژہ دل کو
کبھی ہے خار پہلو میں کبھی گلزار پہلو میں

Kabhī hai dhyān 'āriz̤ kā kabhī yād-i mizha dil ko
Kabhī hai khār pahlū meñ kabhī gul-zār pahlū meñ

Sometimes I contemplate her cheek
sometimes my heart recalls an eyelash.
Sometimes I have a thorn in my side
sometimes a garden by my side.[29]

Of this first example Hali opines that Nasikh employs reasonably natural language, but that the *she'r* cannot be called natural in meaning. He says :

> This verse can only be called natural in terms of vocabulary. But in terms of meaning it cannot be [called natural]. Doubtless contemplation of the beloved can bring the *'āshiq* joy or pain. But when it brings joy, then the contemplation must be of both the cheek and the eyelash. And when it brings pain then the pain must come from contemplation of both [cheek and eyelash]. It cannot be that eyelashes—which resemble thorns—can have the effect of thorns from contemplation; and the cheek—which resembles the rose—cannot have the effect of a garden just by being imagined.[30]

In other words, Hali considers the verse lacking in *aṣlīyat*. The other example of Nāsikh's poetry is:

جائے کافورِ سحر چاہیئے کافورِ حنوط
یہ شبِ ہجر ہے یارو شبِ دیجور نہیں

Jā-i kāfūr-i saḥr chāhiye kāfūr-i ḥunūṭ
yih shab-i hijr hai yāro shab-i daijūr nahīñ

What's needed, Love,
in place of the soothing break of dawn
are embalming salts:
it's not winter's longest darkest night
but the night of separation.[31]

This second *she'r*, says Hali, is perfectly plausible because it elaborates upon the familiar theme of how long a night in separation from the beloved can seem; and because it is quite plausible that, when each minute and each hour seem to take as long to pass by as a whole lifetime, an *'āshiq* might well become agitated enough to desire death.[32] But, says Hali, "Nasikh's expression in this *she'r* is so far removed from regular Urdu parlance that it can in no way be considered a natural expression."[33]

Hali's specific objection to the second of the above pair of *she'rs*, then, is that its language is unnatural because it is not colloquial. Recalling that Azad objected to Nasikh on the grounds that his language was too elaborate and that his admiration of Atish's poetry lay in its colloquialism, it would seem that the primary criterion of analysis for both Hali and Azad is language usage, specifically *sādagī* (simplicity). The word *ḥanūṭ* (embalming) is certainly not colloquial—in fact, it does not even appear in Platts' dictionary. The expression *daijūr* or *shab-i daijūr* is not in common parlance, but is not as obscure as *ḥanūṭ*, and it does appear regularly throughout Nasikh's *dīvān*. Hali does not specify, but one wonders if his objection to the *she'r* doesn't lie more in its slightly macabre visual image than in its actual vocabulary. In other words, is Hali's objection really to the language of this *she'r* or is he, rather, judging the appropriateness of introducing *kāfūr-i ḥanūṭ* into a *she'r* whose basic theme is the highly romantic and charged night of separation?

Except for one verse by Atish, and other examples culled from *marṡiyas* by Anis,[34] Lakhnavi poetry is presented in the *Muqaddma* as deficient. On the other hand, examples of poetry considered to fulfill the requirements of *josh*, *aṣlīyat* and *sādagī* come from Arabic, Persian, and (in Urdu) certain Dihlavi poets.[35] While Dihlavi poets also appear occasionally to illustrate faulty verse, their appearance in other places in a favourable light contributes to a more balanced picture of Dihlavi poetry in general. Overall, except for two *she'rs* by Nasikh and eight by Atish, the Lakhnavi ghazal is ignored altogether. Thus, whether inadvertently or deliberately, Hali's treatise on Urdu poetry may be seen to condemn Lucknow by omission.

A possible explanation for the paucity of Lakhnavi poets among Hali's examples is that he was much less familiar with their work than with that of Dihlavi poets. After all, Hali was educated in Delhi. Not only was he influenced by his patron, Navab Mustafa Khan Shefta (1806-69) as well as the great master, Ghalib; but he would also have had much occasion to hear the verses of the poet laureate, Zauq, and other contemporaries such as Momin and Bahadur Shah Zafar. It is no surprise, then, that these poets figure so prominently in Hali's examples of Urdu poetry. Despite the impressive volume of foreign literature apparently at his fingertips (he quotes Arabic, Persian, and even cites the example of Hebrew poetry in his disussion of *josh*)[36] the dearth of Lakhnavi poetry in the *Muqaddma* suggests that Hali is not as well-read as his critical predecessor; or that he is—even if benignly—prejudiced against Lucknow, that he considers the work of Lucknow's poets generally unworthy of comment. While Azad had little good to say about Nasikh, his remarks did indicate a respectable familiarity with the poet's work.[37]

Despite other differences in outlook, Hali is a product of literary circumstances similar to those of Azad, and they share certain assumptions and attitudes. Hali unwittingly bolsters a number of the same myths and prejudices that are expressed by the Maulana. At the very least, he manifests preferences which have become incorporated into the post-classical tastes of the general Urdu audience. The dearth of Lakhnavi poetry in the *Muqaddma* is the primary reflection of this. Secondary is the fact that Atish is still looked upon with greater favour than Nasikh. Consistent with the standard treatment of both Lakhnavi *ustāds* in Urdu criticism, the *Muqaddma* features considerably less of Nasikh's poetry than of Atish's. Similarly, the one example of Lakhnavi poetry which is called "good" (because of being colloquial) is by Atish rather than Nasikh, the "Imam of the Lucknow School."

Hali follows other points of conventional wisdom, too, sounding the most like Azad when he makes comments such as this:

> In Lucknow the situation was [such that] poetry was heard in greater quantity than in Delhi ... but it is unfortunate that the footsteps [of Lakhnavi literature] have not marched in step with the times. As much as literature has been propagated, that much have Lakhnavis departed from the proper path of progress . . .[38]

A bit further on, using criteria also employed by Azad in *Āb-i Ḥayāt*, Hali discusses defective idiomatic usage in Lakhnavi language, judging that the abandonment of certain phrases is

> exceedingly desirable, because it is along such lines that differentiation between Dihlavi and Lakhnavi language is born. If the people of Lucknow were to discard such words then we could introduce many others, and no great change in the scope of the language would result from discontinuing those words.[39]

An example of Lakhnavi diction discussed is the use of *ujyālā* for *ujāle* (morning brightness). One wonders how significant the employment or absence of this word could be in such a rich lexical sphere as that of the ghazal, and Hali does not elaborate. It is possible that he draws particular attention to this idiom primarily because Azad had pointed it out in *Āb-i Ḥayāt*.[40]

So Hali seems to follow critical convention in implying that where there is a difference between Lakhnavi and Dihlavi idiom, the Dihlavi ought to be preferred. And yet, discussing the decline of straightforward (*sīdhī-sādī*) language, Hali mentions a Dihlavi as well as a number of Lakhnavis:

> It was not that straightforward Urdu was abandoned completely in noble and learned society, rather that such language among intimates came to be seen as faulty, or *bāzārī*. This custom [of elaborate, fancy diction] came to dominate prose and poetry. In verse, in the *dīvāns* of Jur'at and Nasikh; and in prose, in the *Bāgh-o Bahār* and *Fasāna-i Ajā'ib* . . . there is plenty of proof of this. . .[41]

To recapitulate: Hali does not appear to promote the policy of Delhi-Lucknow differentiation in the way that we see it threading in and out of the pages of *Āb-i Ḥayāt*. He says that he does not consider differences between the two cities, at least in terms of idiom, to be significant. He names the major poets associated with Lucknow[42] along with the major Dihlavis, in his exhortation to the new generation to study the work of their predecessors in Urdu literature, and to learn from the meritorious example set by those predecessors.

And yet Hali contributes to the Two School theory by tacitly accepting the validity of Dihlavi idiom over Lakhnavi; by drawing attention to idiomatic usage as a distinguishing feature between Dihlavi and Lakhnavi poetry; and by presenting Dihlavi *ustāds* almost exclusively as the Urdu poets whose work constitutes "*necaral* poetry." Hali quite overlooks Lakhnavi poets except in the few instances already cited. By the time Abdus Salam Nadvi wrote his *She'r-ul Hind* in 1926, it was logical for him to assume that the explicit distinction he drew between Lakhnavi and Dihlavi poetry as two separate schools, (largely because Lakhnavi poetry departed from the older tradition of Urdu and Persian literature) was neither new nor controversial. Rather, it was a succinct statement of a widespread and commonly-held literary judgement that had been made much earlier.

NOTES

1. The edition used for this study was published in Delhi: Maktaba-i Jami'a Limited, 1981.
2. "*Necaral shā'irī.*"
3. While Hali was associated with Sir Sayyid Ahmad Khan's Aligarh Movement, before the formation of the Aligarh Movement there were British-sponsored literary circles in Lahore. Perhaps the most important of these was the Anjuman-i Panjab, whose interest in "vernacular literature impregnated with the spirit of the West" [Sadiq, *Muhammad Husain Azad: His Life and Work*, Lahore: 1965, p. 24] may be seen as kindred in purpose to the Aligarh group. Azad was affiliated with this earlier group but not with the Aligarh Movement *per se*.
4. Recall that Sadiq had said: "*Āb-i Ḥayāt* is a memorial to the old loves and loyalties, doubly sacred because they had ceased to exist." *Azad: His Life and Works*, p. 48.
5. The above discussion focuses on ghazal reform, and neither addresses nor diminishes the separate issue of Hali's ideas on the new poetic form, *naẓm*.
6. See the *Muqaddma*, p. 192, where Hali explains why Western countries are "superior" in art, science and industry.
7. As it happens, Hali was associated with Aligarh. For fuller treatment of these reform movements, see David Lelyveld, *Aligarh's First Generation: Muslim Solidarity in British India*, Princeton: Princeton

University Press, 1978; and Barbara Daly Metcalf, *Islamic Revival in British India: Deoband, 1860-1900,* Princeton: Princeton University Press, 1982.

8. Sir Walter Scott's poetry is given brief discussion, for example; pp. 56-57, as is the work of Oliver Goldsmith, pp. 41-42. Of some interest is Laurel Steele's observation that Hali's exposure to these English classics would have come through versions translated into Urdu. See "Hali and his *Muqaddma*: The Creation of a Literary Attitude in Nineteenth Century India," pp. 1-45 in *Annual of Urdu Studies*, no. 1, 1981, p. 8.
9. *Muqaddma*, pp. 50-58.
10. *Op. cit.*, pp. 67-78.
11. *Op. cit.*, p. 68: "*Milton . . . kahtā hai ki she'r kī khūbī yih hai kih sāda ho, josh se bharā huā, aur aṣlīyat par mabnī ho.*"
12. Cf. Laurel Steele, *op. cit.*, Wahid Quraishi, ed. *Muqaddma She'r-o-Shā'irī*, reprint edition, Aligarh, 1977; Salihah Abid Husain, *Yādgār-i Hālī*, Aligarh, n.d.; Shuja'at 'Ali Sandilvi, *Hālī ba-Haiṣīyat-i Shā'ir*, Lucknow, 1960; Kalim ud-Din Ahmad, *Urdū Shā'irī par Ek Naẓar*; and Saiyid Masu'd Hasan Rizvi "Adīb", *Hamārī Shā'irī*, Lucknow, 1923, 1964; V. Alavi, *Hālī, Muqaddma aur Ham*, Allahabad, 1983; and Salim Ahmad, "*Naī Naẓm aur Pūrā Ādmī*," Karachi, 1962?
13. As will be demonstrated below, he does state that Dihlavi poets do not commit the "sin" of *ri'āyat-i lafẓī*, which he depicts as a primarily Lakhnavi "defect."
14. *Muqaddma*, p. 117.
15. The final chapter takes up the issue of the connection between this call for a reconstituted artistic vitality and the Aligarh Movement's desire to reclaim a favourable political and social position for Indian Muslims.
16. *Muqaddma*, p. 118.
17. Especially the great *ustāds* like Nasikh, Ghalib, Zauq and Shah Nasir, to name a few. These same poets comprise our own sample group in Chapter X's literary test of the Two School theory. See below.
18. *Āb-i Ḥayāt*, p. 81; *Muqaddma*, p.159.
19. *Muqaddma*, p. 183.
20. *Op. cit.*, p. 184.
21. See especially "unnatural" *she'rs* by Ghalib, Amir Minai and Zauq on p. 105 of the *Muqaddma*.
22. *Muqqadma*, p. 85.
23. Ibid.
24. See discussions of Nasikh's *she'rs* below.
25. *Muqaddma*, p. 86.
26. Hali does not divide literary eras quite the same way as Azad and Nadvi, but says that Atish may be considered to be of the fourth or fifth generation—*chauthā yā pānchvāñ ṭabqa*. p. 110.

27. *Muqaddma*, p. 180.
28. The *necural ash'ār* are by Mir Hasan, Zauq, Zafar, Momin, Dagh and Ghalib—all Dihlavis.
29. *Muqaddma*, p.104.
30. *Muqaddma*, p. 104.
31. *Op. cit.*, p. 111.
32. The desire for death is signified in the above *she'r* by the *'āshiq's* call for embalming fluid instead of the arrival of dawn.
33. "*Nāsikh kī tarz-i bayān Urdū kī ma'mūlī bol chāl se is qadar ba'id hai kih us ko kisī ṭaraḥ necural bayān nahīñ kahā jā saktā*". p. 111.
34. For example, see p. 74.
35. His examples include Ghalib, Zauq, Mir; and, secondarily, Dard, Shefta, and Momin, pp. 81-83.
36. *Muqaddma*, pp. 78-79.
37. In fact, it is interesting to note that the *intikhāb* of Nasikh's ghazals in *Āb-i Ḥayāt* draws largely upon the second *dīvān* which is far less known than the first divān, entitled *Daftar-i Pareshān*.
38. *Muqaddma*, pp. 117-118.
39. Ibid.
40. Azad, *Āb-i Ḥayāt*, pp. 371-72.
41. p. 158. *Bāgh-o Bahār* and *Fasāna-i Ajā'ib* were the works of writers Mir Amman, a Dihlavi, and Rajab Ali Beg Suroor, a Lakhnavi.
42. Jur'at, Insha, Mushafi, Nasikh, Atish, Vazir, Rind, Asir, Barq, Anis and Dabir, as well as others, p. 116.

CHAPTER VII

Assessing Nadvi's Exposition of the Two Schools

It will be established now that Abdus Salam Nadvi played a crucial role in the history of the Two School theory by being the first critic to call the poetry of Delhi and that of Lucknow "Urdu poetry's two separate schools."[1] More than that even, Nadvi explicitly enumerated and illustrated eight characteristics which distinguished the two schools. Most of them are criteria which had been suggested several decades before by Azad and Hali, but Hali and Azad had not explicitly stated them as the essential points of distinction.[2]

She'rul Hind's presentation of the Two School theory is the first and most methodical exposition of what literary differences distinguish the *dabistān-i Dillī* from the *dabistān-i Lakhna'u*.[3] Nadvi's explications are the most thorough—and the most concrete—of any in the Two School literature. As such, they provide the best test case for close scrutiny of the critical process in Urdu literature.

This section conducts a full study of the chapter in which Nadvi lays out his Two School theory. It consists of three elements: naming the *k͟huṣūṣīyāt* (special characteristics) of Lakhnavi poetry; illustrations of those *k͟huṣūṣīyāt*; and commentary or elaboration upon those illustrations.

The following are the eight characteristics of *She'rul Hind's* Delhi-Lucknow distinction. The points themselves will first be cited verbatim and later argued as fully as possible:

1. "The influence of the effeminacy which was born into Lucknow's society and population is manifestly apparent in its poetry as well. For example:

کسی کے محرم آبِ رواں کی یاد آئی
حباب کے جو برابر کبھی حباب آیا

Kisī ke maḥram-i-āb-i ravāñ kī yād ā'ī
Ḥabāb ke jo barābar kabhī ḥabāb āyā —Atish

Whenever a bubble
By another bubble rose
I thought of her brassiere
Of finest gauze.[4]

جلد رنگ اے دیدۂ خوں بار اب تارِ نگاہ
ہے محرّم اس پری پیکر کو ناڑا چاہیئے

Jald rang ae dīdah-i khūñ-bār ab tār-i nigāh
Hai muḥarram us parī paikar ko nāṛā chāhiye — Nasikh

Quickly now
O blood-dripping eyes
dye the thread of sight:
It's Mohurram,
That one with a fairy's countenance
Needs a thread to hand round her neck.[5]

and

کافر خطِ استوا بدن کا
تیری سونے کی کردھنی ہے

Kāfir khaṭ-i istivā badan kā
Terī sone kī kardhanī hai — Nasikh

Like the equator, beloved,
Your golden girdle
delineates the axes of your body.

In the case of these three *she'rs* it seems clear that the manifestation of effeminacy lies in the mention of *kardhanī* (girdle), *nāṛā* (drawstring) and *maḥram* (bodice or brassiere)—in other words, in the mention of feminine items of apparel.[6] Nadvi says further that

> These verses are but a handful out of a huge amount. However, if a thorough survey of the *dīvāns* of Lakhnavi poets were made, one could compile a veritable index of women's jewels, dress and adornments, often employing women's idiom—that of the *zanāna*.[7]

Another aspect of effeminacy cited by Nadvi is the occurrence of women's idiom in the verse of Lakhnavi poets just cited. He lists five *she'rs* by Rind—one of the most successful disciples of Atish—as illustrations, pointing out the phrases and words in women's idiom. They are as follows:[8] (1) an idiomatic use of the expression *maut ā'e* (may death come); (2) the phrase *Terī eṛī par karūñ sadqe meñ choṭī ḥūr kī*; (I would sacrifice a fairy's braid for your heel); (3) *'alam-i ḥaẓrāt-i 'abbās hī kī mār paṛe* (X will get a beating with the standard of Abbas, a flagbearer at Karbala); (4) the phrase *jalāpe meñ* (in the throes of pain, grief or envy); and (5) the expression *ānkheñ phūṭnā* (for the eyes to burst and run out, to become blind). Nadvi says, "Those words and phrases which we have underlined are all expressions of the *zanāna*. The poets of Delhi do not speak in women's idiom."

2. "The Dihlavi poets, as can be surmised from the charming *fārsī tarkībeñ* (Persian constructions) which fill their written work, respected and held to the customs established by their literary forebears..."

In substantiation of this claim Nadvi lists three *she'rs* by Ghalib; four by Momin; nine by Sayyid Zakariya Khan Zaki (1839-1903); and seven by Mir Mahdi Majruh. In each case he underlines the words or phrases which reflect charming and delightful *fārsi tarkībeñ*. He concludes this point with the following statement:

> But the works of Lakhnavi poets are completely devoid of these constructions. And even among Dihlavi poets, the work of Zauq and Shah Nasir do not manifest this style of composition, and the poetry of these two masters shows much similarity with that of Nasikh and Atish. Thus their style is not different from the Lakhnavi style; but we do not consider the Lakhnavi poets' style to be faulty for pure language is a thing also worthy of honour.[9]

3. "The poets of Delhi, in accordance with tradition, generally wrote short ghazals and therefore avoided superfluity and 'filler verses.'

But the Lakhnavi poets generally wrote very long ghazals, which resulted in ridiculous resolution of *qāfiyas* and, therefore, degraded themes."[10] Nadvi cites four *she'rs* by Atish—two pairs each of verse in the same *zamīn*—where the *qāfiyahs* and *radīfs* suffer as the result of elongated ghazals. The end-rhymes are *muḥāse paidā*[11] and *batāse* (a sweet):

لب شیریں کی تری چاشنی ممکن نہ ہوئی

رس سے شکر ہوئی شکر سے بتاسے پیدا

Lab-i shīrīñ kī tirī chāshnī mumkin na huī
Ras se shakkar huī shakkar se batāse paidā

It was impossible to savour
the taste of your sweet lips:
Sugarcane crystallized into sugar
and sugar blended into a sweet.

4. "The essential point of distinction between the writing of the poets of Lucknow and those of Delhi is that one finds very little expression of spiritual emotion in the Lakhnavi poets, and in its place [articulation of] the beloved's external attributes and endowments. For example curls, downy cheeks, bodice, brassiere and blouse, etc. are mentioned to such an extent that the pleasure of *taghazzul*[12] is greatly diminished in reading their *dīvāns*."[13]

Nadvi then lists five *she'rs* by Nasikh from the same ghazal. The first mentions a muslin dupatta (*malmal kā dupaṭṭā*); the second the beloved's velvet belly (*makhmal kā shikam*); the third the beloved's mount or conveyance (*gul kī savārī*, *nikahat-i gul*); the fourth a chafing-dish (*minqal*) and the beloved's fiery cheek (*ātish-i rukh*); and the fifth compares the beloved's ink-black eyes to collyrium. Nadvi concludes this point with the following sentence: "These few *she'rs* are just a fleeting example but the *dīvāns* of Nasikh and Atish are replete with this type of verse."

5. "In the matter of *ri'āyat-i lafẓī* [word play], it is the common practice of Lakhnavi poets, and they employed it with excessive baseness..."[14] The four *she'rs* of *ri'āyat-i lafẓī* which Nadvi lists are:

دلا سوتے میں قندِ لب کے خاطر خواہ بوسے لے
مثل مشہور ہے دنیا میں گڑ میٹھا ہے چوری کا

(i) Dilā sote maiñ qand-i lab ke khāṭir khvāh būse le
Maṣal mashhūr hai duniyā meñ guṛ mīṭhā hai chorī kā
—Husain Ali Khan Asar

Heart, as she sleeps
let me take kisses from those sugar lips
to my heart's content:
The whole world knows
how sweet is stolen candy.

Here the phrases *qand-i lab* (sugar lips) and *guṛ mīṭhā chorī kā* (Stolen molasses is always sweet) are noted as objectionable.

جو میٹھی میٹھی نظروں سے وہ دیکھے
کہوں آنکھوں کو میں بادامِ شیریں

(ii) Jo mīṭhī mīṭhī naẓroñ se voh dekhe
Kahūñ ānkhoñ ko maiñ bādām-i shīrīñ —Nasikh

I would call those eyes "sweet almonds"
that look with sweet, sweet glances.

Here the relationship between *mīṭhī mīṭhī* (sweet, sweet) and *bādām-i shīrīñ* (sweet almonds) is objectionable.

کیا لکھوں شورشِ دل کاغذ میں
تاؤ کاکل کی طرح کھائے گا

(iii) Kyā likhūñ shorish-i dil kāghaẓ meñ
Tā'o kākul kī ṭaraḥ khāyegā — Khalil

What can I write on paper
of the tumult in my heart?
It would curl up like her tresses.

In this verse the phrase *kākul kī ṭaraḥ tā'o khānā* (to curl like tresses of hair) is objectionable.[15]

وصل کی شب پلنگ کے اوپر
مثل چیتے کے وہ مچلتے ہیں

(iv) Vaṣl kī shab palang ke ūpar
Miṣl chīte ke voh machalte haiñ —Khalil

On the night of union
atop the bed
She struggles like a cheetah.[16]

6. "Commonness or degeneracy (*mubtaẓal*, the state of being *ibtiẓāl*, or degraded) is also a general characteristic of Lakhnavi poets."[17] Nadvi illustrates that characteristic with the following six *she'rs* by Nasikh and two from the same ghazal by Khalil:

دیکھ کر تجھ کو نہ کیونکر نعرہ زن ہوں سب رقیب
بیشتر کتوں کو بھکواتا ہے جلوہ ماہ کا

(i) Dekh kar tujh ko na kyonkar na'ra zan hoñ sab raqīb
Beshtar kuttoñ ko bhukvātā hai jalva māh kā

Why shouldn't my rivals
raise a hue and cry when they see you?
Dogs, too, go wild
at the sight of the moon.

استرہ منہ پہ جو پھرنے نہیں دیتا ہے بجا
محو دیندار سے کیونکر خطِ قرآن ہوتا

(ii) Ustara munh pe jo phirne nahīñ detā hai bajā
Maḥv dīndār se kyonkar khaṭ-i qurān hotā

It's fitting that no razor
be laid upon his face:
How can a line of the Qur'an
be effaced by a believer?

مجھ سے ہلواتا ہے اب لیزم جنوں زنجیر کی
اور کوہِ عشق کی کہتا ہے تو مگدر اٹھا

(iii) Mujh se hilvātā hai ab lezim junūñ zanjīr kī
Aur koh-i 'ishq kī kahtā hai to mugdar uṭhā

The chains of madness
I have lifted up like a barbell
and raised the mountain of love
in the manner of a dumbbell.

تو نے مگدر ہلائے کیوں نہ کریں
باغ عالم میں افتخار درخت

(iv) Tū ne mugdar hilāye kyoñ na kareñ
Bāgh 'ālam meñ iftikhār darakht

Why shouldn't the trees feel proud
when you practice with dumbbells?

بالوں کو کچھ اثر بغلِ یار میں نہیں
پڑتا ہے عکسِ زلفِ سیہ فام دوش پر

(v) Bāloñ ko kuchh aṣar baghal-i yār meñ nahīñ
Paṛtā hai 'aks-i zulf-i siyah-fām dosh par

It's not really hair
in the beloved's armpits:
The shadow of her blackish locks
falls upon her shoulder.

مجھ کو سودائی بنایا ہے دکھا کر آنکھیں
تم دھتورے کا لیا کرتے ہو بادام سے کام

(vi) Mujh ko saudā'ī banāyā hai dikhā kar ānkheñ
Tum dhatūre kā liyā karte ho bādām se kām

You drove me insane when you showed me your eyes
with almonds you achieved the effect of datura.

معمار ہی سمجھے وہ اگر اپنے محل کا
کیا خوش ہوں کہ حاکم میں ہوا راج محل کا

(vii) Me'mār hī samjhe voh agar apne maḥal kā
Kyā k͟hush hūñ kih ḥākim maiñ hu'ā rāj maḥal kā

If she were to treat me just as
a suitable house-builder
how happy I'd be for I'd be
like the ruler of a palace.

پھرتے ہوئے دن کاٹتا ہے نامہ بری میں
قاصد مرا گویا کہ روانّا ہے محل کا

(viii) Phirte hu'e dīn kāṭtā hai nāmah barī meñ
Qāṣid-i mirā goyā kih ravānnā hai maḥal kā —Khalil

He passes the day
going back and forth
bearing letters:
My messenger is like
the errand-boy of the harem.

7. The seventh characteristic set out by Nadvi is: "The general style of Lakhnavi poets is *mu'āmla bandī* which, spreading over all, created the tenor of the marketplace, and one does not, therefore, find the vigorous and genuine style that is found in the writings of the poets of Delhi..."[18] The three examples of *mu'āmla bandī* are all by Khalil:

ہم کیا قمارِ عشق میں گھاتیں بتائیں گے
وہ خود جواریوں سے بھی زیادہ ہیں چالیے

Ham kyā qumār-i 'ishq meñ ghāteñ batāyenge
Voh k͟hud juvāriyoñ se bhī zyāda haiñ chāliye

What can I teach of her strategies
in the game of love?
She outmaneuvers even the greatest of gamblers.

منہ گال پہ رکھنے سے خفا ہوتے ہو ناحق
مس کرنے سے قرآن کی فضیلت نہیں جاتی

Munh gāl pe rakhne se khafā hote ho nāḥaq
Mas karne se qur'ān kī fazīlat nahīn jātī

Don't be angered
When I rest my fact on your cheek:
One does not erase the Qur'an's sanctity
Merely by caressing it.

دیکھی شب وصل ناف اس کی
روشن ہوئی چشم آرزو کی

Dekhī shab-i vaṣl nāf us kī
Roshan hu'ī chashm ārzū kī

On the night of union I saw her navel:
The eye of my desire lit up.

8. "In the last epoch of Persian poets the employment of delicate similes and elegant figures of speech reached the height of refinement. Its verdance is seen in the writing of Urfi, Naziri and Talib-i Amuli. The early [Urdu] poets Vali, Mir and Sauda followed this tradition and one finds the same refinement in their work as well. And the poets of the Delhi school also added to the stockpile of these figures of speech. For example..." There follow fifteen *she'rs* by Dihlavi poets[19] which display delightful figures of speech. They, in turn, are followed by seven of Nasikh's *she'rs*, introduced by:

> Nasikh's work completely overflows with similes and figures of speech, but what manner of simile has his *nāzuk khayālī* [excessive delicacy or abstruseness of thought] given rise to!... and it got even worse in the era of his pupils...[20]

The first few examples from Nasikh's *dīvān* appear below:

شاخ آہو ہے بھنویں آنکھیں ہیں چشم آہو
مشک نافہ تھا کوئی ناف میں گر تل ہوتا

Shākh āhū hai bhaveñ ānkheñ haiñ chashm-i āhū
Mashk nāfa thā ko'ī nāf meñ gar til hotā

Your eyebrows are soft, fuzzy antlers
Your eyes those of the gazelle:
Were there a mole on your navel
It would be a gland of musk.[21]

خاکِ صحرا چھانتا پھرتا ہوں اس غربال میں
آبلوں میں کر دیے کانٹوں نے روزن زیرِ پا

Khāk-i sahrā chhāntā phirtā hūñ is ghirbāl meñ
Ābloñ meñ kar diye kāñṭoñ ne rauzan zer-i pā

In this sieve I wander hopelessly
straining the dust of the desert:
Thorns have gashed out blisters—
peepholes through the soles of my feet.

کیوں نہ اے کافر کروں سجدہ میں تیرے پاؤں پر
صورتِ محراب ہے حلقہ ترے خلخال کا

Kyoñ na ae kāfir karūñ sajda maiñ tere pā'oñ par
Ṣūrat-i mahrāb hai ḥalqa tire khalkhāl kā

Infidel, why should I
not prostrate myself at your feet?
The link of your ankle bracelet
looks like an Imam's prayer arch.

ہے دہاں میں اس قدر خوشبو کہ اب رکھا ہے نام
عطر کی شیشی تری بلوّر کی مہنال ... کا

Hai dahāñ meñ is qadar khush-bū kih ab rakhā hai nām
'Iṭr kī shīshī tirī billūr kī muhnāl kā

The fragrance of your mouth is so sweet
that the crystal lip of your hookah
is called a phial of attar.

دلِ سخت اس بتِ کافر کا ہے کوہ جودی
کار گر خاک مرے اشک کا طوفاں ہوتا

Dil-i sakht us but-i kāfir kā hai koh jūdī
Kār gar khāk mire ashk kā ṭūfāñ hotā

That idol-infidel's stony heart
is like the Ararat:
what in the world could my storm of tears do to it?

یاد آجاتی ہے ٹکڑی اس کبوتر ناز کی
کیا اڑا دیتے ہیں میری نیند تارے رات کو

Yād ā jātī hai ṭikṛī us kabūtar nāz kī
Kyā uṛā dete haiñ merī nīnd tāre rāt ko

I remember her flirtations, a flock of pigeons:
the scattered stars take my sleep away.

تیری ایسی انگلیاں ہیں استخواں جس میں نہیں
پور پور اُن کی مگر خرمائے تر بے خستہ ہے

Terī aisī ūngliyāñ haiñ ustukhvāñ jis meñ nahīñ
Por por unkī magar khurmā-i tar be-khasta hai

It's as though there are no bones in your fingers
each digit is like a fresh unbroken date.

Nadvi says that "Khvaja Atish certainly created excellent and suitable similes, but there is no lack, either, of base and vulgar metaphors in his work."[22] And two examples of Atish's base and vulgar metaphors are presented. Nadvi then offers a disclaimer reminiscent of those in *Āb-i-Ḥayāt*:

> All these characteristics, as will have been surmised by the examples, though found in the writing of Atish and his disciples, are really the specialty of Nasikh and the disciples of Nasikh...[23]

We have just presented a neutral report of Nadvi's eight listed characteristics which distinguish Lakhnavi poetry from Dihlavi. However, I take certain exceptions to Nadvi's argument, and they now follow.

There are myriad problems, for example, with Nadvi's statement of point 2, 1.1., that the Delhi poets *fārsī tarākīb* evidence a respect for the customs of their literary forebears. In the first place Nadvi does not explain why the verses he has chosen are particularly delightful, appropriate or reflective of the tradition. Nor does he offer any "inappropriate" or "vulgar" examples of Lakhnavi employment of *fārsī tarkīben* for comparison. Then, too, Nadvi lists more than twice as many examples from obscure poets like Zaki and Majruh as from his two famous *ustāds*, Ghalib and Momin. If, indeed, this type of expression was characteristic of Dihlavi poetry, why is the preponderance of his examples from practically unheard-of poets? The reader is left to suppose that either Nadvi's choices are simply idiosyncratic or that the *fārsī tarkīben* which he has in mind are not, perhaps, as readily found in the pages of Dihlavi poets' written works as he had earlier suggested.

The objection is not to Nadvi's claim that Dihlavi poetry is full of charming and delightful *fārsī tarkīben*. But one cannot help but wonder how representative Nadvi's examples are of the *dabistān-i Dillī*; and how illuminating those examples are of the points he argues. A more instructive method of illustration would, perhaps, have been to take a number of verses by both Lakhnavi and Dihlavi poets which contained Persian words or expressions and then to explicitly demonstrate the relative appropriateness and charm of their manner of employment and their patterns of occurrence in each body of poetry. As Nadvi's point now stands, it is unclear what kind of Persian expression is meant by *fārsī tarkībeñ*; what constitutes their appropriate or inappropriate employment; and what are the specific principles of employment that distinguish the Dihlavi poets from the Lakhnavis.

Finally, as regards this second point of distinction, attention must be drawn to Nadvi's mention of Zauq's and Shah Nasir's style as "not different from the Lakhnavi style." Every Two School critic lists both poets unequivocally as Dihlavis. Indeed, as has been noted, Zauq was the *ustād* of the last Mughal emperor, Bahadur Shah Zafar, and was situated at the Red Fort in Delhi. To call Zauq and Shah Nasir "Lakhnavi style Dihlavi poets" in the same manner that Z.A. Siddiqi has called Atish a "Dihlavi style Lakhnavi poet"[24] is to present a grave contradiction to the whole basis of two poetic schools whose styles reflect the times and social conditions of the cities for which they are named.[25]

In point 3, the *batāse paidā* verse is apparently frivolous. One takes no exception to that. However, when placed outside the context of the very long ghazal from which it is presumably lifted, it is impossible to judge the veracity of Nadvi's claim that there is a causal relationship between long ghazals, ridiculous or frivolous *qāfiyahs* and, thus, degraded themes. Furthermore, even a casual survey of the *dīvāns* of Dihlavi and Lakhnavi poets shows that there is no clear pattern of longer ghazals in the Lakhnavi poets' writings than in that of the Dihlavis. It is true that some eighteenth century poets, such as Dard and Sauda, typically wrote shorter ghazals than did many nineteenth century poets like Nasikh, Atish, Zauq or Shah Nasir. But it seems far more likely that factors other than locale determined ghazal length even among this group. Residence in Delhi or Lucknow is not a realistic principle for discussing the ghazal length of large numbers of Urdu poets who composed under different sets of circumstances, without the substantiation of a full-scale ghazal count of all the major Urdu poets. Nobody has yet done this. The question of literary era would seem to suggest itself as a more realistic focal point, although a survey of ghazal length for all eighteenth and nineteenth century poets would not be realistic for the present study.[26]

Nadvi's fourth point of distinction—that spiritual emotion in Dihlavi poetry is replaced by discussion of the beloved's external attributes in Lakhnavi poetry—is also troublesome. In the first place, one is obliged to trust Nadvi's word that the *dīvāns* of Nasikh and Atish—a total of some fifteen thousand verses—are full of such *she'rs*. Furthermore, why does Nadvi claim that this type of *she'r* replaces what would, in the *dīvān* of a Dihlavi poet, be a *she'r* which expressed spiritual emotion (*rūḥānī jaẕbāt*)? There is simply no evidence on which to base such a correlative assertion, without a laborious word-count of all the *dīvāns* of all the major Dihlavi and Lakhnavi *ustāds*. Even then it seems impossible to determine that Lakhnavi poets wrote verses describing the beloved's external appearance *in lieu of* those concerned with spiritual emotion.

The entire verse comparing the beloved to a heaving cheetah is apparently objectionable to Nadvi, since he does not underline any particular words. It would have been very useful for him to specify all that was objectionable in the *she'r* since we must speculate instead. While the theme (*maẓmūn*) itself is profane—in that graphic allusion is made to physical union (*viṣāl, vaṣl*)—the expression is playful in tone and theme as well as whatever word-play it contains. The word-play is based on *palang* (bed) which also can mean "panther or cheetah." He further says:

> Although this sort of figure of speech is present in places in the work of Delhi poets, it is not there to such a degree that it can be fixed as a distinguishing characteristic [of *Dihlavīyat*].[27]

Nadvi's discussion of *ri'āyat-i lafẓī* (word-play) begins and ends here. Considering that *ri'āyat-i lafẓī* is considered to be a major distinguishing characteristic of *Lakhnavīyat*,[28] the topic merits a more thorough explication.

Unlike Hali's explanation for why Nasikh's *she'rs* were "unnatural," Nadvi does not explain what is degenerate about the eight verses he uses to illustrate the characteristic degeneracy of Lakhnavi poets. However he does say that "except for Zauq and Shah Nasir this kind of degenerate verse is not to be found in the poets of Delhi."[29] To speculate, then, on why those eight *she'rs* show baseness, one would guess that verses which depict "vulgar" situations or themes—as in the two *she'rs* by Khalil—and physical union are considered base. The mixing of profane (*majāzī*) topics with sublime topics—such as, in the first of Nasikh's *she'rs*, equating the rivals' contemplation of the beloved with dogs baying at the moon—is no doubt considered to be in poor taste. Even though the beloved is compared with the moon according to convention, to compare her admirers to dogs detracts from the compliment, for it lacks "lofty thought" or seriousness. Even to compare one's rivals to dogs would not be thought proper, or *sharīf*.

One should, rather, treat even one's mortal enemy with elaborate courtesy in the ethos of *sharāfat* which parallels that of the ghazal.[30]

Similarly, the second of Nasikh's verses equates a razor travelling over the beloved's face with the faithful ones (*dīndār*) reading the lines of the Qur'ān. While there are certainly instances where the beloved's face is compared to the Qu'rān, and the down on his face with letters of the Qur'ān, the notion of shaving seems to be distasteful. The presence of the razor as well as the pun on *khaṭ* ("peach fuzz" as well as "writing") leaves no doubt at all as to what sort of beloved the narrator speaks of—it is clearly a young man—and that manner of explicitness as well as the play in *khaṭ* is probably what caused Nadvi to label the verse *mubtaẕal* (degenerate).

Nasikh's employment of weight-lifting terms to refer to the burdens of *'ishq* probably constitute the objectionable elements in the third *she'r*. To refer to the ghazal's great heroes Majnun and Farhad—by alluding to the "chains of madness" (*junūn kī zanjīr*) and the "mountain of *'ishq*" (*koh-i 'ishq*)—in this particular context are probably deemed inappropriate because of the verse's levity of tone. Certainly the accoutrements of wrestlers do little to universalize the legendary sufferings, burdens and feats of Majnun and Farhad because the *'āshiq* is not claiming that he has prevailed over Majnun and Farhad by suffering greater or more intense grief. Rather he is suggesting that he overcomes the burdens of love by sheer brute strength. In the ethos of the ghazal, the narrator's own boastful claims of outdoing these heroes at physical games are appropriate if they communicate a nobility or are placed in the grander scheme of things. That grander scheme of things is not suggested, one speculates, by barbells and dumbbells.

The fourth "vulgar" or "degenerate" verse which Nadvi cites shows the beloved himself/herself practicing with dumbbells. The objection is obvious: the world's trees are supposed to be proud of the fact that the wood of one of them has gone into the making of the bells which this beloved now lays hands upon. The fifth and six verses refer to physical attributes of the beloved, but that in itself is probably not why Nadvi considers them degenerate. The reference to the hair in the beloved's armpit might be thought off-colour. And if the objection to the sixth verse is that the effect of the beloved's almond eyes is narcotic—as opposed to fiercely painful in the conventional sense of the ghazal—then one might claim to understand Nadvi's judgement.[31]

In summary, then, what Nadvi means by the vulgarity or degeneracy (*mubtaẕal*) of *Lakhnavīyat* remains largely unclear. The educated reader of ghazal poetry can speculate as to Nadvi's criteria for judging, extrapolating from individual experience of the genre. But s/he does so only advisedly. The sense of *mubtaẓal* as essential to *Lakhnavīyat* has been thoroughly integrated into not only Urdu critical works of the past century, but also into writings in English on the subject of Lakhnavi poetry, especially Ahmed Ali,[32] Muhammad Sadiq,[33] and Annemarie Schimmel.[34] It would have been of invaluable use to the purposes of this and other studies had Nadvi set an example of explication as well as illustration when he established *mubtaẓal* as a fundamental characteristic of *Lakhnavīyat*. That he did not do so has caused—or contributed significantly to—the increasingly difficult task of elucidating, defending or challenging the Two School theory.

Yet again, the only kind of contrast posited by Nadvi between Dihlavi poetry and the Lakhnavi verses of Khalil in point 7—which are to illustrate *mu'āmla bandī*—is that "[this] could not come from the pen of any Delhi poet."[35] These verses would seem to be better described by Mir's term "*chūmāchāṭī*" than by *mu'āmla bandī*, which—according to one critic— is an entire sub—genre depicting a particular aspect of the nature of the '*āshiq-ma'shūq* relationship. The above three *she'rs* by Khalil might well fit into the category of *mu'āmla bandī* by virtue of their reference to union (in the second and third verses) and by the tone of *shikāyat* (complaint) in the first. But there are numerous other facets of *mu'āmla bandī* than this, and they can be found in far less obscure poets than Khalil. For example, an entire ghazal by the famous Dihlavi poet Momin is built on *mu'āmla bandī* and contains almost none of the explicitness or *chūmāchāṭī* of the verses by Khalil which Nadvi lists.[36] The only exception is to be found in verse 10 of that ghazal. It is a verse whose subject is the same as in Khalil's fourth verse in Nadvi's point 5 above (i.e., *ri'āyat-i lafẓī*), where the beloved eludes the '*āshiq* even when they are physically together. But Momin does not explicitly mention bed, and her refusals are not unequivocally to physical overtures:

وہ بگڑنا وصل کی رات کا وہ نہ ماننا کسی بات کا
وہ نہیں نہیں کی ہر آن ادا تمھیں یاد ہو کہ نہ یاد ہو

Voh bigaṛnā vaṣl kī rāt kā voh na mānnā kisī bāt kā
Voh nahīñ kī har ān adā tumheñ yād ho kih na yād ho

That displeasure of yours
on the night of union

that refusal at every point
that petulant no, no to every entreaty
Do you remember that or not?

Nothing is obscure about the setting of this verse, but the classic reluctance of the beloved to bestow her favours is conveyed in a much broader reiteration of the entire relationship between *'āshiq* and *ma'shūq* than Khalil conveyed by his bedroom scene.

The example above is offered in illustration of Nadvi's questionable argumentation. In the first place, the most famous ghazal of one of the most famous Dihlavis is entirely a poem of *mu'āmla bandī*, contrary to Nadvi's claim that *mu'amla bandī* is the common style (*'ām rang*) of Lakhnavi poets which distinguishes them from Dihlavi poets. In the second place, Nadvi's claim that *mu'āmla bandī* "gives rise to the tenor of the market-place" and inevitably erodes the "vigour and genuineness" of the Delhi style is patently untrue. Despite its entire basis on *mu'āmla bandī* Momin's ghazal is his most famous because it does convey genuine emotion, its language is straightforward, and it fulfills its audience's requirement that the ghazal express the condition of *'ishq* in a romantic fashion.

To summarize this review of Nadvi's argument, there are two primary points to be made which contribute to this study's refutation of the Two School theory. The first is that Nadvi converted Azad's and Hali's general feelings of difference between Lakhnavi and Dihlavi poetry into concrete criteria, neglecting the onus of substantiation which should have been placed on so profound a distinction. One would like to have seen some proof offered of the validity of Nadvi's initial two-school premise, rather than see Nadvi build on that premise as though its truth were self-evident or already established. Nadvi, by establishing as official opinions which were conveyed obliquely and informally by his literary predecessors, irrevocably converted conventional wisdom into "fact."

It is true that the general impression of Lakhnavi poetry conveyed in *Āb-i-Ḥayāt* forms the skeleton of Nadvi's two-school delineation, but the onus of rigorous documentation could not be put upon Azad because he never actually declared two formal schools. Nadvi could cite Azad as his authority, but Azad could not be impeached for a position which he had never specifically taken. Thus the theory entered literary criticism without ever being challenged to defend itself.

Nadvi's overall treatment of Delhi and Lucknow echoes that originated by Azad and continued by Hali in the *Muqaddma*. Most specifically, *She'rul Hind* features the same dual polarisation between Delhi and Lucknow; and Nasikh and Atish—with blatant preferences expressed for Delhi in the first case and Atish in the second—which have been observed in Azad's and Hali's works. While Nadvi's illustrative examples represent a constructive addition to the Two School theory's articulation, Nadvi is scarcely more consistent in his commentary upon cited examples than was Hali in the *Muqaddma*. This lack forms the basis for our second point of refutation: the manner of the Two School theory's argumentation.[37]

Secondly, the illustration and substantiation of Nadvi's eight distinguishing characteristics lack sufficient detail to convince the skeptic. For each illustration of a *khuṣūṣīyat* of Lakhnavi poetry a similar verse—containing the same essential features—can be found by a Dihlavi poet, and a major Dihlavi poet at that. One need not cite the work of obscure poets from either *markaz* to illustrate characteristic features of Urdu poetry. Even when Nadvi offers ample quantities of illustrative *she'rs* he does not specify how they illustrate the particular *khuṣūṣīyat* he is discussing. Therefore, while it is far more helpful to have unclear illustration offered than to have no illustration at all, Nadvi's discourse ultimately leaves serious questions as to how convincing are the tenets of the Two School theory.

Paucity of rigorous substantiation seriously undermines Nadvi's dissertation. Had his analysis been consistently rigorous the methodological problems of coming to terms with the Two School theory would have been greatly diminished. However, the fundamental problem is not with Nadvi—it is with the Delhi-Lucknow distinction itself.

It is well to reiterate here that Lakhnavi and Dihlavi poetry draw upon the very same fundamental aesthetics, structural and thematic conventions. Neither Nadvi nor anyone else has actually argued to the contrary;[38] nor has any Urdu critic shown why separate schools should be formally declared on the basis of more superficial differences than an inherited aesthetic, structure and stock of themes. Certainly none of the critics of the Two School theory has ever specifically established what that distinguishing aesthetic or those distinguishing structures are. The existing general charges of characteristic sensuality and degeneracy in Lakhnavi poetry cannot stand because even some of the Two School critics acknowledge that the elements of both bodies of poetry are the same—the difference, they argue, is one of degree.[39] While this study acknowledges that there may indeed be differences of degree in Lakhnavi and Dihlavi poets' preferred dictions and subject matter at any given time, all the poets write on those same topics in much the same dictions at one time or another. How, then, can the exercise of preferences within the same stock of structural elements and topical themes constitute separate schools of poetry? Chapter X offers an illustration of how poets of Delhi and those of Lucknow, writing in the same literary tradition at roughly the same time in history, can be seen to exhibit greater similarities than differences in their treatment of structural and thematic aspects of the ghazal.

NOTES

1. *"Urdū shā'irī ke do mukhtalif iskūl,"* Nadvi, *She'rul Hind*, Azimgarh: Matba'- i Ma'arif, 1926, vol. 1, pp. 204-215.
2. Except that Hali had claimed that *ri'āyat-i lafẓī* was the domain of Lakhnavi poets and was eschewed by the poets of Delhi.
3. Andalib Shadani, nearly forty years later, presents a similar exposition which obviously borrows heavily from Nadvi's work. It will be discussed in the chapter which follows.
4. Translation by Ahmed Ali, *The Golden Tradition*, New York: Columbia University Press, 1973, p. 214.
5. Women and children apparently were known to wear a red thread around their necks during Mohurram to symbolize the bleeding throat of Ali Asghar, Husain's baby killed at Karbala.
6. This same point is made in Andalib Shadani's *"Lakhnavī Shā'irī kī Chand Khuṣūṣiyāt,"* although he expands it to three characte-istics, specifying *sāman-i ārā'ish* [accoutrements of adornment], *zevarāt* [jewelry] and *zanāna libās aur ajzā-i labās* [feminine garments and accessories]. These are Shadani's second, third and fourth characteristics. See *Tahqīq kī Roshnī meñ*, Lahore: Shaikh Ghulam Ali and Sons, 1963, pp. 250-253.
7. Abdus Salam Nadvi, *She'rul Hind*, vol. 1, p. 204.
8. All five *she'rs* cited on pp. 204-205 of *She'rul Hind*, vol.1.
9. Ibid., pp. 205, 208-9.
10. Ibid., p. 208.
11. The meaning of *muḥāsā* is "a pimple on the face."
12. Literally, "ghazalness." See C.M. Naim, "Ghazal and taghazzul: The lyric, personal and social," in Edward C. Dimock, Jr., *The Literatures of India: An Introduction*, Chicago: University of Chicago Press, 1974, pp. 181-197.
13. Nadvi, p. 209.
14. Ibid., p. 210.
15. S.R. Faruqi explains this verse as follows: he says the point is that *tā'o khānā* means "to be excited, to become curled," but *tā'o* alone

also means "a sheet of paper." Personal communication, New Delhi, 26 December 1985.

16. Platts' *Dictionary of Urdu, Classical Hindi and English*, p. 268 offers as a secondary meaning of *palang* "panther, leopard or tiger." Here there is *ri'āyat-i lafẓī* between the Hindi where *palang* signifies a bed, and this secondary Persian word.
17. Nadvi, p. 210.
18. Ibid., p. 211.
19. Five by Ghalib; four by Zaki; three by Majruh; and three by Khalil.
20. Nadvi, pp. 213-14.
21. This verse was discussed in the opening pages of this study. See Preface, pp. x-xi.
22. Nadvi, p. 214.
23. Ibid.
24. See Chapter V, note 7.
25. Dagh, too, is characterized as displaying the features of a Lakhnavi poet. See Ahmed Ali, *The Golden Tradition*, p. 274.
26. An impressionistic observation is that the average length for an Urdu ghazal by the poets addressed in this study is fifteen *she'rs*. But there are ghazals examined in later chapters which are as short as three verses and as long as twenty-seven.
27. Nadvi, p. 214.
28. An important modern critic, Professor Naiyar Masud of Lucknow University even refers to the so-called Lucknow school as the *dabistān-i ri'āyat-i lafẓī*. Personal communication, Lucknow, February, 1982.
29. Nadvi, p. 211.
30. This point will be discussed in the final chapter.
31. Nadvi's point actually seems to be the equation of eyes with real almonds, and then with datura. It is harmless, playful fancy rather than truly degenerate, one would think.
32. *The Golden Tradition*, p. 56: "In poetry .. the fleshly school, developing in a fast degenerating Lucknow, the second seat of culture, decaying before it had become ripe, gained popularity and subsidized a desperate order floundering in a morass of superficies;" p.76: "... literature of wider appeal to the basic primary emotions, such as was found in the poetry of the fleshly school of Lucknow which had a direct appeal to erotic sensations ..." and p. 274: "[Dagh], though a Delhi poet, displays affinity with the fleshly school of Lucknow in this manner and, like Atish and Nasikh, sacrifices refinement to sensuality, though he does not stoop to the obscenities or vulgarity which are displayed by the fleshly school."
33. *A History of Urdu Literature*, pp. 121: "... in its want of depth, its absence of sentiment, its superficial polish and glitter, its wit, brilliance, persiflage, effeminacy, and dalliance with courtesans, the

poetry of Lucknow presents a faithful reflection of the life of the period."

34. *Classical Urdu Literature from the Beginning to Iqbal*: In addition to referring to "the smooth and refined Lucknow style" of Urdu, [pp. 167 and 157] Schimmel discusses its "decadent and unhealthy culture and its flirtatious poetry, not rarely transgressing the borders of obscenity..." p. 190.
35. "*Dillī ke kisī shā'ir ke kalām se nahīñ nikal saktī.*" Nadvi, p. 211.
36. We refer here to the famous *musalsal* ghazal whose *maṭla*; is "*Voh jo ham meñ tum meñ qarār thā tumheñ yād ho kih na yād ho/ Vahī ya'nī vāda nibāh kā tumheñ yād ho kih na yād ho*—Do you or don't you remember/That understanding we had/That very vow of eternal truth/ Do you remember that or don't you?" from *Kulliyāt-i Momin*, Allahabad: Ram Narayan Beni Madhav, 1971, No. 152, p. 136.
37. Chapter IX's discussion of Ali Javad Zaidi's *Do Abadī Iskūl* shows how troublesome Zaidi, too, finds these standard modes of argumentation.
38. Furthermore this will be illustrated in Chapter X's examination of a controlled sample of Dihlavi and Lakhnavi poetry.
39. See Ali Javad Zaidi, op. cit., p. 16; and M. Sadiq, *History of Urdu Literature*, pp. 121-122. Note: although Zaidi writes on the subject of the Two Schools he cannot be considered a Two School critic, since his writing challenges the Two School distinction.

CHAPTER VIII

Andalib Shadani's *"Lakhnavī Shā'irī Kī Chand Khuṣūṣīyāt"*

As the last chapter reiterated, Nadvi was the critic who bridged the time gap separating Hali and Azad, nineteenth century writers, from the twentieth century critics through whose writing the Two School Theory has come down to us, thoroughly and explicitly integrated into Urdu literary theory. Later critics built upon the platform established by Nadvi.[1]

One such twentieth century critic is Andalib Shadani. His essay entitled "*Lakhnavī Shā'irī kī Chand Khuṣūṣīyāt*" or "A Few Characteristics of Lakhnavi Poetry" (1963) lists twelve special characteristics (*Khuṣūṣīyāt*) of Lakhnavi poetry, four more than Nadvi. In general, they resemble the major features outlined by Nadvi. The essay is discussed here briefly because it is mentioned by Ali Javad Zaidi as a direct motivation for *Do Adabī Iskūl*, which came some eight years later.[2] The *khuṣūṣīyāt* are listed below:

1. Lakhnavi poets focused on a veiled female beloved (*parda nashīn*), while "in the twelfth century Hijri the beloveds of Dihlavi poets were foppish boys..."[3]

2. Cosmetics: "Lakhnavi poets give all the particulars of feminine adornments and cosmetics."[4]

3. Jewelry: "One finds more detailed descriptions of female jewelry than anywhere else."[5]

4. Clothing: Lengthy descriptions of feminine raiment and apparel.[6]

5. Nudity: "Nudity, lewdness, and description of the beloved's limbs and organs, though written about in every language of every epoch, is not found to this extent anywhere else."[7]

6. Mention of song, dance and dancing girls.[8]

7. "Notwithstanding the fact that Lakhnavi poets expurgated many Hindi words and expressions which were part of common parlance in Delhi; and that they drew heavily upon Persian vocabulary and practiced *fārsī tarkīben* (Persian constructions); still, there is a great influence of Hindu society, customs and manners in Lakhnavi poetry..."[9]

8. Lakhnavi poets use the word *parī* (fairy) a great deal, and sometimes change its gender from feminine to masculine.[10]

9. Lakhnavi poets love to make jests (*phabtī kahnā*) and draw attention to their own cleverness.[11]

10. A special affliction of Lakhnavi poets is *dāgh-i junūn*, or the brand of madness.[12]

11. Exaggerated drollery which, rather than serving to reinforce or elucidate the meaning of a figure of speech, renders it ridiculous.[13]

12. *Tavassul* (the evocation of Shi'ite martyrs Ali, Hasan and Husain) in the ghazal's *maqṭa'* in order to attain some grace or blessing by association.[14]

Shadani's first point, that the beloved in Lakhnavi poetry is female, whereas in Dihlavi poetry he had been a young "foppish" boy, is very provocative. While the beloved in Lakhnavi poetry is often clearly female, it is quite overstating the case to say that Dihlavi poets of the eighteenth century were enamoured only of young boys. Recent scholarship in English corroborates Shadani's assertion that some Dihlavi poets did refer unambiguously to young male beloveds some of the time,[15] despite the attempts of English-educated and reformist Indian Muslims to suppress or deny this fact. But one could cite as many cases in opposition, indicating a female beloved, or the Divine beloved. However, Shadani's main argument here is that ambiguity of gender in the ghazal's beloved gave way in Lucknow to an unambiguously female beloved. Even among the examples of Lakhnavi poetry that Nadvi cited in the last section to illustrate his own *khuṣūṣīyāt* of Lakhnavi poetry there were clear references to male beloveds. And one wonders how Shadani can say, on the one hand, that Lakhnavis wrote exclusively of a female beloved and say as he does in his eight Lakhnavi *khuṣūṣīyāt* that in describing the beloved as a *parī* (fairy), they sometimes changed the gender of *parī* from female to male. This would appear to be a contradiction. Shadani's point cannot, therefore, be accepted as stated.

However, had the identification of the beloved actually made the transition from young boy to mature woman, as suggested by Shadani, the implications of such a development for the entire ghazal genre would have been significant. Certainly a discussion of those implications would have been of great interest here.

Points 2-5 can all be grouped together into one broad statement which parallels Nadvi's first point: that the particulars of the (unambiguously female) beloved's body and clothing often appear in the verse of Lakhnavi poets. Again, however, it is not at all clear that particulars of the beloved's external appearance are more characteristic of the Lakhnavi ghazal than the Dihlavi, without a word count to determine relative frequency in the two bodies of poetry.

Shadani's seventh point can be broken up into two. His primary argument is that Lakhnavi poetry is greatly influenced by Hindu society (rites, customs and manners). Secondarily Shadani broaches the issue of Persianized constructions, or *fārsī tarkībeñ*. On this point he would appear to differ with Nadvi, who says that the Dihlavis employ Persian constructions but that the Lakhnavis do not. Shadani says that "*notwithstanding the fact that Lakhnavis Persianized their language*[16] their poetry still reflects the influence of Hindu society."

Points 8-11 may well be accurate observations of discernible subject matter, as may be his sixth point regarding the mention of song, dance and dancing girls, but there is nothing in them which supports the idea that Lakhnavi poetry constitutes its own literary school: even in such *she'rs* as those, Lakhnavi poets observe the standard conventions of the ghazal. There is nothing in song, dance, dancing girls, drollery, *phabtī kahnā* or mention of brands of madness (*dāgh-i junūn*) which goes against the established format of the Urdu ghazal.

Shadani's outline generally emphasizes topics of observable features in Lakhnavi poetry which are objectionable because they indicate rather forcefully the physical aspect of the '*āshiq's* relation to the beloved. It may be inferred that Shadani finds Lakhnavi poetry to be frivolous because of what he sees as an emphasis on external attributes of the beloved. It is further inferred that he would have wished to see, in the Lakhnavi ghazal, a showcase for more abstract, spiritual, "noble" (*sharīf*) facets of Indo-Muslim identity. In short, Shadani's unfavourable characterization of *Lakhnavīyāt* is based on moral and cultural, rather than literary, judgements.

Nadvi's characterisations were based far more on literary criteria. This is not to say that he favours *Lakhnavīyat*, or that he does not share Shadani's implied moral objections to it; few Urdu critics do not express these moral objections. Still Nadvi, in his attempt to elucidate the differences between *Lakhnavīyat* and *Dihlavīyat*, generally confines himself to literary criteria, to structural rather than thematic elements in the poetry. The "moral" vs. "literary" bases of Shadani's and Nadvi's arguments reflect a widespread, and fundamental, emphasis in the literary scholarship addressed to Lucknow, starting as far back as Hali's *Muqaddma*.

Shadani also emulates Nadvi in the matter of illustrating his points. However like Nadvi he often culls his examples from lesser-known poets. If the features cited by Two School critics are in fact characteristic of Lakhnavi poetry then there should be ample illustration of them in the founding poets of the so-called *dabistān-i Lakhna'u*. The persuasiveness of Nadvi's and Shadani's arguments would be greatly enhanced were they to cite the major poets of either *markaz*.

A final point which emerges from this examination of Shadani is that conceptions of what constitutes *Lakhnavīyat* and *Dihlavīyat* in literature neither changed significantly nor became more sophisticated in their articulation from 1926 with *She'rul Hind* to 1963, despite a proliferation of literary scholarship in Urdu which attempted to break away from the rigidity of the Two School theory.[17]

In recent years there has been one particular dissenting Urdu critic. His name is Ali Javad Zaidi, and his book *Do Adabī Iskūl*, which challenges the Two School theory, is discussed in the next chapter.

NOTES

1. When Abul Lais Siddiqi and Nurul Hasan Hashmi undertook full-fledged studies of Lakhnavi and Dihlavi poetry in the early 1940s, for example, they took for granted that the existence of the Delhi and Lucknow "schools" was proven and uncontroversial. Their works, *Lakhnau kā Dabistān-i Shā'irī* and *Dillī kā Dabistān-i Shā'irī*, in turn have served as the standard reference for critics of the past four decades.
2. See the next chapter.
3. Shadani, "*Lakhnavī Shā'irī kī Chand Khuṣūṣīyāt*" in *Taḥqīq kī Roshnī meñ*, Lahore: Shaikh Ghulam Ali and Sons, 1963, p. 249.
4. Ibid., p. 250.
5. Ibid., pp. 251-253.
6. Ibid., p. 253.
7. Ibid., p. 254.
8. Ibid., pp. 255-258.
9. Ibid., pp. 259-261.
10. Ibid., p. 261.
11. Ibid., p. 262.

12. Ibid., p. 263.
13. Ibid., pp. 264-269.
14. An example of this can be seen in Atish's *maqṭa'*:

نزع کی مشکل بھی آساں ہوتی ہے آتش نہ ڈر
شاہِ مرداں سے طلب کر ہمتِ مردانہ آج

Naz' kī mushkil bhī āsāñ hotī hai Ātish na ḍar
Shāh-i mardāñ se ṭalab kar himmat-i mardāna āj
Fear not death's affliction, Atish/it, too, is made easy/ Seek manly courage/ from Ali, King of Men. *Kulliyāt-i Ātish*, {I: 203. 261}, Shadani, p. 351.
15. See C.M. Naim, "The Theme of Homosexual [Pederastic] Love in Pre-Modern Urdu Poetry," in *Studies in the Urdu Ghazal and Prose Fiction*, Ed. M.U. Memon, Madison: South Asian Publication Series, No. 5., 1979, pp. 120-142; and Frances W. Pritchett, "Convention in the Classical Urdu Ghazal: The Case of Mir," in *The Journal of South Asian and Middle Eastern Studies*, vol. 8, no. 1, Fall 1979, pp. 60-77.
16. Emphasis mine.
17. We refer here to the work of such critics as Abdul Haqq, Masud Hasan Rizvi 'Adīb,' Shamsur Rahman Faruqi, and Gopi Chand Narang.

CHAPTER IX

Zaidi's Challenge to the Two School Theory

In 1970 Ali Javad Zaidi published a book called *Do Adabī Iskūl* (Two Literary Schools),[1] which challenged the Two School theory. He writes, on the first page of the first Preface, "In this study I have made so bold as to state that I do not accept the idea that there are two separate literary schools of poetry in Delhi and Lucknow."[2] Zaidi claims that what moved him to write the book was reading Shadani's "*Lakhnavī Shā'irī kī Chand K͟husūṣīyāt*," although this school-designating problem had concerned him for about three decades. His primary concern is "with the truth and intelligence of Shadani's arguments," writes Zaidi.[3] What struck him most of all was that the theory of Two Schools seemed just as muddled and unpolished in 1963 as it had been in 1926 when Nadvi first published *She'rul Hind.*[4] Because it is beyond the scope of his book to analyse in detail all the features of *Dihlavīyat* and *Lakhnavīyat*, says Zaidi, he will confine himself to the particular features which Shadani, Nadvi and Abul Lais Siddiqi consider to be especially characteristic:[5]

> For convenience I have named it *Do Adabī Iskūl* but I must make it clear from the outset that this is not a comparative study of Delhi and Lucknow, nor is it a detailed study of the two alleged schools. My entire thesis should be read in light of the "school designators"—especially Andalib Shadani's—writings...[6]

According to Zaidi, Shadani's list of Lakhnavi poetry's *k͟huṣūṣīyāt* (distinguishing characteristics) left him with many questions and responses. He observes that Shadani practically copied his *k͟huṣūṣīyāt* verbatim from Nadvi; that the new *k͟huṣūṣīyāt* outlined were quite superficial in nature, reflecting a very cursory study of Lakhnavi poetry at best;[7] and that the discourse of the two-school designators is completely unscientific, or *nā-sāyinsī*.[8]

Zaidi also argues that cities or *marākiz* do not determine literary schools. Elements of this argument are made in detail. In the Delhi *markaz*, he writes, poetry was written and recited continuously for over two hundred years. Poets like Shah Hatim, Sauda, Dard, Shah Nasir and Momin could hardly be grouped together according to any criteria other than that they were all Urdu poets and all lived in Delhi (albeit over a span of four or five generations). Why, since their styles admittedly differ, he asks, should they all be considered members of the same literary school? And why, if Shah Nasir and Sauda seem to resemble Nasikh and Insha in poetic style, should the first pair be members of the Delhi "school" and the latter belong to the Lakhnavi *dabistān*?[9]

Furthermore, there is the problem of designating poets "Dihlavi" or "Lakhnavi" even when the majority of their lives were lived in other places. In the section called "*Shahr aur Shā'ir*" (City and Poet)[10] Zaidi recounts the peregrinations of a number of major Urdu poets, observing, for instance, that the Dihlavi poet par excellence, Mir Taqi Mir, was born in Agra, moved to Delhi when he was nine years old, returned to Agra during the invasion of Nadir Shah in 1739, returned to Delhi thereafter, and spent the last thirty years of his life (1781-1810) in Lucknow. Similarly Khan-i Arzu, reputedly the first great Urdu *ustād*, was born and educated in Gwalior of a family from Avadh—Faizabad in Ayodhya district—moved to Delhi at the age of twenty-one, and after thirty-five years in Delhi moved back to Faizabad and finally to Lucknow, where he died. Similarly, both Lakhnavi *ustāds* Nasikh and Atish were born in Faizabad and moved to Lucknow as young men. Even Nasikh—the quintessential Lakhnavi poet in many eyes—was forced to spend a number of years in exile due to the political climate in Lucknow and his personal affiliations with certain officials. Insha, whom Nadvi named as the early sculptor of the Lucknow *rang* (style), was born in Bengal and achieved the status of *ustād* in Delhi before migrating to Faizabad and, finally, Lucknow. Zaidi's point is this: If the school-designation is based on affiliation of poets with a particular city, how can it hold up under the inconsistencies of most poets' habitation and peregrinations? How many years' residence in a particular city qualifies one for a "Dihlavi" or "Lakhnavi" title? In other words, how can it really be determined—and justified—who is a Dihlavi and who a Lakhnavi?

Additional points raised by Zaidi are that literature develops over time, and there can be no singular *rang*[11] in Delhi or Lucknow over a span of several centuries.[12] In other words when Shah Hatim and Shah Nasir—or Ghalib, Momin, Zauq and Shah Nasir—are all Dihlavis and it is accepted that their styles differ dramatically from one another, whose style can most judiciously be called exemplary of *Dihlavīyat*?[13]

Zaidi's final objection to the methods of the school-designators is that they confine themselves to discussion of the ghazal. This does Lucknow a grave injustice, argues Zaidi, since the ghazal was a relatively small portion of the literary output in the Lakhnavi *markaz*. In fact, he goes on to say, the greatest Lakhnavi *ustād* was not Nasikh at all, but were Mir Hasan and Mir Babar Ali Anis whose *maṣnavī Siḥrul Bayān* and *marṣiyas*, respectively, were the greatest literature produced in Lucknow.[14]

The arguments Zaidi raises are very well taken: in the first place, he says, all the so-called *khuṣūṣīyāt* named by Nadvi, Shadani and Abul Lais Siddiqi can easily be found in Dihlavi poetry as well, and in amplitude:

> If there is a difference it is one of quantity rather than quality. From a scientific point of view a difference in quantity also becomes a difference in quality. But even the qualitative differences between Delhi and Lucknow seem very slight.[15]

He goes on to say that if these so-called differences form the basis of the "school-designators' thesis," and can be proved spurious, then where is the fundamental merit in their distinction between the two schools?[16]

Nadvi's eight points are recapitulated before Zaidi undertakes his discussion of Shadani. Perhaps to show the nature of Nadvi's choices of substantiating verse, he cites a solitary example of Nadvi's illustration of *zanānapan* in Lakhnavi poetry,[17] but no others. He refutes the claim that Lakhnavis' use of language was vulgar, saying that, on the contrary, Nasikh improved Urdu as a poetic language by chastening it,[18] and that Nasikh expanded the entire scope of the ghazal in his introduction of new *maẓāmīn*, or poetic themes.[19] He repeats his point that there is *khārijī shā'irī* (poetry enumerating or concerned with external, physical attributes and phenomena) in Delhi; and a *dākhilī andāz* (introspective mode) in Lakhnavi poetry; again, by showing that there is no one *rang* in either body of poetry, citing the examples of Nasikh and Atish as poets of generally divergent temperaments to whom critics attribute individual schools of disciples,[20] Zaidi repeats the question of how there can be two separate schools within a distinct Lakhnavi school, as Nadvi and others have suggested.

Do Adabī Iskūl is a remarkable assay at arguing against the Two School designation from a logical, scientific point of view. Its refutation of Shadani opens with the following remarks:

> Maulana Abdus Salam Nadvi declared the characteristics of the Lucknow School and Andalib adopted them. Those fundamental defects in the Lucknow School designation which were first displayed by Nadvi were copied, with understandable confidence. Having established an edifice on limitlessly weak foundations, Shadani then gave it strange and wondrous embellishment. . .[21]

Thereafter is launched a point-by-point exposition.

During the course of nearly three hundred pages, Zaidi painstakingly presents a number of *she'rs* by Dihlavi poets which manifest the various so-called *k͟huṣūṣīyāt* of Lakhnavi poetry; and other verses by Lakhnavi poets which bear the mark of so-called *Dihlavīyat*. It is not within the scope of the present study to fully recount Zaidi's examples: for that the reader is referred to *Do Adabī Iskūl* itself. But Zaidi's counter-arguments and counter-examples disprove soundly and convincingly Nadvi's and Shadani's asserted delineation of the characteristics which particularly distinguish the Lucknow school of poetry from the Delhi school of poetry.

In summary, Zaidi raises very logical and plausible objections to the Delhi-Lucknow *dabistān* distinction. His objections are addressed to the school-designators' methods of argumentation as well as to the fundamental logic of equating Urdu *marākiz* with literary schools.[22] He demonstrates the near-impossibility of assigning most major poets to one school or the other with accuracy, given the facts of their lives and movements in search of patronage. He raises the question of the Two School theory's inability to account for developments in literary style and genre over time. And he demonstrates amply that the characteristics attributed to one *dabistān* or the other are to be found in the poetry of the opposite "school," rendering the fundamental distinction by *markaz* fallacious.

And yet there have been a number of critical works published in the 1970s and 1980s which continue to operate on the assumption that two separate *dabistāns* exist and which do not appear to take Zaidi's work into account.[23]

Since one of the two-fold purposes of this study is to present and critique the literature relevant to the Two School theory, respect for the contribution of *Do Adabī Iskūl* calls.for a substantial response to its critical content. One the one hand it has been amply recorded that Zaidi makes a genuine attempt to place poetic trends in their historical context, and that he amply supports his point-by-point refutation of Shadani with numerous poetic samples of his own choice. On the other hand certain questions do arise in studying Zaidi's treatment of the topic.

In the first place, *Do Adabī Iskūl* hints at the treatise of a Lucknow apologist, whose reiterated message seems to be that "Delhi was just as bad as Lucknow," or "Lucknow wasn't any worse than Delhi," because, after all, the whole Mughal Sultanate was in decline. A great part of Zaidi's refutation of the Two School designation appears to be motivated by a desire to defend Lucknow against the aspersions cast by the Two School theory's tenets.[24] At one point Zaidi argues that because the Shi'i '*ulemā* were so much stronger an influence in nineteenth century Lucknow than they were in contemporary Delhi, they exerted stringent moral discipline on literature.[25] He even goes so far as to reject the conventional wisdom that Ĺakhnavi poetry was degenerate because of the influence of the whole Lucknow environment, saying that the *ulemā* kept the general populace in line, and that it was only the nobility who were degenerate;[26] and that, in fact, during Lucknow's heyday, the political and economic conditions were not at all as depicted by the Two School-designating critics, and the rivers of wealth were no longer flowing.[27] These points may be well taken, but they do not particularly advance the basic thesis that there is no sound literary basis for the Two School theory.

Secondly, the rigorous scientific method whose lack Zaidi laments in the "school designators" proves itself to be more elusive, perhaps, than Zaidi himself had anticipated. While claiming to limit himself to addressing "the Two School designators, especially Andalib Shadani," Zaidi devotes more than a hundred pages to recounting the history of Urdu's development as a language as well as to the general political history of eighteenth century Avadh.[28] On the basis of this recounted history, he concludes that politics and culture all over Muslim India were in decline, that any degenerate tendencies in Lucknow had been inherited from Delhi anyway, and that the influence of Hindu customs on Lakhnavi poetry was no greater than those of Avadhi, Braj Bhasha, Sanskrit and Indo-Persian *sabk-i Hindī*.[29] Unfortunately—regardless of their essential merit with which we do not quibble at all—

these arguments are unsupported by corroborative samples of poetry. Such corroboration would have been most welcome. It might even have inspired a more satisfactory response from the Urdu literary establishment, though that is by no means certain.

Zaidi's objections to the Two School designators are very sound, but are perhaps diminished by his apologetic stance with regard to Lucknow. Furthermore, he appears to repeat certain methodological practices which he considers to be mistakes on the part of Shadani and Nadvi. He says in the beginning:

> After enumerating each *k͟huṣūṣīyāt* Shadani and Nadvi have illustrated their point by presenting several *she'rs*. In each place I have offered a few more *she'rs* from Dihlavi poetry to prove that these characteristics are also present in Delhi poetry and thus cannot be called special characteristics of Lucknow. .[30]

While observing that is impossible to get the measure of an entire body of poetry from only a few verses[31] he appears to overlook the fact that the admittedly more numerous *she'rs* which he offers in refutation of Nadvi and Shadani might be considered equally inconclusive by skeptics because they are presented out of direct context; and because they represent only a fraction of all Dihlavi and Lakhnavi poetry. When he discusses "the other aspect of Delhi" (*Dillī kā dūsrā rūp*)—meaning other than the lofty, spiritual aspect—Zaidi offers a fifteen-page *intik͟hāb* of ghazals by Dihlavi masters from Shah Hatim through Bahadur Shah Zafar which include *she'rs* containing *k͟hārijī* (external) poetry.[32] While he does not simply extract incriminating *she'rs* from the whole ghazal—as he correctly accused Shadani and Nadvi of doing—he offers no commentary on which of the *she'rs* in his *intik͟hāb* are examples of Delhi's *dūsrā rang*, and why. Once again, this presents problems similar to those which arose for Zaidi in the *nā-sāyinsī* (unscientific) method of argumentation employed by the Two School critics.

The one traceable review of *Do Adabī Iskūl* was published by S.R. Faruqi in *Shab K͟hūn*.[33] In his estimation Zaidi made the same severe methodological error made by all the Two School critics. All are "illogical and unrealistic," argues Faruqi, in that they set up the paradigm of "Delhi is good and Lucknow is bad." Lakhnavi poetry need not be legitimated by showing how much it resembles Dihlavi poetry: to employ such a strategy, as Zaidi largely does, only serves to perpetuate the myth of Delhi's exclusive cultural authority. Faruqi and Zaidi seem to agree, however, on the problem of designating who is a

Dihlavi and who a Lakhnavi, especially in the case of the interim generation of poets between Mir, Sauda, etc. and Nasikh and Atish:

> The fact is that the poetry of the émigré generation [Jur'at, Insha, Mushafi, etc.] is different from that of those poets born and brought up in Lucknow. . . There certainly are similarities between Lakhnavi and Dihlavi poetry but they won't be proven by talking about combs, jewels, moles, noserings, etc.[34]

Also in his review, and more recently, Faruqi has declared that it is necessary "to make a comparative study of large chunks of verse by the major poets from both cities," using perhaps ten thousand *she'rs* and counting the frequency with which the *khuṣūṣīyāt* enumerated by the "school designators" occur on both sides. Then, he argues, if the occurrence is "more or less the same between Dihlavi and Lakhnavi poetry, one can say that *in these specific aspects* Delhi and Lucknow are not different."[35]

The crux of Faruqi's arguments is that there do exist perceptible differences among the poets of the three generations (Dihlavis like Mir, Sauda and Dard; the émigrés; and Nasikh and Atish, the Lakhnavis) but they have yet to be pinpointed by literary critics. To discuss the pros and cons of "qualitative and quantitative" differences, as Zaidi assays at one point, does not solve the problem.

The comparative study of ten thousand *she'rs* which Faruqi suggests in his review of *Do Adabī Iskūl* comes as close as possible to the sort of scientific method presumably envisioned by Zaidi. It would certainly be of interest to see the results of a frequency count of specified *maẓāmīn* in Dihlavi and Lakhnavi poetry. This has yet to be undertaken, no doubt due in some part to the arduousness of such a task. But even so, argues Faruqi, there is no guarantee that those results would solve the problem of defining what distinguishes Dihlavi and Lakhnavi poetry in literary terms.

Faruqi seems to argue that it would be more appropriate to identify the distinguishing factor between various poets as one of generation, rather than of which *markaz* they inhabited. As was mentioned earlier, Zaidi makes this same point in *Do Adabī Iskūl* . He even reiterates it in a later essay, "*Mafrūẓah Adabī Iskūl* (Supposed Literary Schools)."[36] Certainly this is the present study's assessment,[37] since attributing distinctions with reference to poetic generation would acknowledge, at least tacitly, that Urdu continued to develop as a literary language over a long period of time. Therefore one expects to find similarities between poets of a single generation that are not necessarily shared by poets of different generations, even in the same *markaz*. It is perplexing that the point has not yet been driven home, and that Hashmi's and Siddiqi's conception, not to mention that of Andalib Shadani, apparently continues to carry greater weight than that of Zaidi.[38]

As with theologians who are want to support whatever is their particular point of view by citing chapter and verse from scriptures, there is ample support for almost any kind of assertion about the nature of Urdu poetry when the same method is employed. In short, with a great enough volume of authoritative material at hand—such as the millions of *she'rs* in the established Urdu canon—Urdu poetry can be proved to have almost any tendency or special characteristic at all. This cannot be called "scientific method," and will ultimately fail to convince those whose dissent is based on intuition. The fact is that whatever differences exist or have been argued by critics are perceived intuitively, since nobody has read all of the poetry which they have attempted to characterise.

As has been acknowledged throughout this section, most of the points of refutation advanced by Zaidi have been raised and corroborated during the course of our own research. Of especial merit are his arguments that Nadvi and Shadani, the two most explicit school-designators, often point to superficial thematic content and back up their declarations with verse selected, apparently, at random; and that just assessment of the literary questions which arise from designating separate literary schools for Lucknow and Delhi must be made with attention paid to the historical context in which literature is produced, patronised and received by its audience.

It is hoped that the present study in developing some of these arguments raised by Zaidi offers some complement to his pioneering challenge. In the following chapter a model for literary analysis of a controlled sample of poetry[39] is suggested which might serve to deflect claims of randomness : or irrelevance if employed in addition to the method used by Nadvi, Shadani and Zaidi.[40]

And with regard to the issue of placing Dihlavi and Lakhnavi poetry in historical context in order to best understand the Two School theory, the last chapter of this study attempts to develop a discussion of the interlocking relationship between culture, political history, and literary criticism in Indo-Muslim culture. It is not of present concern to try to legitimise Lucknow within the terms set by Urdu culture, as other critics have tried. Whether Delhi was as degenerate as Lucknow—

or Lakhnavi morals as lofty as those in Delhi—is of far less interest than why a literary theory which can easily be refuted, even in its own terms, continues to dominate Urdu critical literature; and why serious analytical attempts, such as Ali Javad Zaidi's, apparently cannot dissuade the Urdu audience—nor Urdu literary culture—away from the Two School theory.

NOTES

1. In addition to *Do Adabī Iskūl*, see Zaidi's essay's, "*Mafrūẓa Adabī Iskūl*," (Supposed Literary Schools) and "*Dillī aur Lakhna'u Iskūl*," (Delhi and Lucknow Schools) in *Fikr-o Riyāẓ*, Delhi: Maktaba-i Jami'a Limited, 1977, pp. 41-53; and 54-101.
2. *Do Adabī Iskūl*, Preface to the First Edition, 1970, p. 13: "*Maiñ ne is maqāle meñ 'arẓ karne kī jur'at kī thī kih maiñ Lakhna'u aur Dillī ko alag adabī iskūl nahīñ māntā.*"
3. "*Maiñ ne zyādatar 'Andalīb Shādānī hī ke ḥaqā'iq-o daqā'iq se sarokār rakhā hai,*" p.15.
4. Zaidi, *op. cit.*, pp. 15, 175.
5. Ibid., p. 16.
6. Ibid.
7. Zaidi, p. 177: "*In khuṣūṣīyāt par sāthī naẓar daurāne vālā bhī yih maḥsūs kiye baghair nahīñ rah saktā kih tamām khuṣūṣīyāt ek manfīyāna aur munāẓirāna nuqtah-i naẓar se muntakhab kī gayī haiñ...*"
8. Ibdi.: " *Sach to yih hai kih Lakhna'u aur Dillī ko alag alag adabī dabistānoñ meñ bānṭ-nā hī sarāsar nā-sāyinsī fe'l hai.*"
9. Zaidi, *Do Adabī Iskūl* , pp. 21-22.
10. *Op. cit.*, pp. 83-88.
11. Literally, "color," but also used to mean "aspect, style, manner, character, nature." See Platts' *Dictionary of Urdu, Classical Hindi and English*, London: Oxford University Press, 1974, p. 601.
12. Zaidi., p. 21.
13. Ibid., p.154. Elsewhere he challenges the sub-division of the Lucknow school into two further schools—those of Nasikh and Atish—on the same grounds, [p.88].
14. Ibid., pp.159-60.
15. Ibid., p.16.
16. Ibid.
17. The *she'r* is Atish's "Whenever a bubble/by another bubble rose/ I thought of her brassiere/ of finest gauze."
18. Zaidi, *Do Adabī Iskūl*, pp. 169-70.
19. Ibid.

20. Ibid., pp. 173-74.
21. Ibid., p. 175.
22. Zaidi also observes that there were *marākiz* in Rampur, Hyderabad, and Azimabad but no separate schools have been designated for them. Ibid., p. 17.
23. Cf. Shabihul Hasan, *Nāsikh: Tajzīya-o Taqdīr*, Lucknow: U.P. Urdu Akedmi, 1974; Rashid Hasan Khan, *Intikhāb-i Nāsikh,* Delhi: Maktaba-i Jami'a Limited, 1972; Shah Abdus Salam, *Dabistān-i Ātish*, Delhi: Maktaba-i Jami'a Limited, 197; Abul Lais Siddiqi, *Tanqīd-o Tabṣire*, Hyderabad: Urdu Book Centre, 1971; and Khalil Ahmad Siddiqi, *Rekhtī kā Tanqīdī Muṭāla'a*, Lucknow: Nasim Book Depot, 1974.
24. In this context Zaidi cites other defenders of Lucknow. Cf. Abid Ali Abid, *Tanqīdī Mazāmīn*; Rashid Hasan Khan, *Intikhāb-i Nāsikh*; Khalilur Rahman Azami, *Muqaddma-i Kalām-i Ātish*; Al-i Ahmad Suroor, "*Lakhna'u Iskūl ne Nahīñ, Lakhna'u ne.*"
25. Zaidi, *Do Adabī Iskūl* , pp. 95-97.
26. Ibid., p. 93: "*Avām kī akhlāqī hālat durūst thī. Rang raliyāñ umarā tak mahdūd thīñ.*" However, since it was almost solely the upper classes who produced Urdu literature until very recently; and since the custom of conspicuous consumption as a means of articulating the élite in India has been seen by historians to outlast the resources required for it, this particular point of Zaidi's does little to advance his overall position.
27. Ibid., p. 91.
28. Only on page 175 does Zaidi actually begin his close examination of Shadani's designated Lakhnavi *khuṣūṣīyāt*, the stated purpose and domain of the book.
29. Ibid., p. 171.
30. ZIbid., p. 16.
31. *Sāyinsī nuqta-i naẓar se yih tarīqa ghalaṭ hai.*" Ibid.
32. Ibid., pp. 125-140.
33. *Shab Khūn*, No. 81, February 1973, pp. 74-75. Zaidi also refers to a radio response by Gopi Chand Narang on pp. 54 of *Fīkr-o Riyāẓ*, New Delhi: Maktaba-i Jam'ia Limited, 1975. However, I have not been able to locate a text of this response.
34. Ibid.
35. Personal communication, Berkeley, 20 November 1984.
36. *Fikr-o Riyāẓ* pp. 41-42.
37. It will be illustrated in the next chapter's controlled study of Dihlavi and Lakhnavi poetry.
38. Indications that this is so are that both Hashmi and Siddiqi are quoted in nearly every published work on the Two Schools; whereas Zaidi is not. Even Shah Abdus Salam's *Dabistān-i Ātish*, one of the few books that lists *Do Adabī Iskūl* in its Bibliography, does not quote Zaidi in

its discussion of the dubious differences between *Dihlavīyat* and *Lakhnavīyat* on pp. 39-40. This is all the more surprising in view of the fact that Abdus Salam's discussion here appears to coincide almost completely with that of Zaidi in *Do Adabī Iskūl*.

39. The sample is offered as an illustration of how comparative studies of Urdu ghazal poetry might be made, and in no way claims to address all the aspects of a question as large as how to accurately determine and designate schools of poetry for a literature like the ghazal.

40. In fact, it is quite legitimate—if not essential—to question the appropriateness of attempting "objective, scientific" analysis of something as inherently subjective as literature. One insight it does substantiate, however, is that structural demands such as metre and end-rhyme can play an important role in the thematic choices of any given poet in a given compositional context. For example, in a *mushā'ira*, where a number of poets are all given a set *zamīn*—metre and rhyme-scheme—several or more will often choose similar rhyming words. This, in turn, results in a number of *she'rs* with similar thematic features.

CHAPTER X

Comparison of Lakhnavi and Dihlavi Poetry in the Same *Zamīn*

Introduction

The last chapter's exposition of *Do Adabī Iskūl* by Ali Javad Zaidi showed that a reader familiar with the Urdu poetry of both Delhi and Lucknow can quite easily find numerous examples in Dihlavi poetry that display the characteristics described by Two School critics Nadvi and Shadani, as typically Lakhnavi—and vice versa. The fact that characteristics of *Lakhnavīyat* were readily apparent in Dihlavi poetry—and that characteristics of *Dihlavīyat* were also manifest in Lakhnavi poetry—formed Zaidi's fundamental objection to the delineation of two literary schools for Delhi and Lucknow. Zaidi also cited a number of other arguments which further challenged the logical premises of the Two School theory. Yet the challenge represented by *Do Adabī Iskūl* appears to have had little impact on the theory's overwhelming prevalence as conventional wisdom among the Urdu literary establishment.

One wonders if there might not be additional fruitful alternatives to Zaidi's particular approach to the Two School theory, other possible methods of comparison for the Urdu ghazal that might illuminate the thorny problem of what distinguishes one style of Urdu ghazal poetry from another. The primary problem is that any comparison of poets or groups of poets would necessarily involve an enormous volume of poetry. Zaidi condemned as "unscientific" (*nā-sāyinsī*) other critics' "proof" of Dihlavi or Lakhnavi characteristics (*k͟huṣūṣīyāt*) that were based on the citation of a few individual *she'rs*—or sets of *she'rs*—out of the context of their ghazals. In light of this, Zaidi made a point of citing greater numbers of *she'rs* in his refutation of Nadvi and Shadani than they had originally offered as examples of Dihlavi and Lakhnavi *khuṣūṣīyāt*.

The question still remains of how one can apply the scientific method alluded to by Zaidi—dependent as it is on quantification—to arguing what characterises topical differences in such a subjective field as literature. Until such time as the field of Urdu criticism has complete access to computer technology—and the inclination to apply it—it is highly unlikely that a truly scientific word-count of the Two School theory's distinguishing *khuṣūṣīyāt* will be effected.

In this chapter we propose to employ a method of comparing different bodies of ghazal poetry that does not appear to have been applied in critical literature concerned with the Two School theory. Since the ghazal has a rigid technical structure, it strikes us as promising to base poetic comparison on choices made within the context of the genre's structural parameters. All the critics discussed so far—including Zaidi—have based their comparative samples largely on allegedly "Lakhnavi" or "Dihlavi" themes, and their assumption has been that poets will gravitate to certain themes as a result of the social or economic or political environment in which they are composing. The role of structural features on the thematic outcome of a *she'r* has been debated in Urdu criticism[1] and encourages an examination of Dihlavi and Lakhnavi poetry on the basis of end-rhyme. If there were different Dihlavi and Lakhnavi approaches to poetry, one would expect to see *Dihlavīyat* and/or *Lakhnavīyat* reflected in how Delhi and Lucknow poets evoked various associations suggested by the same word in *qāfiyah* position. Therefore *qāfiyah* words are emphasized in the analysis below. Furthermore, by also restricting the metre (*baḥr*) and *radīf*, the only fluid structural feature in the ghazal excerpts examined will be the *qāfiyah*. In some instances a particular *qāfiyah* word will seem to give rise to *she'rs* displaying more characteristics associated with *Lakhnavīyat*, while certain other *qāfiyah* words will tend to give rise to *she'rs* which more closely resemble the *Dihlavīyat* described by the Two School critics. It is important to note that, on the whole, most *she'rs* will manifest a mixture of these characteristics, and that no particular Delhi-type or Lucknow-type patterns of choice are apparent. The reason for this is simply that all Urdu poets subscribe to the same essential literary values and aesthetic. Only one or two verses in the pages to come will appear to epitomise *Dihlavīyat* or *Lakhnavīyat* as they have been articulated by Nadvi, Shadani and others—and, ironically, even then a characteristically Lakhnavi *she'r* will often have been written by a Dihlavi *ustād.*

The poetic samples which appear in the following pages have been selected on the basis of *zamīn*, that is, according to their meter and rhyme-scheme.[2] They have all been drawn from a pool of seven poets: Nasikh, Atish and five of their contemporaries from Delhi—Momin, Zauq, Shah Nasir, Zafar and Ghalib. All seven poets are discussed in the context of Azad's *pānchvāṅ daur* (Fifth Epoch) in *Āb-i Ḥayāt*, which is the age Nadvi points to as the time when the two separate schools were established.[3] A comparison of Dihlavi and Lakhnavi poetry restricted to poets of a single era further reduces the number of variables contributing to the circumstances in which they wrote. For this reason we have not included such Dihlavi *ustāds* as Mir and Sauda, nor such Lakhnavi *ustāds* as Mushafi, Jur'at or Insha.[4]

It was not possible to cull numbers of *she'rs* by all seven poets in a single *zamīn*—which would probably have been ideal to a truly *sāyinsī* method—but all the poets have been represented with the comparative basis expanded to two *zamīns*. Those two *zamīns* are (1) rhyme scheme "*āb meṅ*" in the metre *muzāri'*[5] and (2) the rhyme scheme "*- ūr kā*" in the popular *ramal* metre.[6] In the first *zamīn* six of the seven poets are compared, leaving out only the Dihlavi Shah Nasir, whose *kullīyāt*[7] includes no ghazal in that particular *zamīn*. In the second *zamīn* Ghalib and Momin are not represented for the same reason; their published works include no ghazals in that *zamīn*, although there are a number written in that particular *baḥr* (metre).[8]

The following experiment should be seen as an illustration rather than an attempt at definitive or conclusive argument. The poetic sample upon which it draws is very small in relation to the total output of all the seven represented poets, and cannot possibly serve to prove or disporve—on the basis of statistical analysis—as complicated and comprehensive a literary theory as the Two School theory. As we have said, that would be quite impractical and not necessarily conclusive in any case. Yet even a cursory comparison of poetry by contemporaneous Lakhnavis and Dihlavis confirms that, in general, all Urdu poets follow the same fundamental rules of structure and adhere to the same system of literary aesthetics. No matter where a ghazal poet dwells, the technical structure of the ghazal remains the same.

For example, the presence of a strongly-loaded term such as *sharāb* (wine) in the first *zamīn* below or *ḥūr* (heavenly nymph) in the second can be seen as a word-choice made to fit the demands of the *qāfiyah* -"*āb*" or -"*ūr*". Such words will often exert great influence on the *she'r's* central theme or image and, thus, on the verse's overall flavour.[9] It is therefore extremely difficult to lend credence to the notion that poets' thematic choices are any reflection at all of their geographic or societal surroundings. Rather, the thematic choices are being exercised from within the *she'r*, in accordance with the formal demands of Urdu ghazal composition.[10]

When these dynamics are observed in the context of neutral *radīfs* such as *meñ* (in) or *kā* (of), all the more persuasive is the notion that the *qāfiyah* works to bring together structure and theme in the ghazal.[11] Again, the following experiment is offered as an illustration of this point of view rather than a hard and fast proof of it.

The comparison begins with four sets of *she'rs* in the first *zamīn*, starting with those which employ the word *naqāb* (veil) for their *qāfiyah*. Other sets in the first *zamīn* will feature *she'rs* with *qāfiyah* words *sharāb* (wine), *māhtāb* (moonlight) and *javāb* (answer, reply). We will see that the verses in this first *zamīn* have *qāfiyah* words which represent key terms in the ghazal lexicon and therefore provide layers of connotation and allusion which the poets can exploit without having to specifically cite them.

The four sets of *she'rs* in the second *zamīn*, on the other hand, will feature the *qāfiyah* words *kāfūr* (camphor), *ḥūr* (houri, heavenly nymph), *angūr* (grape) and *dūr* (distant). Except for *ḥūr* these words carry far less specific connotations in the world of the ghazal, and their poets must therefore create associations which bridge that distance and draw them into the stock realm of the genre. This being the case, the verses in the first *zamīn* will tend, overall, to reiterate familiar themes, while the second set of verses will include much more creation of new themes (*maẓmūn āfirīnī*).

Choices of diction and tone, while sometimes exercised in accordance with the associations suggested by the *qāfiyah* word, will still tend to reflect, overall, the specific whim or mood of the poet at the time of composition. Thus there will be instances where the *qāfiyah* word has given rise to *she'rs* by more than one poet on a similar theme, but the tone or diction might vary from *she'r* to *she'r*. The point remains, however, that if *maẓmūn* and specific topical concerns are said to distinguish *Lakhnavīyat* from *Dihlavīyat*, then there ought to be a reflection of this in *she'rs* by poets of both *marākiz*, even emanating from employment of the same *qāfiyah* word.

Naqāb meñ

Five poets—Zafar, Nasikh, Momin, Atish and Ghalib—ended at least one *she'r* in their ghazals in this *zamīn* with the *qāfiyah* word *naqāb*, meaning "veil," or "hood." All five poets build on the meaning of *naqāb* to reiterate the conventional theme of the beloved's inaccessibility. Since Zafar's *she'r* with this *qāfiyah* is a *maṯla'* it is appropriate that it be studied first:

اللہ ری شرم آئے جو وہ شب کو خواب میں
پنہاں رکھا حجاب سے منہ کو نقاب میں

Allah rī sharm ā'e jo voh shab ko khvāb meñ
Pinhāñ rakhā ḥijāb se munh ko naqāb meñ

{Zf: II. 153.1} God, what modesty!
that even in my dreams at night
she kept her face hidden
behind the veil.

This is a playful verse in which Zafar simultaneously praises and teases the beloved's modesty in keeping her face veiled from admiring eyes—even those of a dreamer. Word-play (*ri'āyat-i lafẓī*) gives the verse its punch, especially plays on the various connotations and interrelationship between night (*shab*), veils (*pinhāñ*, *naqāb*), concealment and modesty (*sharm*). The pivotal word in this play is *ḥijāb*, which carries all those connotations. The poet also employs assonance (*shab* and *sharm* in the first *miṣra'*, and the long vowel sound *ā* in the second syllables of *pinhāñ*, *rakhā*, *ḥijāb* and *naqāb*). At first glance the occurrence of *ḥijāb* and *naqāb* in the same *miṣra'* might appear to be redundant, since the primary meaning of *ḥijāb* is "veil." However, it also can mean "curtain, night, concealment, modesty,"[12] and all those connotations are clearly intended here.

The elusive aspect of the beloved which permeates this verse might well lend itself to a mystical (*ḥaqīqī*) interpretation. In a mystical statement of *'ishq* the *'āshiq* refers to—or beseeches—the divine beloved. Such an interpretation is possible, but not compulsory, here especially given the verse's ironic tint. The beloved is not present during the *'āshiq's* discourse, as he complains about her elusiveness. Since both God and human beloveds elude the hungry eyes of their admirers, the question of the beloved's identity remains deliciously ambiguous.

Nasikh drew upon the ghazal's conventional associations with Sufi motifs to remind the reader that the divine beloved, as well as a human, is hidden from the sight of earthly lovers and also unattainable. This next verse depicts the *'āshiq's* deluded condition, brought on by his vain struggle to catch a glimpse of the beloved who obsesses him:

غفلت سے اپنا طالبِ دیدار آپ ہوں
میرا ہی چہرہ ہے جو نہاں ہے نقاب میں

{N: I . 140.5} Ghaflat se apnā ṭālib-i dīdār āp hūṅ
Merā hī chahra hai jo nihāṅ hai naqāb meṅ

I'm so foolish:
I seek a glimpse of myself
when it's my own face
concealed behind that veil.

This *she'r* is undoubtedly intended to be read for its mystical message. On the Sufistic plane, it is God who conceals Himself behind the veil of this temporal world. Because the Sufi is filled with *'ishq*, or love for God, he seeks the same union which an *'āshiq* normally seeks with his earthly beloved. In deep contemplation of the object of his love, and in the disorientation brought on by that contemplation, the *'āshiq* perceives that there is no distinction between himself and God—they are one and the same.[13] Therefore the face of the beloved (God) is none other than the *'āshiq's* own. Another interpretation might be that the *'āshiq* is reporting his inability to transcend the phenomenal world, and his efforts lead him only back to images of his own making.[14]

According to the *khuṣūṣīyāt* delineated by Two School critics, the *taṣavvuf* which predominates in this verse—and its simple, straightforward diction—might lead one to guess that its author was a Dihlavi. Enumerations of feminine beauty and apparel; song, dance, effeminacy and frivolousness; lascivious banter and *mu'āmla bandī*; and complicated, extremely refined diction—in other words, characteristics which one might well expect to encounter in a verse by the *Imam of Lakhnavīyat*—are nowhere to be found in this verse.

In the next three *she'rs*, those of Atish, Momin and Ghalib, the *'āshiq* reports on images of the beloved which he glimpses fleetingly through the opening in her veil. Atish and Momin describe effects of those glimpses on the '*āshiq*, referring to the hunt, or battle:

ٹٹی کی اوٹ میں وہ کیا کرتے ہیں شکار
منہ کو چھپائے رکھتے ہیں اپنے نقاب میں

{A: II. 35.4} Ṭaṭṭī kī oṭ meñ voh kiyā karte haiñ shikār
Munh ko chhupā'e rakhte haiñ apne naqāb meñ

She always hunts
from the shelter of a screen:
she keeps her face hidden in her veil.

This verse likens the beloved's veil to the bamboo or grass screen (*ṭaṭṭī kī oṭ*) commonly used by hunters stalking game. It is also a *she'r-i tams̤īl*, wherein the first *miṣra'* makes some sort of statement or proposition. The beloved here might be divine or human, since God does hide His face from the world, and is often considered to be everywhere, all around humans as we move through our temporal days, thus "stalking" the '*āshiq*. Light in tone, this *she'r* by Atish makes perhaps the most superficial *maẓmūn* of the *naqāb*-set of verses in its equation of *naqāb* with a bamboo-screen.[15] It would be difficult to argue persuasively that this *she'r* manifests either greater *Lakhnavīyat* or *Dihlavīyat*: mostly it strikes us as a "garden variety" verse of the Urdu ghazal genre.

چینِ جبیں کو دیکھ کے دل بستہ تر ہوا
کیسی کشودِ کار کشادِ نقاب میں

{M: 140.4} Chīn-i jabīñ ko dekh ke dil-basta tar huā
Kaisī kushūd-i kār kushād-i naqāb meñ

Seeing her frown
my heart was twisted and wrung anew:
how could my heart's knots unravel
when she untied her veil?

This *she'r* by Momin, a Dihlavi, relies a great deal upon *ri'āyat-i lafẕī*. Its language is neither simple nor colloquial, especially in the second *miṣra'*, whose only two non-Persian words are *kaisī* (how, what sort [of]) and *meñ* (in). The verse's assonance and alliteration are pleasing, and the vocabulary itself impressive, if not easily comprehended (*kushūd* and *kushād* are both Persian participles not commonly found in conversational Urdu). In its long Persian constructions (phrases strung together with *izāfat*) this verse contains the most *fārsī tarākīb* seen so far. There is also an element of *ri'āyat-i lafẕī* in the paradox that the beloved's unloosening of her veil results in tying the '*āshiq's* heart up in knots. It was already constricted in anticipation, but now the actual attainment of a glimpse of her annoyed frown tightens the noose even more, so to speak.

Ghalib's *she'r*, like Atish's *she'r* in this *qāfiyah*, is a *she'r-i tamṡīl*, conveying its message in two parallel statements. From the outer surface of the beloved's veil, the '*āshiq* "reads" what is going on inside: from the wrinkle which mars the surface of her veil he deduces that she is frowning, and announces it to all and sundry:

ہے تیوری چڑھی ہوئی اندر نقاب کے
ہے اک شکن پڑی ہوئی طرفِ نقاب میں

{G: 109.9} Hai tevarī charhī huī andar naqāb ke
Hai ik shikan parī huī ṯarf-i naqāb meñ

She's scowling inside her veil:
A crease has wrinkled the surface of the veil.

The tone is light, and the '*āshiq's* teasing of the beloved is rather daring. If the narrator appeared to be the '*āshiq* speaking indirectly to the beloved, this verse might be considered a *she'r* of *mu'āmla bandī*. However, the narrator is likelier one of a group of admirers speaking to his peers, so one hesitates to push the label of *mu'āmla bandī* on this verse.

The technical accomplishment of this verse creates a pleasing effect, though I would suggest that its technical intricacy relates directly to its lightness of tone and relative absence of *josh*. In support of the *she'r's tamṡīlī* nature (the two *miṣra's* contain complete, parallel assertions), the verbal construction of the two lines is also parallel. For example, the word *hai* (is) begins both lines. In the middle of both lines the sound *arhi* serves as a sort of secondary *qāfiyah*,[16] with the participial *huī* acting as a secondary *radīf*. Furthermore, Ghalib plays on the antonymous meanings of *charhī huī* (arisen, risen up) and *parī huī* (lying, fallen).

Its playful tone discourages a Sufistic reading, for if the message were mystical, God's frown (presumably of displeasure rather than of coquettish pique) would be an object of fun and irony. One can well imagine Hali frowning at the inappropriateness of such an image, although such a scenario is not totally implausible in the context of the ghazal. In fact it should, technically, be perfectly legitimate. Still, one expects a *haqīqī* verse to be more serious in tone than this *she'r* by Ghalib: God should not be depicted as a woman frowning behind a veil.

It is not always the case that technical intricacy and *mazmūn āfirīnī* create verses whose tone is light and which lack *josh*. For instance, Momin created an essentially emotional effect based on the creation of a *mazmūn* equating the beloved's veil with the *'āshiq's* heart—the opening of the former (the veil) caused the latter (the heart) to constrict—though he employed difficult vocabulary and complicated Persian constructions. Still, two of the five *she'rs* in this group—those of Ghalib and Zafar—displayed some technical intricacy involving *ri'āyat-i lafzī*, and were essentially light and playful in tone. Both verses were written by Dihlavi poets.

To summarise the first set of verses in this first *zamīn*: the word *naqāb* in *qāfiyah*-position seems clearly to have inclined all five *she'rs* to centre around the "aloof-beloved theme," for the veil is a very connotative, concrete symbol in the realm of the ghazal. It carries with it an entire setting, evoking a *bazm* or assembly, with the aloof beloved in the centre and the *'āshiq* and his rivals clustered around her, vainly hoping for a glimpse of her face from behind the veil. The *bazm*, in turn, readily allows for—but does not dictate—the quality of banter associated with *mu'āmla bandī*. When Zafar claims that she would hide her face from even the dreamer, that "even" means "not only does she elude all of us clustered around her during the day, she hides from us at night as well." "All of us" are, in this case, her admirers. Atish's, Momin's and Ghalib's verses evoke the *bazm* even more directly than Zafar's *she'r*. The stalking and hunting from behind her bamboo-screen-like veil—referred to in Atish's *she'r* —in turn evoke another stock image: the beloved's arrow-like glances that pierce the *'āshiq's* heart. Finally, her frown of displeasure, observed through the veil in Ghalib's and Momin's *she'rs* could only be caused by the beloved's apprehension of some new deficiency in the tiresome *'āshiq(s)* who cluster(s) around her.

In the next set of *she'rs*, whose *qāfiyah* word is *māhtāb*, or moonlight, we will see an even stronger example of the influence exerted on a verse's theme by its end-rhyme.

Māhtāb meñ

Many of the romantic associations of moonlight are evoked by Momin, Nasikh, Atish and Ghalib in the following set of *she'rs*, whose *qāfiyah* word is *māhtāb* (moonlight). In fact, all four poets precede the *qāfiyah* with *shab-i* (night of) so that the situation in each of these verses is a moonlit night. Like the word *naqāb*, only even more so, the word *māhtāb* has extremely strong connotations and, in the *qāfiyah* position especially, carries with it an entire train of allusion. Were the mood and tone of such a *she'r* not romantic, melancholy and longing, and did that mood not arise from *shab-i māhtāb's* allusion to the separation of *'āshiq* from his beloved; most of the ghazal audience would probably be surprised. Similarly, though it is theoretically possible to find *māhtāb* by itself—moonlight connotes nighttime in any case—it would be highly unlikely to see a *she'r* which did not mention or evoke "*shab*" (the night) when the *qāfiyah* word was *māhtāb*. Aside from these thematic reasons for the conjunction of *shab* and *māhtāb*, the pattern of stressed and unstressed syllables in this metre (*bahr*) lends itself very well to a preceding *shab-i* leading into *māhtāb meñ*.

The idea of wine is closely associated with moonlit nights, as we will see: Momin finds a moonlit night so intoxicating in and of itself that he declares wine to be superfluous—he is drunk without imbibing wine, no doubt because his memories (presumably of past union with his beloved) provide a headiness of their own. Nasikh and Ghalib, on the other hand, affected by a similar mood, feel moved to drink on this kind of night. Only Atish, in this instance, speaks of union but does not speak of wine.

کیا جلوے یاد آئے کہ اپنی خبر نہیں
بے بادہ مست ہوں میں شب ماہتاب میں

{M: 140.16} Kyā jalve yād āe kih apnī khabar nahīñ
Be-bāda mast hūñ maiñ shab-i māhtāb meñ

In reminiscence of glories
I'm lost to myself;
I get drunk without wine
on moonlit nights.

ہے رات چودھویں مجھے ساقی پلا شراب
روشن ہو آفتاب شب ماہتاب میں

{N: I. 140.18) Hai rāt chaudhvīñ mujhe sāqī pilā sharāb
Roshan ho āftāb shab-i māhtāb meñ

It's the fourteenth night (full moon)
Saqi, pour me some wine!
Let the sun shine
on this moonlit night.

آجائے شام سے تو نہ جانے دوں صبح تک
اس ماہِ چاردہ کو شبِ ماہتاب میں

{A:I . 35.25} Ā jāe shām se to na jāne dūñ ṣubḥ tak
Us māh-i chār-dah ko shab-i māhtāb meñ

Were she to come this evening,
that one with the full-moon face,
I would not let her leave till dawn
on this moonlit night.

غالب چھٹی شراب پر اب بھی کبھی کبھی
پیتا ہوں روزِ ابر و شبِ ماہتاب میں

{G :13} Ghālib chhuṭī sharāb par ab bhī kabhī kabhī
Pītā hūñ roz-i abr-o shab-i māhtāb meñ

Ghalib, I've renounced wine
but still, from time to time,
I drink on cloudy days
and moonlit nights.

Three of the four poets rely on conventional devices with this *qāfiyah*: Momin submerges himself in ecstatic reverie centred, we assume, around the beloved; Atish compares the beloved's face to the full moon; and in Nasikh's *she'r* the narrator is inspired by the full moon's splendour to drink enough to "glow like sunshine (*roshan-i āftāb*). In fact, here he makes a clever play on words, since *āftāb* can connote wine as well as sunshine. Ghalib strikes an individual note here, making fun of his addiction to wine and inability to stick to his renunciation of drink. He especially gives in to the desire for it on classically romantic occasions like cloudy days and moonlit nights. By citing such occasions he reminds us that it is, after all, the travail of *'ishq* which drives him to drink in the first place.

None of the verses except Nasikh's employs *ri'āyat-i lafẓī*, or *mu'āmla bandī*, and the only instance of *fārsī tarākīb* is Ghalib's *roz-i abr* (cloudy day). None describes the beloved's clothing, though Atish's *she'r* does mention her "full-moon face." His *she'r*, because of that description, lends itself the least readily of the four to mystical interpretation, though it could be pushed in that direction. None of them, however, really seems to be specifically concerned with *'ishq-i ḥaqīqī*: all the poets are trying to describe a more general aspect of *'ishq*. Moonlit nights are highly charged because they drive the *'āshiq* to think of the beloved, especially of union (*viṣāl*) with her, be it remembered or optimistically contemplated.

Nasikh's verse here manifests a certain bravado that is easy to associate with wine, but occasional bravado on the part of the *'āshiq* is quite conventional. Also, in its equation of the *'āshiq's* sunshine-like wine-glow with moonlight, Nasikh comes closer to creating a verse of *maẓmūn āfirīnī* than any of the other poets using this *qāfiyah* word. In creating a *maẓmūn* where he renounces wine but does not stop drinking, Ghalib creates some *ma'nī āfirīnī*.[17] These two features might cast a slightly different tint to Nasikh's and Ghalib's *she'rs* than we saw in the other two *she'rs* of this set, but the overall mood of all four is similar; and in the emotion they all evoke, these verses more closely fit the Two School notion of *Dihlavīyat* than *Lakhnavīyat*.

Sharāb meñ

Four of the six poets compared in this *zamīn* composed *she'rs* whose *qāfiyah* word was *sharāb* (wine). They are Nasikh and Atish—the two Lakhnavis—and the Dihlavis Zafar and Ghalib. Wine is something very much a part of the ghazal lexicon, but it does not necessarily call up as concrete a setting as the *bazm* evoked by the presence of *naqāb* or *māhtāb* in *qāfiyah*-position. Thus the tone of a *she'r* centred around a *maẕmūn* involving wine can be more varied than those focused on moonlight or the beloved's veil. Although a tavern scene will often be evoked in a verse that mentions wine—and that potential is exploited by Nasikh in the verse below—"*sharāb*" as *qāfiyah*-word lends itself as easily to *maẕmūn āfirīnī's* elaborate flights of fancy as to subdued, spiritual rumination; or to melancholy langour as well as to *mu'āmla bandī*; or even to sensual frivolousness. In this set of four *she'rs* all these diverse facets of wine's connotations will be seen, and the mood and tone will differ more from verse to verse than they did in the first two sets of *she'rs* in this *zamīn*. Nasikh's *maṭla'* will be examined first.

مستوں کا عیش تلخ ہے دہرِ خراب میں
یہ رمز ہے جو ہوتی ہے تلخی شراب میں

{N: I. 140.2} Mastoñ kā 'aish talkh hai dahr-i kharāb meñ
Yih ramz hai jo hotī hai talkhī sharāb meñ

In this devastated world
a drunkard's pleasure is bitter:
that is the secret
in the bitterness of wine.

Nasikh's verse is paradigmatically ambiguous: it can easily be read as light or ponderous in tone; the tavern and wine of which the narrator speaks might be construed as real, physical, tangible—or as metaphorical.

Layers of meaning are packed into this *she'r* through the device of *ri'āyat-i lafẕī*, or word-play. Playing on the multiple meanings of words like *dahr* and *kharāb*, the narrator conveys the sense of the tavern as a temple of iniquity, where a melancholy pleasure is attained. One word for tavern is *kharābāt*. Nasikh suggests this word without actually naming it. He suggests it by building a scene with *mastoñ* (the intoxicated, drunks), '*aish* (living, pleasure, delight), and *kharāb* (ruined, spoiled, bad, desolate, drunken). All these words qualify the word *dahr* (time, the world, the times), which is where those who are *mast* (i.e. the '*āshiqs*) are gathered. The pleasure attained in this place is bittersweet, just as walking among ruins often creates a melancholy mood—especially in an intoxicated lover—as he contemplates death and decay, and the vicissitudes inherent in the passage of time. According to the narrator, contemplation of the bitter dregs at the bottom of a wine-cup is all that one gets of the pleasure of drinking.[18] As in Momin's *she'r* "*Chīn-i jabīn*..." the typically Dihlavi tone of emotion not only co-exists with, but is achieved through, the typically Lakhnavi device of *ri'āyat-i lafẓī*.[19]

وہ مست ہوں خمار سے جب دردِ سر ہوا
صندل لگایا میں نے رگڑ کر شراب میں

{A:II. 35.2} Voh mast hūñ khumār se jab dard-i sar huā
Ṣandal lagāyā maiñ ne ragaṛ kar sharāb meñ

I'm the kind of drunk
who cures a hangover's headache
by applying to his throbbing temple
a paste of sandalwood and wine.

The tone of this *she'r* by Atish is clearly light. Its message is "I—the *'āshiq*—am an unrepenting sinner (drinker)." He is so enamoured of forbidden fruit (wine) that even when he has drunk to excess and is suffering the ill effects he cannot bear to be parted from it. Instead, he uses it as a balm to soothe his headache, acting on the familiar adage, "a hair of the dog that bit him."

Or the verse could conceivably be read as a defiant statement of idolatry, which is also conventional to the ghazal. As a defiant statement it would read something like: "Even were I to be punished for my sins (with a hangover) I would flaunt the punishment as a denial of remorse or penitence."[20] Such a reading of this *she'r* would almost certainly be secondary, but legitimate nonetheless.

Only in this last instance, that of its apparently sensual orientation, does Atish's *she'r* fit any characteristics of the *Lakhnavīyat* described by Nadvi and Shadani. Its language has the straightforwardness which they and Hashmi characterise as Dihlavi, but language is not as obvious a feature of this *she'r* as it was in the previous *she'r* by Nasikh. This verse of Atish's is completely conventional within the context of the Urdu ghazal, and could have been written by just about any poet at all.[21]

یوں آنسوؤں کے ساتھ پیا ہم نے خونِ دل
جیسے ملا کے پیتے ہیں پانی شراب میں

{Zf:II. p 153.5} Yūñ ānsūoñ ke sāth piyā ham ne khūn-i dil
Jaise milā ke pīte haiñ pānī sharāb meñ

We drank our heart's blood
mixed with tears
just as wine is drunk
diluted with water.

Zafar makes a melancholy play on words in this *she'r* as he summarises the standard plight of all *'āshiqs*, who suffer intense grief (*khūn-i dil pīnā*). He suggests that, just as wine's richness is often diluted with water for drinking, so too must the intensity of the heart's blood be diluted (this time with a readily available diluting agent—one's own tears). The language is idiomatic Urdu, and the diction simple (*sāda*), just as we imagine Azad and Hali would have Urdu poetry be.[22] Containing no profound statement about the human condition—very few *she'rs* truly do, no matter what their aspirations—it is yet a pleasant enough verse, the kind which pleases without challenging its audience and is therefore very popular.

مجھ تک کب ان کی بزم میں آتا تھا دورِ جام
ساقی نے کچھ ملا نہ دیا ہو شراب میں

{G:109.5} Mujh tak kab un kī bazm meñ ātā thā daur-i jām
Sāqī ne kuchh milā na diyā ho sharāb meñ

When, in her assembly,
did the flask ever get around to me?
The *sāqī* must have
mixed something in the wine.

This verse of Ghalib's is an ironic observation against the beloved, and comes as close to *mu'āmla bandī* as any in the present group. Ostensibly, the *'āshiq* is complaining that the wine-cup which is traditionally passed around the circle of gathered admirers never seems to reach his own lips, though others, his rivals, drink from it. Similarly, it is meant to say that the beloved passes out a few favours within her circle of admirers, but never to him, the narrator. In the second *miṣra'*, he attributes the reason for this present exception to the likelihood that the *sāqī*—who symbolizes, in this case, the beloved—has mixed something (i.e. poison) in the wine. In other words, "I know her unkind ways—if she seems to be doing me a favor (by offering me wine) she probably has something up her sleeve. Favours from her must ultimately be suspect." The apparently urbane but inwardly ironic tone of this *she'r* runs somewhat contrary to the conventional stance of the ghazal's *'āshiq*.[23]

Of this set of verses, the melancholy tone of Zafar's and the glib tone of Atish's satisfy conventional notions of what to expect from a Dihlavi and Lakhnavi poet, respectively. Nasikh's verse contained both the *ri'āyat-i lafẓī* supposedly expected from a Lakhnavi *she'r* and the languid melancholy, the *gham pasandī* which Nurul Hasan Hashmi claimed characterised *Dihlavīyat*.[24] And Ghalib's verse of *mu'āmla bandī* might have been expected of a Lakhnavi poet, although his *sāda*, colloquial diction is claimed by Azad, Hali and others to be the domain of Dihlavi poets. Interestingly, these *she'rs* were not based on *maẓmūn āfirīnī's* or *ma'nī āfirīnī's* elaborate flights of fancy, although they would certainly have been compatible with the various associations carried by wine.

All in all, a broad spectrum of compositional choices was exercised in this set of *she'rs* with the *qāfiyah* word of *sharāb*; and those choices did more to challenge than to confirm Nadvi's and Shadani's designated Dihlavi and Lakhnavi *khuṣūṣīyāt*. The poets combined elements of both, depending on the particular associations they chose for wine.

Javāb meñ

The word *javāb* has very direct and specific connotations, in the ghazal, especially of verbal or written exchanges between the *'āshiq* and beloved. However, it does not dictate setting as strongly as did "*māhtāb*," and once again, like *naqāb* and *sharāb*, there is variation amongst the four *she'rs* with this *qāfiyah* word insofar as mood, tone and specific setting go.

Those connotations of *javāb* lend themselves readily to the composition of *she'rs* of *mu'āmla bandī*, as we will observe in the first two verses which follow. The second pair, while not verses of *mu'āmla bandī*, also speak of stock situations wherein the '*āshiq* has sent a missive to the beloved and awaits, or has already received, a very predictable response from her. First, Zauq's *maṭla*' :

یاں لب پہ لاکھ لاکھ سخن اضطراب میں
واں ایک خامشی تری سب کے جواب میں

{Zq: 126.1} Yāñ lab pe lākh lākh sukhan iẓṭirāb meñ
Vāñ ek khāmushī tirī sab ke javāb meñ

Here a million utterances
crowd my agitated lips
while there you observe
one silence in answer to them all.

This *she'r* touches upon the hopelessness and the blend of frenzy and frustration in the '*āshiq's* situation with his beloved: he barely contains the world of desires within him struggling to pour forth from his lips while she remains unmoved, perhaps even ignoring him. The verse is colloquial, employing the *yāñ..vāñ* construction ("here ... there"; or "on the one hand . . . and on the other") so well-suited to a *she'r-i tamṣīl* presenting two contradictory statements. Together with the hyperbolic *lākh lākh* (lit. hundreds and hundreds of thousands) of unspoken speeches on the '*āshiq's* lips, *yāñ* ... *vāñ* also emphasizes how remote the beloved is, both physically and psychically, from his suffering.

Overall Zauq's *maṭla*' manifests *sādagī* and reiterates the melancholy condition of the universal '*āshiq*. The poet manipulates language to build this verse's impact, employing the soft sounds of Persian words like *lab*, *sukhan*, and *khāmushī*; the drama of *iẓṭirāb*; and the intimacy of colloquial language in vocabulary like *lākh*, *javāb* and Urdu grammatical constructions. Such language use does not constitute *fārsī tarākīb* or *ri'āyat-i lafẓī*, however.

This is certainly an example of *mu'āmla bandī*, despite its plaintive tone—not all *mu'āmla bandī* is glib. The beloved is present, referred to in the second person by the '*āshiq*, and his tone of complaint or dissatisfaction as well as the fact of dialogue between '*āshiq* and *maḥbūb* in this *she'r* strengthens such a categorisation.

On a similar note, Momin also writes about the difference between the '*āshiq's* agitation (*iẓṭirāb*) and how it impedes his verbal progress with the beloved:

کہتے ہیں تم کو ہوش نہیں اضطراب میں
سارے گلے تمام ہوئے اک جواب میں

{M: 140.2} Kahte haiñ tum ko hosh nahīñ iẓṭirāb meñ
Sāre gile tamām hue ik javāb meñ

You say:
You seem so distraught,
have you taken leave of your senses?
All my complaints were thus
disposed of in a single reply.

This verse, too, is essentially simple in concept and colloquially stated, using common Urdu vocabulary (with the slight exception of *iẓṭirāb*) and no Persian construction. The beloved is needling the '*āshiq*, and he is helpless to defend himself against her taunts that he seems so ill at ease. The element of complaint (*shikāyat*) is even more subdued in this verse than it was in the last, but its presence is strongly enough suggested to warrant a claim for this *she'r* as a verse of *mu'āmla bandī*. The second *miṣra'* carries a double sense: it can be read as a statement made by the '*āshiq*—as a report on the first *miṣra'*—or it could be a statement by the beloved. Critics might well consider this *she'r* to be a paragon of *Dihlavīyat* in its simplicity, eloquence and conventional stance of '*āshiqī*.

Atish says:

جب اشتیاق لکھا ہے خونخوار یار کو
قاصد کا کشتہ آیا ہے خط کے جواب میں

{A: II. 35.8} Jab ishtiyāq likkhā hai k̲h̲ūñ-k̲h̲vār yār ko
Qāṣid kā kushta āyā hai k̲h̲aṭ ke javāb meñ

When I wrote of my passion
to that blood-thirsty beloved
the messenger's slaughtered body
came back in reply.

Here Atish departs from the "I . . . you" constructions of the previous two verses, eliminating the tone of *mu'āmla bandī*, but gaining force in his complaint against her injustice and heartlessness. Unlike the previous two *she'rs* the reader cannot assume any direct contact between the '*āshiq* and the *ma'shūq*, be it present or past. In this way Atish once again relates the standard plight of the common '*āshiq*, who is quite unsuccessful and cannot justify harbouring any hope of improvement in his lot. The language is more Persianised than in the two preceding verses, and employs a poetic idiom to the extent that Atish uses secondary epithets like *khūn-khvār* and *kushta* to refer to the beloved and the messenger; but the verse on the whole is colloquial and *sāda*. There is no *ri'āyat-i lafẓī* or *fārsī tarākīb*, and the *she'r* strikes the reader neither as particularly Lakhnavi nor Dihlavi in nature, though it certainly fits into the common pool of Urdu ghazal poetry.

The last *she'r* in this set is by Ghalib:

قاصد کے آتے آتے خط اک اور لکھ رکھوں
میں جانتا ہوں جو وہ لکھیں گے جواب میں

{G:109.4} Qāṣid ke āte āte khaṭ ik aur likh rakhūṅ
Maiṅ jāntā hūṅ jo voh likhenge javāb meṅ

I should write another letter
while waiting for the messenger's return:
I know already what she will have written in reply.

This verse is apparently so colloquial as to seem almost prosaic. It states the typical situation of the '*āshiq* in relation to his beloved, but adds no new information, nor does it offer new nuance or character to that familiar situation by virtue of any unique manner of expression. Rather, in its reiteration it calls up the countless times before that the '*āshiq* must have awaited some response from the *ma'shūq*. While there is no *ri'āyat-i lafẓī* or *fārsī tarākīb*, there is a blend of hope and resignation in the '*āshiq's*, "I already know how she will reply," and the audience knows very well that the reply will not be satisfying. One would hesitate to call this *mu'āmla bandī*. It is a subtle *she'r* in that the '*āshiq* is inwardly laughing at himself and his hopeless passion.

All the verses composed in this "*javāb*" *qāfiyah*—even the *she'r* by Atish Lakhnavi—seem to match more closely the criteria of literary *Dihlavīyat* outlined by Two School critics than did the other three sets of *she'rs* in this *zamīn*. They are neither very unusual in their technique nor in their evocation of pathos, and they manifest the "virtue" of being easily accessible to a broad stretch of the Urdu-speaking audience (Hali's "*necaral*" quality of *sādagī)*. The verses tend to be fatalistic in tone rather than frivolous or sensual, and when they employ *ri'āyat-i lafẓī* the word-play does not become the *she'rs*' most prominent feature, but serves a primary purpose of relating a message.

That message tends to take the shape of reiterating the basic relationship between the ghazal's principal characters the '*āshiq* and his beloved, and the *qāfiyah* word *javāb* inclines these *she'rs* overwhelmingly toward that topic or theme. Turning on a *qāfiyah* which means "answer, response," the verses could not help but allude to—if not mention directly—some communication calling for response. As the ghazal audience is well aware, the beloved's response— or lack thereof— to her admirer(s)is one of the primary themes in the genre. Since the nature of the '*āshiq-ma'shūq* relationship forms the central topic of the *she'rs* in this *qāfiyah*, it was more than likely that the *she'rs* display "traditional" characteristics: no matter how the genre varies in its development over time, this theme must remain fundamentally the same. If these qualities are what the critics have in mind when they speak of traditional literature, then all the verses in this group should be considered essentially Dihlavi in character.

Summary of the First *Zamīn*

In the preceding section we have examined five sets of *she'rs* by six reasonably contemporaneous Urdu poets of the nineteenth century, two from Lucknow and four from Delhi. Whenever the crucial criteria comprising *Lakhnavīyat* and *Dihlavīyat*— as they have been described by Two School critics—played a significant part in the *she'rs* they were discussed. Criteria given special attention were *taṣavvuf*, or mysticism; *ri'āyat-i lafẓī* (word-play); *mu'āmla bandī* (amorous banter); and *fārsī tarākīb* (Persian constructions). *Taṣavvuf* and *fārsī tarākīb* are considered to characterise literary *Dihlavīyat*, while *ri'āyat-i lafẓī* and *mu'āmla bandī* have been called the determinants of literary *Lakhnavīyat*. Yet we saw that all four qualities occurred, in varied degree, in the work of all six poets, Dihlavi and Lakhnavi alike.

From the examples of *she'rs* in this *zamīn* we saw that the qualities discussed by Urdu literary critics, in the context of the Delhi and Lucknow *dabistāns*, do describe much that is to be found in Urdu ghazal poetry; but that such descriptions apply generally to verses by all Urdu poets, be they Lakhnavi or Dihlavi. Of far more causal significance in determining a given verse's theme than factors of geographical setting was the *qāfiyah* word, especially when it was as highly charged and evocative as *māhtāb*. A wider range of mood was offered by the less influential *qāfiyah* words *sharāb* and *naqāb*, but in all cases the topic of the *she'r* was overwhelmingly influenced by its *qāfiyah*, and there was no apparent pattern of choice amongst the Dihlavis or Lakhnavis as discrete groups of poets.

Many of the examined verses tended to defy the Two School critics' assertions: both Ghalib's *she'r* (*Hai tevaṛī chaṛhī*) and Zafar's *maṭla'* (*Allah ri...*) were smooth, playful, and hinted at *mu'āmla bandī*, and employed or were based on *ri'āyat-i lafẓī*, while more or less reiterating the conventional position of the '*āshiq* and the beloved in the ghazal scenario. All these characteristics would be expected from Lakhnavi poets, rather than Dihlavi, according to the critics' assertions.

Further examples of discrepancies between the critical characterisations and actual poetic examples included Nasikh's *she'r* with *naqāb* (*Ghaflat se apnā ṭālib-i dīdār āp hūñ*) which was mystical, colloquial and made up of some *fārsi tarkībeñ*—in other words, manifesting all the "proper qualities of *Dihlavīyat*," as one critic has written.[25] Also Momin Dihlavi's *she'r* (*Chīn-i jabīñ ko dekh ke . . .*) manifested the *ri'āyat-i lafẓī*, difficult Persian vocabulary, and discussion of the beloved's physical features—characteristic signs of *Lakhnavīyat*—while its tone echoed the *gham-pasandī* and emotion more closely associated by critics with the so-called Delhi *dabistān*.

In many of the cases just cited distinguishing characteristics of *Lakhnavīyat* and *Dihlavīyat* could be attributed, to a great extent, to the themes and tone suggested for a *she'r* by its *qāfiyah* word (especially words like *māhtāb* giving rise to *she'rs* which spoke of the melancholy longing of an '*āshiq's* love in separation; and *javāb* giving rise to a verse of *mu'āmla bandī*). On the other hand, given all the different connotations of wine in the ghazal, the *qāfiyah* word *sharāb* gave rise to several moods and tones.

In the following pages we will examine several more groups of *she'rs* in another *zamīn*. We will contine to see a mixture of fulfillment of the expectations set up by critical characterisations of *Lakhnavīyat* and *Dihlavīyat* as well as departures therefrom.

Second *zamīn* —"*-ūr kā*"

As was noted, the verses in the first *zamīn* seemed to strike reasonably conventional notes. In this second *zamīn*, whose end-rhyme is *ūr kā* and whose metre (*baḥr*) is *ramal*[26], a different kind of *qāfiyah* word is seen. All four—*kāfur* (camphor), *ḥūr* (heavenly nymph, houri), *angūr* (grape) and *dūr* (distant)—have far less specific connotations in the ghazal than did the moonlight, veil and wine of the first *zamīn*. Because of this the poets need to create a relationship between the *qafiyāh* word and the ghazal's stock of conventional themes, resulting in numerous *she'rs* of *mazmūn āfirīnī*, the creation of unusual images. The poets featured in this *zamīn* are Nasikh, Atish, Zauq, Zafar and Shah Nasir. We begin with verses whose *qāfiyah* word is *kāfur*.

Kāfūr kā

This *qāfiyah* seems to incline poets toward *maẓmūn āfirīnī*, and also toward the topic of first-aid: almost every single *she'r* associates camphor with dressings or bandages (*marham*). First, Atish's *she'r*:

داغ سینے ہوتے ہیں گل کھاتے ہیں عاشق ترے
گرم بازار ان دنوں ہے مرہم کافور کا

{A:I: 58.5} Dāgh sīne hote haiñ gul khāte haiñ 'āshiq tire
Garm bāzār in dinoñ hai marham-i kāfūr kā

Branding rosy scars across their breasts
your lovers testify fidelity:
There's a hot trade these days
in camphor dressings.

While the underlying purpose of this verse is praise of the beloved—the "hot trade in camphor" attests to how many men are enamoured of her—the primary *maẓmūn* of this verse attests to the degree of devotion in her '*āshiqs*: they are willing to cauterise their breasts (*gul khānā*) in order to demonstrate their love.

This *she'r* is in colloquial Urdu, turning on the idiom *gul khānā* in the first *miṣra'*, and on *garm bāzār* (lit. "hot market," suggesting fast and furious trade) in the second. Although the vocabulary manifests about as much *sādagī* as Hali could hope for, and although there is no *fārsī tarākīb*, there is some *ri' āyat-i lafẓī*, in that camphor (*kāfūr*), which is cold in the medicinal system, is set in opposition to the "hot trade" (*garm bāzār*). The image evoked by *gul khānā*, although graphic, cannot be construed as *maẓmūn āfirīnī* because it is not unique, nor even new to the ghazal aesthetic.[27]

Although the beloved is directly addressed (the narrator says, "Your lovers brand their breasts"), the narrator's wry observation on the flourishing camphor trade does not constitute *mu' āmla bandī*. The general thrust of the verse is a glorification of the '*āshiqs*' plight whether or not it includes a bantering complaint against the beloved by one of her assembled admirers.

This *she'r* could withstand a *ḥaqīqī* interpretation, since the gender and identity of the beloved are not specifically indicated, but a mystical reading would not lend any particular depth to the verse's *maẓmūn*.

The following *she'r* by Nasikh which uses *kāfūr* for its *qāfiyāh* shows very "Dihlavi" characteristics:

دل ہمارا اس قدر سوزش طلب پروانہ ہے
شمع سے بھاگے جو اس میں میل ہو کافور کا

{N:I .58.9}
Dil hamārā is qadar sozish ṭalab parvāna hai
Shama' se bhāge jo us meñ mel ho kāfūr kā

My heart is such a flame-seeking moth
It would reject any candle
that showed a trace of camphor.

There is some *ri' āyat-i lāfẓī* here, with Nasikh perhaps suggesting—though not explicitly using—the phrase *kāfūr honā* as "to vanish, disappear, decamp."[28] It serves to reinforce the overall meaning of the verse, however, which is to demonstrate how hot is the '*āshiq's* heart and its desires. The image is as follows: in the first line the narrator compares his heart's desire for heat to that of the moth (which is so drawn to the candle's flame that it immolates itself). To take the claim a step further, the '*āshiq* implies that his impulse toward heat is even greater than that of the moth, because the moth overlooks the presence of camphor, while this '*āshiq's* heart cannot: camphor, in addition to being a fuel, is also known to contain cooling properties.

In the following verse Zauq associates wounds with burning heat:

تفتہ دل وہ ہوں کہ میرے داغ سوزن کے لیے
گرمی مرہم سے اڑ جائے اثر کافور کا

{Zq: 35.13} Tafta dil voh hūñ kih mere dāgh-i sozan ke liye
Garmī-i marham se uṛ jāye as̤ar kāfūr kā

My heart burns so,
the stifled heat inside these bandages
destroys the cool relief of camphor balm.

This is an elaborate exaggeration, typical of the ghazal's '*āshiq*. The heat emanating from his love-wounds is meant to indicate to the narrator's audience just how intense is his love. The image works as follows: the '*āshiq* has suffered a wounded heart in the vicissitudes of '*ishq*, and the wound has been bandaged. Yet the dressings fail to soothe the '*āshiq's* pain, because his wounded heart gives off waves of heat so intense as to neutralise the expected cooling effects of the camphor balm in which they are soaked.

The whole verse turns on *ri'āyat-i lafẓ̤ī*, especially plays on the various connotations of *tafta dil*. By itself, the word *tafta* means "heated, burning, hot, melted."[29] By extension, the phrase *tafta dil* also means "displeased" or "grieved at heart."[30] The two meanings are similar and reinforcing but not the same. Zauq's use of the phrase *tafta dil* allows the senses of grief, anger and frustration, as well as simple pain, to come into the '*āshiq's* expression. Similarly, the purely "hot" sense of *tafta dil* is reinforced by the burning wounds (*dāgh-i sozan*) at the end of the *miṣra'* which *tafta dil* begins; and both lead comfortably into the *garmī* with which the second line commences.

While the significant vocabulary is Persian, there is a strong presence of Urdu-Hindi grammar, so there is no real *fārsī tarākīb*, and the verse has the sound of colloquial Urdu. The beloved is neither present nor addressed, so there is no *mu'āmla bandī*. Even so, the poetic personalities of Zauq and Nasikh seem similar in these two *she'rs*, and both *she'rs*, because of their word-play and *maẓ̤mūn āfirīnī*, might strike the average Urdu critic as characteristically Lakhnavi. The only key element missing is the *dabistān-i Lakhnau's* alleged preoccupation with feminine apparel and accoutrements.This section concludes with discussion of Shah Nasir's *she'r* employing *kāfūr* in its *qāfiyah*:

ہوگیا داغِ تنِ ماہی اثر سے جس کے خشک
کیا کفِ دریا ہے نسخہ مرہم کافور کا

{ShN:I.113.6} Ho gayā dāgh-i tan-i māhī asar se jis ke khushk
Kyā kaf-i daryā hai nuskha marham-i kāfūr kā

Under its influence
the fish's body wound dried up:
Is the ocean's spume a recipe
for camphor bandages?

Shah Nasir is the second Dihlavi in this section to have composed a *she'r* based on *ri'āyat-i lafẓī* and *maẓmūn āfirīnī*. It is also rather obscure, likening the ocean's foam to a medicinal plaster and a fish's scales to the wounds with which an '*āshiq* is inflicted in his quest for love.[31] The *fārsī tarākīb* are interesting here, especially because the words joined together by *izāfat* do coin a new phrase, "the wound of the body of a fish;" but it does not meet the standard of elegance touted by critics who saw *fārsī tarākīb* as a great virtue in Dihlavi poetry. It is true that the fish was a symbol of honour and rank in Mughal politics, but there is no reason to believe that such a connotation of *māhī* was intended here. So the image itself is an anomaly. The only possible connection between Shah Nasir's fish-imagery and the conventions of the ghazal would be his comparison of the fish's scars to a wounded and scarred '*āshiq*, in the manner that other poets compared the markings on a peacock's tail to wounds. But this connection is remote indeed, and does not really justify the *she'r*.

In this group of verses we saw how the presence of camphor in *qāfiyah* position gave rise to several verses which spoke of bandages and dressings. The images of bandages, in turn, returned the poets to the conventional theme of the '*āshiq's* wounded heart and suffering condition. Even so, among those *she'rs* Atish and Zauq effected similar moods of proud suffering. Nasikh and Shah Nasir created very individualistic—even obscure—verses, also based on *maẓmūn āfirīnī*, the former evoking camphor's other context (as lamp fuel) and the latter evoking the bandage-and-dressing aspect of camphor but applying it to a fish's scales rather than to an '*āshiq's* burning heart.

To reiterate the connection between *qāfiyah* and the mood of a *she'r*, evocation of bandages in the context of the suffering, wounded '*āshiq* created moods of bravado rather than languor, although they ultimately served to maintain the *'āshiq's* conventional role in the ghazal. That mood is also apparent in Nasikh's verse. It is difficult to speak of the mood in Shah Nasir's puzzling *she'r*, although it is clear that the tone is light, and that the ultimate effect of the verse is one of cleverness rather than an expression of emotion.

Ḥūr kā

The four *she'rs* to be discussed in the following pages have the word *ḥūr* (houri, heavenly nymph) as their *qāfiyah* word. All four display elements of so-called *Lakhnavīyat* to a degree we have not yet seen. In this section some attempt will be made to discuss that *Lakhnavīyat* in terms beyond those provided by the Two School critics.

The word *ḥūr* has such specific, stock connotations in the ghazal that it would seem to have dictated a certain kind of verse. That verse is *tamṡīlī*, is based on *maẓmūn āfirīnī*, and compares certain of the beloved's attributes to those of a *ḥūr* or ḥouri, who is the personification of beauty in a woman.[32]

In terms of the Two School theory, the *she'rs* from this set which contain the greatest degree of sensaulity and concern with feminine adornment—and thus *Lakhnavīyat*—are by Atish and Zauq, respectively,[33] while Zafar's evokes the greatest sense of flirtation. We begin with Zauq's verse:

اس نزاکت پر نظر کرنا کہ وہ رشکِ پری
بال بھی باندھے جو مسّے پر تو زلفِ حور کا

{Zq: 35.11} Is nazākat par naẓar karnā kih voh rashk-i parī
Bāl bhī bāndhe jo masse par to zulf-i ḥūr kā

Look at the delicacy of this one
whom even the fairies envy:
She seeks to remove a pimple
by circling it with a houri's hair.

This verse ostensibly celebrates the beloved's delicacy (*nazākat*) but must really be construed as having a joke at her expense, since the example of her delicacy is that she removes blemishes with such fine tools as *houris*' locks.[34] The very mention of a wart (*massā*) lends the *she'r* a ridiculous—or at least jesting—tone, and would probably be considered in poor taste by some critics.

There is *fārsī tarkīb* here, in *rashk-i parī* and *zulf-i ḥūr*, though they are not newly coined phrases. Still the language is predominantly Persianised, with the exception of the third quadrant of the *she'r* (the first half of the second *miṣra'*), where one Urdu grammatical post-position delineates a semantic unit (*is nazākat par*). *Naẕar karnā kih* is common in Urdu, but has the look and sound of Persian to it. The poet made the verb "to look" by joining a Hindi verb (*karnā*) to a Persian noun (*naẕar*), which might indicate that the poet deliberately chose a "loftier" diction than use of the colloquial verbs would have rendered.[35]

The most graphic description of the beloved's physical attributes is mention of her facial wart, and the word *massā* is Hindi, while the less specific comparison with a *ḥūr*, in the last quadrant of the verse, is in higher, Persian diction (*par to zulf-i ḥūr kā*.) In choosing the "lower" diction of Hindi, Zauq makes a play on words which strengthens the *she'r* technically: as well as meaning "to bind or braid the hair, *bāl bāndhnā* indicates doing something minutely, precisely, dextrously, with a fine eye to detail.[36] While ostensibly referring back to the *nazākat* of the beloved, the ultimate reference is to the beloved as a witch. The *'āshiq* is clearly taking his revenge.

The first *miṣra'*'s reference to the beloved as *rashk-i parī* (envy of the fairies) sets up the expectation for *ḥūr* in the *qāfiyah*. That expectation is fulfilled, albeit with the irony of comparing the beloved *ḥūr* to a witch. Although Zauq is a Dihlavi, this verse might well have appeared in Nadvi's list of illustrations of Lakhnavi "degeneracy" along with dumbbells and heaving cheetahs.

Atish's verse advertises an austerity not normally associated with Lucknow. Yet the verse is expressed in a rather airy fashion. Its basic theme is the adverse lot of an *'āshiq*; its elaboration is contained in the claim that difficulties which would stymie lesser men are so commonplace to the lover as to be rendered inconsequential. Atish says:

سختیٔ ایام ہے میرے لئے سامانِ عیش
خشتِ بالیں کو سمجھتا ہوں میں زانو حور کا

{A:I. 58.2} Sakhtī-i aiyyām hai mere liye sāmān-i 'aish
Khisht-i bālīñ ko samajhtā hūñ maiñ zānū ḥūr kā

The trials and tribulations of the times
are but the stuff of pleasure to my mind:

I find in the brick of my pillow
the gentle softness of a houri's lap.

This *she'r* is light in tone and based on *maẕmūn āfirīnī*. The image equates a brick pillow with softness of a heavenly nymph's lap. Complementing the airiness of this *'āshiq's* disclaimer about the effects of difficulty upon him, the diction of this verse is lofty. It is vocabulary is mostly Persian (*sak͟htī, bālīn, zānū*) with a little Arabic (*aiyyām*), although the grammatical items are, of course, Urdu. The light, airy tone helps to accommodate *k͟hisht-i bālīn* (brick pillow) which could otherwise be obstreperous. In fact, there is a glimmer of self-teasing and fun in this phrase.

The third *she'r* in this group is a *maṯla'* by Zafar:

ہے تو انساں پر ہے یہ عالم بتِ مغرور کا
جلوۂ شوخی پری کا سا ہے چہرہ حور کا

{Zf:I. 25.3} Hai to insāñ par hai yih 'ālam but-i mag͟hrūr kā
Jalva-i shok͟hī parī kā sā hai chahra ḥūr kā

She's human, yet
that arrogant idol has
mischievous brightness like a fairy's—
her face is that of a houri.

This *she'r* too fits many of the criteria put forth by Nadvi and Shadani in their lists of what constitutes literary *Lakhnavīyat*. The verse is entirely concerned with describing the attributes of the beloved (especially her face which is, of course, like a fairy's). It is sensual rather than spiritual; and it celebrates the beloved's devilish mischievousness.

It would be very difficult to push a claim for reading this *she'r* on the *ḥaqīqī* level as well as the *majāzī*, even though the Divine beloved is elusive, and does perhaps tease the *'āshiq* with momentary glimpses before flitting off into invisibility again. There are too many other specific attributes to the beloved in this verse for such an interpretation to be likely. For example, the narrator states unequivocally that "she is human" and uses the word *insān*, which emphasizes the beloved object's mortality. But perhaps the most important reason to reject a mystical reading for this *she'r* is that the beloved is described as a "proud idol" (*but-i maghrūr*), "fairy," and houri. It does not characterise the human-Divine relationship.

This verse by Zafar contains *fārsī tarākīb* in the literal sense of the term, but one of the *izāfat* constructions coins a new phrase or is complex. There is a bit of word-play in the *she'r*, but this degree of word-play is normal for any Urdu *she'r*, and does not lend the verse its overall character (whereas the *maz̤mūn* does).

In summary, then, Zafar's *maṭla'*, which might at first seem to fit the stereotype of *Lakhnavīyat* because of its frivolous and sensual tone, lacks the important identifying criteria of either so-called *dabistān* (*ri'āyat-i lafẓī*, *mu'āmla bandī*, *taṣavvuf* and *fārsī tarākīb*). Yet it is certainly a solid example of the "garden variety" Urdu *she'r*.

The final *she'r* in this group is Nasikh's:

اس پری کے چہرے کو تشبیہ کس سے دیجئے
جس کا ہر نقش قدم دکھلائے نقشہ حور کا

{N: I.15.4} Us parī ke chahre ko tashbīh kis se dījiye
Jis kā har naqsh-i qadam dikhlā'e naqsha ḥūr kā

With what can one compare
the face of that fairy
whose every footprint
displays a houri's portrait?

Once again, a verse of *maz̤mūn āfirīnī* has been built around the *qāfiyah* word *ḥūr*; and once again, the *maz̤mūn* is an elaborate, exaggerated statement of the beloved's beauty. Nasikh's narrator says that his beloved is so beautiful that no simile exists for her face (and then he proves his assertion correct by creating one for her footprint).

The image created is rather obscure: the verse compares the footprint of the beloved to a ḥouri's outline. The logic is as follows: my beloved is so beautiful that she cannot be compared. However, if comparison must be made, then make it between her footprint and the outline of the face of a ḥouri, who is exemplary of beauty in the ghazal. In other words, a comparison might be made between the face of a ḥouri (the face being, presumably, the most beautiful part of the most beautiful creature conceivable); and the most base, inconsequential part of the beloved's physical attributes (not just the sole of her foot—

which is base enough—but merely the outline it leaves behind as it moves on).

The verse uses *ri'āyat-i lafẓī* in its explicit and implicit use of simile (the explicit is his use of the word *tashbīh* and the implicit is the *tashbīh* created by the narrator in the second *miṣra'*). Furthermore, the *tashbīh* drawn in the second *miṣra'* plays on the two related, but slightly different, words *naqsh* (imprint) and *naqsha* (which in this context means "state, picture, portrait").

Despite its element of *ri'āyat-i lafẓī*, there are no *fārsī tarākīb* in this *she'r*. *Naqsh-i qadam* is a very common expression in the ghazal, and is used here by Nasikh in its stock context.

The central theme, the incomparable beauty of the beloved, does lend itself to mystical interpretation (if one focuses on the imponderable elements in that beauty), but the verse should be read primarily on the *majāzī* level because God cannot be conceived as leaving footprints.

To summarise the *she'rs* in this group, we found that because of the specific and heavily-laden connotations of *ḥūr* all the verses were concerned with comparing the beloved to ḥouris and *parīs*; and, since those beings exemplify beauty, all the verses were elaborate and/or exaggerated declarations of the beloved's beauty. This kind of verse tends to rely on *maẓmūn āfirīnī*: since the beauty of the beloved is a stock condition in the genre, comments upon it ought to be justified by unexpected or unusual illustrations. Such *maẓmūn āfirīnī* also tends to, but need not, be sensual.

Finally, because of the sort of conditions which such heavily-connoted *qāfiyah* words are inclined to impose on *she'rs*, we saw in this group (as we have seen in others) that the characteristics of *Dihlavīyat* and *Lakhnavīyat* named by Nadvi, Shadani and other Urdu critics are found in the poetry of all Urdu poets at one time or another, depending on the particular structural demands of any given *she'r*.

Angūr kā

Though it is not a word especially common in the ghazal's lexicon, *angūr* (grape), because of its close association with wine, offers little obstacle to the Urdu poet. It appears in every ghazal selected for this *zamīn* except that of Zafar.[37] The following section discusses *she'rs* by Shah Nasir, Atish, Nasikh and Zauq.

The influence which *angūr* exerts on a *she'r* when it appears in the *qāfiyah* is reminiscent of the impact which we saw *ḥūr* exert in the last section. All the *she'rs* in this section are based on *maẓmūn āfirīnī*, and a few of them are extremely far-fetched. The *mazmūn āfirīnī* so inspired has given rise, in two of the four *she'rs*, to uncommon employment of *angūr's* meaning, as will be seen. We begin with a *matla'* by Shah Nasir:

ہے عجب جھومر کا عالم اپنے رشکِ حور کا
سرو میں خوشہ لگا دیکھا نہ تھا انگور کا

{ShN:I .113.1} Hai 'ajab jhūmar kā 'ālam apne rashk-i ḥūr kā
Sarv meñ khosha lagā dekhā na thā angūr kā

It's strange
the state of that ornament
on the head of my beloved,
envy of the fairies:
One has never seen a bunch of grapes
growing on a cypress tree!

The reader will, no doubt, recognise a certain carryover from the previous section, where elaborate descriptions of the beloved's attributes figured in so many verses, and where the beauty of those attributes was compared favourably with the attributes of fairies and ḥourīs.

In this *she'r* Shah Nasir Dihlavi praises the elegant ornament of his beloved as well as her tall, graceful, willowy (only in Urdu, it is "cypress-like" instead) stature. The likeness between *sarv* (cypress) and the beløved's stature is completely stock, but the comparison of the ornament to a bunch of grapes on a cypress tree is unusual. The irony of such an association is not at all lost on the poet, in fact he exploits it. That is where the verse's *mazmūn āfirīnī* lies. When the narrator says, "One has never seen a bunch of grapes like that," (meaning like the chain-link effect of the *jhūmar*) the poet is also claiming that no other poet has likely ever drawn the *tashbīh*, or simile, between a *jhūmar*[38] and a bunch of grapes. He goes further in indulging his flight of fancy by putting the *angūr* on an unlikely genus of tree, the *sarv*. It is justified, however (as noted above) by the stock equation between *sarv* and the *ma'shūq*.

So much for the *mazmūn āfirīnī*. This verse's *riāyat-i lafzī* is two-fold. In the first place, the *khosha*, or cluster (which can refer to grapes or dates, according to Platts) hints at the *angūr* which is to come in the *she'r's qāfiyah*. In a more intricate manner, there is also word-play in the poet's use of *jhūmar* for headdress. *Jhūmar* is derived from the verb *jhūmnā* (to sway, weave, undulate, walk gracefully, as an elephant) and comes originally from a kind of line dance.[39] The crowning reason why this word is such an apt choice here is that the graceful, swaying gait evoked by *jhūmnā* is echoed in the associations of the word *sarv*, especially as it relates to the beloved.

The vocabulary in this verse is a blend of all the elements which make up Urdu—Persian, Arabic and Hindi (*'ajab*, *'ālam*, *sarv* and *ḥūr* are Arabic, though used extensively in Persian; *rashk*, *k͟hosha* and *angūr* are Persian; and *jhūmar* as well as the grammatical morphemes are Hindi).

Finally, there is no question of a mystical reading for this *maṭla*'' by Shah Nasir. It is strictly *majāzī*, if for no other reason than its complete concern with "descriptions of feminine costume and jewelry," as Andalib Shadani described a primary *k͟huṣūṣīyat* for the Lucknow School.[40]

Atish's verse, too, offers a convoluted image crowned by a cluster of grapes:

رنج سے راحت نصیبِ طبعِ شیریں کار ہے
بار لاتا ہے قلم ہونے سے نخلِ انگور کا

{A:I . 58.12} Ranj se rāḥat naṣīb-i ṭab'-i shīrīñ kār hai
Bār lātā hai qalam hone se nak͟hl angūr kā

Experience of pain gives comfort
to things which are sweet in nature:
From being cut, a grape sapling
bears a load of grapes.

In this *she'r-i tamṣil* Atish opines that bitter experience cannot compromise things which are sweet in nature. His "proof" is the observation that a grape tree, having endured the pain of pruning, ultimately bears sweet fruit.

In keeping with the ponderous, pontificatory nature of its message, the *she'r* complements its own gravity by using the "lofty" diction of Persian and Arabic words (*ranj*, *rāḥat*, *shīrīñ*, *nak͟hl*, *naṣīb*, *ṭab'*, *qalam* and *angūr*). The only *izāfat* construction is *naṣīb-i ṭab'-i shīrīñ kār*, which is quite an unusual conjunction of its two discrete elements. There is, therefore, *fārsī tarākīb*, though somewhat obstreperous.

Neither the beloved nor *'ishq* is even mentioned in this verse.[41] Because it is nonetheless philosophical in nature, the verse would stand up to *ḥaqīqī* interpretation,[42] but it is difficult to believe that the poet's intention was to express a truly mystical insight.

Overall, this verse by Atish probably fits more closely the character drawn by critics for literary *Dihlavīyat* than for *Lakhnavīyat*.

In the next two *she'rs* Zauq and Nasikh create *maẓāmīn* around the secondary meaning of *angūr*, "scab, cicatrice":

زخم میرا ہے وہ ایذا دوست خوں رونے لگے
منہ سے گر جرّاح کے سن پائے نام انگور کا

{Zq: 35.17} Zakhm merā hai voh īẓā dost khūn̈ rone lage
Munh se gar jarrāḥ ke sun pā'e nām angūr kā

My wound is so fond of pain
it would begin to weep blood
the moment it heard "scab"
emanate from the doctor's mouth.

and

ہجر میں ساغر سے آئی مجھ کو ساقی بوئے خوں
بادہ کھنچوایا ہے شاید زخم کے انگور کا

{N:I.15.14} Hijr men̈ sāghar se ā'ī mujh ko sāqī bū-i khūn̈
Bāda khinchvāyā hai shāyad zakhm ke angūr kā

Saqi, in separation
there wafts from the goblet
the smell of blood:
Have you perhaps drawn your wine
from thc grape of my wound?

In both the above verses the poets exploit the secondary meaning of *angūr* while retaining the semantic connection between "scab of a wound" and "grape." They do so by reiterating the process of liquid seepage from both: Nasikh refers specifically to "the grape of his wound" (*zakhm ke angūr*), while Zauq implies the wound/grape equation by setting up a scenario wherein a doctor "reminds" the narrator's wound (*zakhm*) of its simlarity to a grape and causes it to pour from the '*āshiq's* own wound. Both *she'rs* clearly rely on *ri'āyat-i lafẓī* in order to be at all comprehensible, and word- and image-play are closely intertwined in both.

In Zauq's *she'r* the subject is his wound, and the beloved is nowhere even alluded to, much less addressed. In Nasikh's *she'r*, things are not quite so straightforward, given that the *sāqī* is, conventionally, *ma'shūq* and is directly addressed by the narrator. Furthermore, there might be a very subtle tone of complaint against the beloved construed here, what with the narrator's suggestion that he is being served blood/wine squeezed from his own wound. After all, the *sāqī*, in his guise as *ma'shūq*, would not be above such cavalier treatment of the '*āshiq*. In these respects there are faint elements of *mu'āmla bandī* in Nasikh's verse, but neither of these last two *she'rs* is based on *mu'āmla bandī* in the clear-cut manner of those *she'rs* whose end-rhyme was *javāb meñ*.

Another possible complexion to be put on the narrator's query would be as follows: it might well be that, with his suggestion that the *sāqī* is serving "wine" squeezed from the "grape" of his (the '*āshiq's*) own wound, he is indulging in the also conventional self-aggrandisement of an '*āshiq*. His claim would read something like, "So exemplary is my suffering in love that the very blood of my wounds is fit to serve as wine to other '*āshiqs*." With this reading one would also have to recognise the *ḥaqīqī* possibilities of the *she'r*. In this instance, the *sāqī* (*pīr*, spiritual preceptor) would be serving wine (mystical, divine knowledge) to other drinkers/'*āshiqs* (seekers after mystical knowledge) which had been gleaned from the exemplary blood/wine of this particular '*āshiq*. Such an interpretation is complicated and rather far-fetched, but within the acceptable realm of ghazal convention.

All in all, this pair of *she'rs* is complicated and far-fetched because of the ways both verses incorporate the *qāfiyah* word *angūr*. Both are conventionally acceptable, and can be related to the ghazal's express concern with '*ishq* and '*āshiqī*, though neither one directly speaks of that general condition, focusing rather on circumstances extrapolated therefrom. This pair is a good example of how verses based on *maẓmūn āfirīnī* result from a particular kind of word in the *qāfiyah* position. They can rely to quite some degree on word-play, and yet fit easily into neither so-called *dabistān*. The two poets—in this case one Dihlavi and one Lakhnavi—created remarkably simlar *maẓmūns*.

In this set of four verses employing *angūr* for their *qāfiyah* word there was a heavy emphasis on *maẓmūn āfirīnī* and very little emotional impact.[43] The two verses which explored *angūr's* secondary meaning of "scab or cicatrice," not very surprisingly, came, closer to touching upon the suffering inherent in an *'āshiq's* condition.

The strongest example of how the *qāfiyah* word influences the theme, tone and mood of a *she'r* was seen in Shah Nasir's *maṭla'*, where there were two *qāfiyah* words. The first word, *ḥūr*, set up an expectation from the second. We have already seen how influential the presence of *ḥūr* can be in a *she'r*—especially how it tends to create verses which contain mention or enumeration of the beloved's beauty. Thus, the creation of a *maẓmūn* using *angūr* to relate back to the ḥourī and, thus, the beloved's beauty—which was accomplished by making the grape into some item of adornment—was not only logical, but also much to be expected. The flight of fancy necessary to accomplish this certainly took the audience away from the set stock of key ghazal-words and their connotations and allusions, and so the poet had little stock of emotion or mood to rely upon. Therefore the overall impact of the verse was wonder, but not the sort of wonder which was evident in those verses whose *maẓmūn* was more conventional.[44]

Dūr kā

The final set of *she'rs* in this second *zamīn* all contain the *qāfiyah* word *dūr* (far, distant). The set consists of verses by all five poets Zauq, Nasikh, Zafar, Atish and Shah Nasir, making *dūr* the most popular choice for a *qāfiyah* word in this *zamīn*. This is the case, no doubt, because of how extremely common is the word *dūr* in Urdu speech. Also, it is an adjective that can modify countless nouns, and is therefore versatile as a *qāfiyah* word. There is far less *maẓmūn āfirīnī* among these verses than in the others from this *zamīn*; but there is greater variety of mood and tone from verse to verse. Most of the poets in this group have drawn out something more than the ordinary meaning or use of *dūr* in their *she'rs*, in contrast to the rather ordinary ways in which they used the word *javāb*. The section opens with a *maṭla'* by Zauq:

وادیٔ ظلمت میں اپنی دخل ہے کب نور کا
ہر اک شعلہ سا ہے سو بھی چراغِ دور کا

{Zq: 35.5} Vādī-i ẕulmat meñ apnī dakhl hai kab nūr kā
Mihr ik sho'la sā hai so bhī chirāgh-i dūr kā

How could light possibly enter
my valley of darkness?
The sun is but a single flame
and that, too, from a distant lamp.

Whereas in previous *she'rs* Zauq has often struck a note of clever fancifulness, in this *maṯla'* there is the tone of wistful languor with which the ghazal audience identifies classic '*āshiqī*.

Zauq's *maṯla'* does not rely on *ri'āyat-i lafẕī* to make sense, but there are complicated relationships between the words in the phrase *vādī-i ẕulmat* which add depth to the verse's mood. Translated here as "valley of darkness," *vādī-i ẕulmat* could conceivably be taken to mean "dark place where the river of immortality flows." Secondary meanings of *vādī* are "river" and "desert;" and the related word *ẕulumāt* is "a dark place where the water of immortality is said to be.[45] *Vādī-i ẕulmat* and *chirāgh-i dūr* are the verse's *izāfat* constructions, but they really don't bring together two words which would not otherwise be related to one another.

The question of *taṣavvuf* is not of crucial importance in this *maṯla'* because the relationship between '*āshiq* and *ma'shūq* is not at its forefront: although the narrator is assumed to be an '*āshiq*; and although his "valley of darkness" is an indirect reference to the difficulty of his state of '*āshiqī*; whether he is in love with a human or divine beloved still has no special bearing on his statement. Therefore, though the verse would stand up to both *majāzī* and *ḥaqīqī* interpretations, its potential "mystical content" is not of primary interest to our inquiry.

The next *she'r* by Shah Nasir also builds an image around a candle flame and a visual/emotional sense of perspective:

شمع کے زیرِ قدم ہے منزلِ اقلیمِ عشق
سر سے جو گذرے اسے کیسا سفر ہے دور کا

Shama' ke zer-i qadam hai manzil-i iqlīm-i 'ishq
Sar se jo guẕre use kaisā safar hai dūr kā

The objective of the lands of love
is beneath the candle's foot:
He who journeys from the "head"
has a far-out trip indeed!

This *she'r* is mainly concerned with *maẕmūn āfirīnī* and features some *ri'āyat-i lafẕī* as well. The basic image is that of a candle, with wax dripping down its side into a pool at the candle's base. The wax's journey down the side is equated with the *'āshiq's* journey on the path of love—both end in *fanā*, they melt into extinction.

Despite its *maẕmūn āfirīnī* and *ri'āyat-i lafẕī*, this *she'r* has strong mystical connotations. The critical literature has tended to place *taṣavvuf* and those two major characteristics of so-called *Lakhnavīyat* in polar opposition, but Shah Nasir shows, in this *she'r*, that they are not at all incompatible. In fact, the many layers of meaning suggested by the poet's choice of words serve to draw out the verse's mystical meaning.

For example, the word *manzil* is a key term in Sufistic vocabulary. It simultaneously refers to a stage in travelling (say, a day's projected destination on a long journey) and "a stage in the divine life," in the words of John Platts (P.1076): *Manzil karnā* means "to end or finish a task or journey." Simlarly, the word *qadam* can be read two ways, both of which make sense in this context: its most usual definition is "foot, footstep, sole of the foot;" but the word *qidam*—which is spelled the same way in the absence of diacritical marks—means "the being before, preceding (in point of time), etc."[46] While it seems fairly clear that *qadam* is the intended reading, the nuances of *qidam* were surely not lost on Shah Nasir when he chose the word for this *she'r*. And the sense of a passage of time complements the sense of the candle's foot" representing the destination to be reached at the end of a long journey.

Heavily Arabicised vocabulary in the first *miṣra'*, as it states its mystical message (*shama'*, *qadam/qidam*, *manzil*, *iqlīm*, *'ishq*), is complemented by the second *miṣra's* more colloquial Urdu as it steps back and offers what sounds to the ears like a far more plainly stated "proof."

Perhaps the most significant manipulation of language in this verse is the sense Shah Nasir draws out of the very ordinary *qāfiyah* word, *dūr*. Not only does it indicate that it's a long journey from the "head" (*sar*) of the candle/journey *(safar)*, but it also suggests that the journey into *fanā*, which lies in the "land of love beneath the foot of the candle," is remote in the sense of strange, far-fetched, "far out" as one says in recent colloquial American English.

Fārsī tarākīb are here in abundance, although the words joined together, as we noted above, are mostly Arabic rather than Persian. *Manzil-i iqlīm-i 'ishq*, especially, is a phrase joining its component words together in a fairly novel and complex fashion, although *zer-i qadam* is quite ordinary.

All in all, one might say that this verse by Shah Nasir has "almost everything" in the way of common ghazal conventions, and could neither be called typically Lakhnavi nor typically Dihlavi.

Nasikh, too, in his *she'r* with the *qāfiyah* word *dūr*, lends a bizarre, remote sense to *dūr*:

ہے بجا نزدیک والے مجھ سے گر واقف نہیں
میرے شہرے نے کیا ہے اب ارادہ دور کا

{N:I.15.11} Hai ba-jā nazdīk vāle mujh se gar vāqif nahīn̄
Mere shuhre ne kiyā hai ab irāda dūr kā

It's fitting that I remain unknown
to those close to me:
My renown has set its sights
on more distant horizons.

The sense of this verse is that the creative merits of Nasikh's narrator are so extraordinary as to be unrecognised by his intimates. Literally, he "has fixed on a more distant goal or objective." In other words, "I am not surprised that these people of inferior conception who surround me should not recognise my greatness—my intended audience is far more exalted than they."[47] The statement is clever and witty, though it contains no elaborate verbal constructions. The vocabulary is a blend of Persian (*ba-jā, nazdīk, gar*) and Arabic (*vāqif, shuhra, irāda*) quite common to Urdu ghazal.

Nasikh casts a mystical tint to this verse. The elusive identity of the narrator mirrors the elusive but unignorable presence of the Divine Being. When, as we saw in Nasikh's *she'r* (*Ghaflat se apnā ṭālib-i dīdār āp hūn̄*) the *'āshiq* seeking mystical knowledge gains a flash of that special recognition, he perceives that God, or the Divine Entity, is not separate from himself. In that context, this verse's declaration could be read on a *ḥaqīqī* plane. This verse is a sample of the illustration that there is not necessarily a direct relationship in the ghazal between mysticism and "lofty or spiritual thought," although this was strongly implied by Nurul Hasan Hashmi.[48]

Zafar, too, concentrated on matters of visual perspective when composing his *she'r* around the *qāfiyah* word *dūr*:

دور ہے دل سے جو دیکھے تو وہ نزدیک ہے
تجھ میں اس میں ہے بظاہر ایک عرصہ دور کا

{Zf:I.25.6} Dūr hai dil se jo dekhe tū voh nazdīk hai
Tujh meñ us meñ hai baẕāhir ek 'arsa dūr kā

Things that are distant
from the heart
if you look
are really quite close:
Only apparently
a great distance
separates you and him.

In this verse Zafar considers the phenomenon of perspective as his narrator offers encouragement to the despairing *'āshiq*. The language is colloquial, and the *nazdīk ... dūr* equation between the two [*miṣra's*] is quite predictable. There is the hopeless optimism in this *she'r* which reaffirms the status quo of *'āshiqī*, though for the moment optimism holds the upper hand. There are none of the *khuṣūṣīyāt* focused upon in Nadvi and Shadani to help distinguish this verse as either particularly Lakhnavi or Dihlavi, although it would certainly lend itself to a mystical interpretation because of the unspecific identity of the beloved and the "so near and yet so far" element of desired union. Ultimately, though, it is a standard kind of Urdu *she'r* which is popular and undemanding.

Atish's *she'r* stands slightly apart from the others in this group, although he, like Nasikh, ends with the words *irāda dūr kā*. He does not specifically mention the beloved, but the situation he depicts is almost certainly that of an aspiring *'āshiq*, tongue-tied and nearly desperate in the presence of his beloved:

آ کے سینے سے لبوں پر دم اٹکتا ہے عبث
ٹھیرنا اچھا نہیں جب ہو ارادہ دور کا

{A:I.58.7} Ā ke sīne se laboñ par dam aṭaktā hai ’abaṣ
Ṭhernā achhā nahīñ jab ho irāda dūr kā

How futile,
my breath rising up from my breast
only to stick to my lips:
It’s no good to tarry
when one’s goal is so remote.

Here the ’*āshiq* is suffering unto the point of death, but death eludes him. For breath to get stuck on one’s lips (*dam laboñ par aṭaknā*) means for one to be about to die. In this *she’r* the ‘*āshiq* is looking forward to passing his last breath from his body, but fate foils him, and that breath sticks to his lips, refusing him the reprieve of final extinction. This *she’r*, therefore, relies on *ri’āyat-i lafẓī*, playing on the literal and idiomatic meaning of *dam aṭaknā*. Even so, it is neither light nor hopeful in tone.

In its conventional tone of ‘*āshiqī*, the *she’r* is fairly straightforward, or *sāda*. Its imagery is not paramount by any means, so this would not be considered a verse of *maẓmūn āfirīnī*. Furthermore, the vocabulary and diction are completely colloquial Urdu, and this *she’r* would require almost no explication at all to most audiences.

The beloved could be conceived of as divine, but the verse is neither mytical nor spiritual in tone: rather, it is merely fatalistic albeit in an ironic way.

To summarize this set of *she’rs*, all the poets used *dūr* to generally reiterate the untenable situation of the ‘*āshiq*. Only Zafar’s verse offered a clear contrast, suggesting that there is indeed hope for the aspiring ‘*āshiq*. Atish concentrated on the most familiar aspect of ‘*āshiqī*: no matter what means he tries to effect fulfillment of his desire for the beloved (or for death), it is bound to remain beyond his grasp. The other two poets used *dūr* in a slightly different way, drawing out its sense of the absurd or bizarre. Shah Nasir had the ‘*āshiq* referring to how ulitmately absurd his aspirations are with regard to the beloved; while Nasikh, in keeping with what we now know so well about his poetic personality, stepped back away from the more confining persona of '*āshiq*, to include a reminder of his unusual reputation as a poet as well.

None of the verses in this group was sensual or frivolous, and only Nasikh's was the least bit glib. The connotations of the word *dūr* seem to have set a tone of fatalism, and this fatalism is synonymous with the plight of the conventional '*āshiq*.[49] Even when the distance is negated—as in Zafar's *she'r*—its message ultimately works to keep the '*āshiq* on the path of '*āshiqī*. In a way it could be argued that all five verses reiterate the ideal ghazal.

Chapter Summary

The purpose of this chapter has been to present a sample of Urdu ghazal *she'rs* by contemporaneous poets of Lucknow and Delhi which shared the same structural constraints. The sample illustrated the range of choices available to, and exercised by, the majority of *g̲hazal-go* poets in this classical literary tradition.

Zaidi has demonstrated that the *k̲huṣūṣīyāt* of *Lakhnavīyat* and *Dihlavīyat* which were designated by Abdus Salam Nadvi and Andalib Shadani occur in both Lakhnavi and Dihlavi poetry. Zaidi argued, on the basis of this demonstration, that the Two School theory's fundamental distinction between Lakhnavi and Dihlavi poetry was invalid; and that the theory itself was therefore invalid.

What this chapter offered—in conjunction with the present study's own refutation of the Two School theory—was a method of comparison which approached *she'rs* from the structural context of their ghazals. Neither Zaidi, nor Nadvi or Shadani, had examined differences between Dihlavi and Lakhnavi poetry from the point of view of structural influences on poets' thematic choices. *Qāfiyah* can be seen as the strongest structural element by far in terms of how a *maẓmūn* develops in accordance with the formal parametres of ghazal composition. By comparing ghazals in the same *zamīn*, keeping other structural elements like *radīf* and *baḥr* (metre) constant, this point was highlighted here. Furthermore, all the poets compared were general contemporaries, which decreased the possibility that individual choices might be attributed to trends, or the manifestation of literary fashion over time. In thus delimiting our comparative parametres we came as close as we could envision to an objective or "scientific" (*sāyinsī*) method, and this goal had been inspired by Ali Javad Zaidi's objection to the comparative methods of Two School critics.

Although Zaidi's examples of *Lakhnavīyat* in poetry written by Dihlavis—and of Dihlavi characteristics in poetry written by Lakhnavis—were offered without the benefit of a simlar "scientific" method, they were of sufficient amplitude to cast grave suspicion on Nadvi's and Shadani's categories.[50] This comparison complements Zaidi's challenge to existing categories of distinction between Lakhnavi and Dihlavi poetry.

My own point of view is as follows: if in fact, characteristic differences do separate Dihlavi from Lakhnavi poetry, the categorical differences claimed by Two School critics are far too rigid, and are based on spurious, extra-textual influences. Vulnerable as Zaidi's method of disputation may be, I would still support the essential justice of his claims. One benefit of the method employed here is that it can illustrate the same point of dispute also made by Zaidi, but do so in a fashion which is not vulnerable to accusations of subjectivity or of quoting verses out of context.

In addition to the relative objectivity of the method used here, its perspective on the question of differences in theme or subject matter departs from that of Two School criticism: in some of the *she'rs* the dictates of structure, rather than the aesthetic tastes dictated by social environment, have influenced the verse's central *maẓmūn* and thus its overall flavour. In other words the experiment presented in this chapter challenges the conception held by all the critics—Zaidi included—that popular taste, historical events and economic conditions are the greatest influences on the poetic characteristics of theme, imagery (*maẓmūn*) and diction.

It may be true that *k͟huṣūṣīyāt* claimed for *Dihlavīyat* and *Lakhnavīyat* by critics of the Two School theory do distinguish the two bodies of poetry in terms of degree. Even if the frequency count envisioned by S.R. Farqui were to demonstrate that Delhi-Lucknow differences are more quantitative than qualitative,[51] it is important to establish tangible and plausible causes for these quantitative differences. Exploring the possibility of structural influence as a cause is a step in that direction.

I cannot share the belief that different moral, spiritual, political and socio-economic climates in Delhi and Lucknow engendered poetic differences profound enough to warrant the designation of two discrete literary schools. As long as ghazal poets address the theme of *'ishq*, draw upon the same essential stock of images, and adhere to the same fundamentals of structure, external events and environments cannot impose profound enough variations in theme and diction to justify "school" distinctions between contemporary Urdu ghazal poets on the basis of geography.

If various groups of poets identified their particular structural approach or intended message as different from that of their contemporaries, then perhaps school-distinctions would be better justified or more appropriate. But all ghazal poets—by definition—address themselves to the subject of *'ishq* as an encapsulisation of the human condition: they would not be ghazal poets otherwise.[52] Nor would they be ghazal poets if they did not adhere to the genre's rigid structure: for it is the series of two-line verses composed in a set *zamīn* which ultimately defines the ghazal itself. Disparate structures and purposes are what separate *maṡnavīs* from ghazals; and *maṡnavīs*, ghazals and *qaṣīdas* from one another.[53] Not even the Two School critics have argued that the Delhi and Lucknow "schools" work consciously toward such different purposes.

This is not to suggest that the ghazal is stiflingly rigid in structure despite the strong influence often exerted by structure upon the thematic content of certain verses. On the contrary, the unique appeal of this genre is its potential for play between set structure and individual poetic interpretation.[54] In some of the *she'rs* presented in this chapter the influence of structure on *maẓmūn* appeared to be stronger than in others. In some *she'rs* it seemed to exert little impact on factors other than topic tone, diction, mood, etc.

Evidence does exist that Urdu critics have debated just how much influence the *qāfiyah* exerts, and whether or not it constrains the poet's range of thematic choices. Two passages referring to this debate are to be found in the writings of Sayyid Masud Hasan Rizvi "*Adīb*" and Muhammad Sadiq. Sadiq has written in English:

> It is maintained that in the ghazal the thoughts and feelings of the poet are governed by the *qāfiyah*; he cannot say what he wishes to say; he says only what the *qāfiyah* permits him to say...[55]

Sadiq goes on to argue that the Urdu poet is no more constrained by the *qāfiyah* than other poets working within a range of other forms, conceding beforehand however that "there is a large element of truth in the argument because in the ghazal the idea is suggested by the rhyme, which has the pivotal position in the line."[56]

Sadiq's discussion seems to draw upon a passage from Sayyid Masud Hasan Rizvi's *Hamārī Shā'irī* (1928),[57] on the role of *qāfiyah* and *radīf* in the Urdu ghazal. Rizvi asserts that

> Each and every word can direct the human mind toward countless ideas or thoughts. In the mind of a poet the power of associations, reflections and insights is all the stronger. From among those many notions to which the *qāfiyah* directs the poet's thoughts, he creates his own particular verse. Therefore it will always remain the case that in the ghazal the constraint of *qāfiyah* does not *force* its own ideas on the poet.[58]

In other words, it is the mark of a successful poet to honour the constraints of the ghazal form without being so fettered to it that s/he is unable to express individual thoughts and emotions. Drawing a further conclusion, I would say that Urdu poets, in making the individual choices available to them within the structural constraints of the ghazal form, are responding to influences far more concrete and immediate than those suggested by geographical location.[59] It is not made clear in either Rizvi's or Sadiq's discussion whence such aspersions had been cast on the Urdu ghazal, and I know of no other printed discussions on the topic. Nonetheless their tone of defence does seem to indicate some sort of literary debate. Both critics are almost certainly referring to the issue of *qāfiyah paimā'ī*, which was an accusation sometimes levied against classical poets. A fascination on the part of some classical poets with manipulating all the possibilities suggested by a particular *qāfiyah* was said by others to result in long ghazals with ridiculous resolutions of rhyme and, thus, to a general degradation of theme. This practice they called '*qāfiyah paimā'ī* or the "senseless enumeration of *qāfiyah*."[60]

Ultimately it remains that the seven Dihlavi and Lakhnavi poets compared in this chapter exercised essentially the same range of compositional options; and that there was no discernible pattern of choice amongst them as Dihlavis or Lakhnavis. It is of less importance here to judge whether the *qāfiyah's* influence on the *she'rs* in a ghazal is detrimentally strong—as seems to have been the position of the reformist critics to whom both "Adib" and Sadiq respond—than it is to demonstrate that the influence of the *qāfiyah* is indeed strong, that its strength is an integral structural feature of the ghazal, and that such structural features as the *qāfiyah*, *radīf* and perhaps metre (*baḥr*) are far likelier candidates than social milieus for the study of what might determine fundamental distinctions in different poets' approaches to the Urdu ghazal.[61]

NOTES

1. Two passages from Sayyid Masud Hasan Rizvi "Adib's" *Hamārī Shā'irī*, 8th edition, [pp. 51-53] and Muhammad Sadiq's *A History of Urdu Literature*, 2nd edition, [p.22] refer to the role of *qāfiyah* in influencing the poet's choice of *mazmūn*.
2. *Zamīn*, as was noted in the Introduction, literally means "earth, land, soil, region, etc." but by extension, in poetic parlance it refers to the structural elements of a given poem such as metre—*bahr*—and rhyme scheme—*qāfiyah* and *radīf*. See John T. Platts, *A Dictionary of Urdu, Classical Hindi and English*, London: Oxford University Press, 1974, p. 617.
3. *She'rul Hind*, vol. 1, p. 204.
4. This restriction is intended to minimise the possibility of differences in style perceived between poets—or groups of poets—from different generations being interpreted as "school" distinctions.
5. Represented as follows: [- - ˘/ - ˘ -/˘ ˘- - ˘/ - ˘ -] where a long syllable is represented by [-] and a short syllable by [˘].
7. Ed. Tanvir Ahmad Alvi, Lahore: Majlis-i Taraqqi-i Adab, 2 vols., 1971, 197.
8. See *Kullīyāt-i Momin*, ed. Dr. Masih uz-Zaman, Allahabad: Ram Narayan Lal Beni Madhav, 1971; and the *Divān-i Ghālib*, Arshi edition, New Delhi: Anjuman Taraqqi-i Urdu, 1982, second printing.
9. In the second *zamīn* especially the *qāfiyah* words *hūr*, *angūr*, and *kāfūr* give rise to *she'rs* based on *mazmūn āfirīnī*, or the creation of unusual images, often involving subtle deviations from accepted themes.
10. To compare the relative frequency of the various *zamīns* in which individuals and/or groups of Urdu poets compose would indeed be fascinating. Such an enquiry might shed new light on the Two School debate: it is possible that differences in nuance presently perceived as reflections of societal differences between Delhi and Lucknow *marākiz* do somehow reflect the popularity of various metres and rhyme-schemes at certain times and places. But in the absence of such a study—quite beyond the scope of this present study—further speculation along this line would be inappropriate.
11. Another line of enquiry might be developed at some time which measured the impact of *qāfiyah* on both *mazmūn* and overall mood of whole ghazals when there was not a fairly neutral *radīf*. For example, the presence of the *radīf* "*tumheñ yād ho kih na yād ho*—do you remember or not?" might well exert extra influence on both individual *she'rs* in the ghazals as well as on the overall mood of the ghazal; and *qāfiyah* words leading into this long and semantically significant *radīf* might be seen to exercise relatively less influence on theme than in the present examples. Again, however, it is not within the present scope of this study to conduct such an experiment.

12. John T. Platts, *A Dictionary of Urdu, Classical Hindi and English*, p. 474.
13. Perhaps the most famous incident of this divine revelation was that of Mansur al-Hallaj, who was executed in 922 A.D. for his ecstatic exclamation, "'*anal-Haq*—I am the Ultimate truth [i.e. God]." See Annemarie Schimmel, *Mystical Dimensions of Islam*, Chapel Hill: University of North Carolina Press, 1975, pp. 62-77 and passim.
14. Thanks to Frances Pritchett for pointing out this secondary interpretation.
15. If the purpose of the two objects being equated was ostensibly different, then the *tamṡīl* would be considered more striking.
16. The technical term is *ham-qāfiyah*.
17. *Ma'nī āfirīnī* works rather like *maẓmūn āfirīnī*, only the novel creation is in meaning rather than image or theme.
18. This verse reiterates the orthodox notion that there is only one true God and one true religion: ultimate ruin is the destiny of other paths. Or, on a more mundane level of interpretation: the bitter aftertaste in wine presages the ruinous end to which drunks come; or that the pleasure experienced in wine-drinking is transitory at best: just as bitter dregs lie at the bottom of a glass, so do wine's effects leave a bitterness in the drinker's mouth. And he often experiences bitter thoughts when the wine is gone and he is left with a hangover.
19. According to Nadvi's and Shadani's lists of Lakhnavi *k͟huṣūṣīyāt*.
20. Rubbing sandal-paste on the forehead even suggests Hindu ritual.
21. We do note, however, that Atish as a poet seems particulary fond of wine imagery, though we will see only a few examples of it in these pages.
22. In fact, this might well be the sort of *she'r* critics had in mind when they coined the term *Dihlavīyat*. While it does not exude the "spirituality and loftiness of thought" described by Hashmi in *Dillī kā Dabistān-i Shā'irī*, neither is it completely devoid of them.
23. See M.A.R. Barker's description of conventional '*āshiqī* in *A Reader of Modern Urdu Poetry*, Montreal: McGill University, Institute of Islamic Studies, 1960 (Introduction).
24. *Dillī kā Dabistān-i Shā'irī*, p. 13.
25. Z.A. Siddiqi, p. ل in the Introduction to *Kullīyāt-i Ātish*, Allahabad: Ram Narayan Beni Madhav, 1972.
26. Scansion for metre *ramal*: - ˘ - -/ - ˘ - -/ - ˘ - -/ - ˘ -
27. The phrase is a part of colloquial speech, according to Platts' *Dictionary of Urdu, Classical Hindi and English*, p. 911: "*gul khānā*— to cauterize oneself [a practice among lovers, who burn themselves with heated peices of coin, etc. as a proof of their love]."
28. Platts, p. 802.
29. Ibid., p. 328.
30. Ibid.

31. Fish scales are supposed to be dry, because water doesn't affect them. Wounds also have "scales" when they dry and scab over. So the fish here is supposed to have wounds which left scales. I am indebted to S.R. Faruqi for explaining this verse to me.
32. In general *ḥūr*, or ḥourī, is not translated. In Platts' dictionary, a *ḥūr* is defined as "a virgin of Paradise, a black-eyed nymph, a very beautiful woman." p. 482.
33. Zauq's ghazal in this *zamīn* includes another *she'r* with *ḥūr* as its *qāfiyah* word. Though the *maẓāmīn* differ slightly, both *she'rs* compare the beloved's beauty to that of a ḥourī, and both are based on *maẓmūn āfirīnī*. This observation is made in substantiation of the argument that a *qāfiyah* word like *ḥūr* will indeed tend to exert great influence on the kind of *she'r* a poet is likely to compose.
34. In fact, the suggestion is that she is a witch, for they characteristically bear fleshy warts on their faces!
35. It is conceivable that such a choice would be construed as pretentious by some critics in some circumstances.
36. See Platts, p. 124.
37. We note that Zafar's is the shortest of all ghazals in this *zamīn*; and that, two of the four poets whose ghazals do contain *angūr* as a *qāfiyah* word wrote more than one *she'r* with *angūr*. So it is by no means an obscure choice for the *qāfiyah*.
38. Platts, p. 140: "An ornament consisting of a number of chains forming a fringe, which is attached to the top-knot [of a woman's head] and falls on the forehead."
39. Ibid.
40. See *Taḥqīq kī Roshnī meñ*, p. 253; cited earlier in Chapter VIII.
41. The audience is expected to recognize the relation between an *'āshiq's* typical condition and the urge to philosophize on the nature of adversity or *ranj*.
42. However, distinction can also be drawn between the *'āshiq's* philosophical reflection and actual mysticism.
43. However, the two qualities are not necessarily mutually exclusive.
44. The reader may refer, for example, back to Momin's *she'r* "Seeing her frown..." (p.154) whose *qāfiyah* word was *naqāb*, in order to get the different sense of a verse whose *maẓmūn* is more central to the standard topic of expressing the *'āshiq's* internal condition.
45. Platts, p. 755.
46. Platts, p. 789.
47. I am indebted to Ken Bryant for clarifying this verse for me.
48. Recall his characterization of *Dihlavīyat, D.D.S.*, p.13.
49. Except, as we just noted, in the case of Nasikh. On the other hand, Nasikh's *'āshiq* stands alone, feels an outsider to his social group, and in that sense is a conventional *'āshiq*.

50. Even so an antagonist might well claim that Zaidi merely cited a small number of *she'rs*—relative to the total corpus of Dihlavi poetry—which happen to represent exceptions to an essentially valid rule of distinction. There can be no resolution to such a controversy as long as *she'rs* are chosen and cited on the basis of their thematic content, as Zaidi as well as the Two School critics, have all done.
51. This has been suggested by critics like Zahir Ahmad Siddiqi and Ali Javad Zaidi.
52. See M.A.R. Barker, *A Modern Urdu Poetry Reader*, Introduction, p. xiv.
53. For example, *'ishq* tends to form the subject of *masnavī's* as well as of the ghazal, but their structures differ: a *masnavī's qāfiyah* and *radīf* can change from one *she'r* to the next, while a given ghazal's end-rhyme is invariable by definition. Similarly, the *qaṣīda* and the *masnavī* are both narrative poems, but their structures differ: *qaṣīda* tends toward panegyric themes rather than romantic tales and has a rhyme-scheme more similar to that of the ghazal than to the *masnavī*. Yet, it is critically different from the ghazal because of its definition as a narrative form. The ghazal is by definition, a lyric.
54. As we saw in the case of *she'rs* containing the word *naqāb* in the first *zamīn*, the *qāfiyah* word formed the pivot around which one central theme emerged in all five verses—that of the beloved's inaccessibility. Even so, there was variation in the tone and treatment of that *mazmūn* from poet to poet. Nasikh expressed a certain mystical insight into the nature of Divine revelation; Momin's *'āshiq* spoke in a voice of wonder at the calamitous affect which even a mere glimpse into the fold of his beloved's veil had on him; and Atish, Ghalib and Zafar created verses which were light, teasing, ironic, and even facetious in tone.
55. *A History of Urdu Literature*, 2nd edition, Delhi: Oxford University Press, 1984, p. 22.
56. Sadiq, Ibid.
57. Sayyid Masud Hasan Rizvi, *Hamārī Shā'irī*, 8th edition, Lucknow: Nizami Press, p. 53.
58. Ibid. *Ek ek lafz insān ke zahn ko beshamār khyāloṅ kī ṭaraf muntaqil kar saktā hai. Shā'ir ke zahn meṅ mushāhie aur tafakkur ke ba'is intiqāl kī quvat aur bhī zyāda hotī hai. Qāfiyah jin khayāl kī ṭaraf shā'ir ke zahn ko muntaqil kar degā un meṅ se jis khayāl ko voh nazm kar de voh usī kā khayāl hogā. Is ṣūrat meṅ yih qaul kyonkar ṣaḥīḥ ṭhahregā kih ghazal meṅ qāfiye kī pābandī shā'ir ko apne khayālāt nazm nahīṅ karne detī.* Emphasis mine.
59. Rizvi appears to be defending the role of *qāfiyah* in the ghazal as being no more inhibiting on a poet's creative impulse than in other genres of Urdu poetry (specifically *nazm*).

60. The term is based on the Persian verb *paimudan*, "to count or measure." Platts, *A Dictionary of Urdu, Classical Hindi and English*, p. 301.

61. "Adib" acknowledges that *qāfiyah* often serves as a pivot for the bundling of associations in a ghazal on p. 52 of *Hamārī Shā'irī*: *"Agar yih farẓ kar liyā jā'e kih ghazal meñ shā'ir kā ẓahn qāfiyae se maẓmūn kī ṭaraf jātā hai to bhī kyā qayāmat hai?*— Even assuming that the intellect of the poet is drawn toward a theme by the *qāfiyah*, even so, what is wrong with that?" This role of the *qāfiyah* is widely acknowledged. Another Urdu scholar affirms that the bundling of associations around *qāfiyah* was the way he was taught to read the verses of a ghazal, and that is how he has taught his own students. Professor C.M. Naim, personal correspondence, 25 May 1986.

CHAPTER XI

Comparison of Nasikh and Atish

Nasikh and Atish were a pair of contemporary poets whose individual styles often differed discernibly from one another, though both conformed sufficiently to the prescriptions of the Urdu ghazal to have been acknowledged *ustāds* during most of their creative lives. Their polarisation, which has been consistently maintained by critics, is certainly justified to a degree, but has contributed to a fundamental irony in the Two School theory. Take, for example, the two following critical assessments of Atish, the first by an Urdu critic, Zahir Ahmad Siddiqi; and the second by Ahmed Ali, writing in English:

> Lakhnavi poetry, in reality, became separated from the Delhi style in a single age and forged a path of its own, of which the foremost exponent was Nasikh. *On the other hand, it is not proper to call Atish, in whose writing there is such an abundance of "true poetry"... a Lakhnavi poet* or a standard-bearer of the Lucknow style of literature. *He is not Lakhnavi*, rather, after a fashion, *he was a porter of the correct elements of Dihlavi poetry living in Lucknow...*[1]

and

> He [Atish] escaped many pitfalls [common to the Lakhnavi poets] by virtue of his aesthetic nature and religious background. *In fact, he founded a rival school to Nasikh...*[2]

If the two founders of the "Lucknow School" of poetry manifest different enough styles to warrant polarisations which effectively deny that one of them is a member of the poetic school which he is credited with co-founding, then there is a serious problem with the manner in which that school has been designated.The above point of logic provides the background for the present comparison between the two main Lakhnavi *ustāds*. The following comparative discussion is prefaced with brief biographical notes—unfortunately, very little is really known about the lives of these poets.

Shaikh Imam Bakhsh Nasikh—"he who obliterates"—(d.1838) was probably born in Faizabad in 1771, and was adopted and raised by a tentmaker from Lahore.[3] Brought to Lucknow as a boy, he received instruction at the Firangi Mahal, where he learned Persian and Arabic. As a young man with poetic aspirations, he petitioned to enter the tutelage of Mir Taqi Mir (d. 1810), but the great *ustād* from Delhi refused to take him on. Nasikh then determined to school himself in the art of poetry.[4] He is said to have been intellectually inclined and enamoured of displaying his learning. He is also credited with having achieved the elegance and chasteness of expression for which Lakhnavi Urdu is still renowned and cherished, by "cleansing the language of awkward Hindi and Sanskrit expressions"[5] and then infusing it with Persian and Arabic instead. It is for this reason, as well as for his poetic prowess, that he earned the title of "Imam of the Lucknow School."

Khvaja Haidar Ali Atish (1774?-1846)—whose pen-name means "fire" or "flame"—was Nasikh's only real rival in Lucknow. Born into a family of dervishes and religious men of Delhi who had emigrated to Faizabad during the repeated sacks of Delhi in the middle part of the eighteenth century, Atish is credited with having introduced Sufistic themes into Lakhnavi poetry.[6] Because his father died before Atish's education had been completed, Atish was not a particularly learned poet (in contrast with his rival, Nasikh). After the death of his father, Atish was taken under wing by a nobleman from Faizabad named Mir Muhammad Taqi Taraqqi, who brought the young man with him when he migrated to Lucknow. There Atish is reported to have "passed his youth in wildness and brawling"[7] before entering the tutelage of the poet Mushafi. He then underwent a change of heart, apparently, for he began to shun the court, subsisting on the verge of penury and living at the outer fringes of Lakhnavi society. Nonetheless, he was well-respected and attracted numerous *shāgirds* (pupils), who acted as his representatives in the mainstream of literary society. They are said to have engaged in heated disputes with the followers of Nasikh regarding the principles of proper poetry.[8] Unfortunately, we have no transcripts of these debates. They would have proved interesting and enlightening reading.

Although Nasikh was given the impressive-sounding epithet "Imam of the Lucknow School," it is Atish to whom the tradition has proved kinder, exempting him from most of the harsh judgements against Lakhnavi poetry. This has been effected by more than one critic calling him a "Dihlavi-style Lucknow poet". In large part Atish's favourable reputation is based on the mystical bent with which he is credited; and on his family's known Sufi (and Dihlavi) heritage. To be considered a Sufi poet is to be guaranteed a special place in the Urdu literary canon.[9] Furthermore, Atish is considered a paragon of *sādagī*. An example of how he is perceived by twentieth century literary critics is presented in Ahmed Ali's introduction to Atish:

> ...his works are characterized by a simplicity of style, in spite of an occasional vulgarized use of Persian idiom and of Urdu. He is less flamboyant, and even achieves nobility of thought in a period of effeteness. His imagery is more sensuous than sensual; and he displays a naturalness in his descriptions of the fashionable paraphernalia of a woman's toilet [that were] popular in his day ...while Nasikh employed them with exuberance and erotic pleasure...[10]

The contrast in poetic personalities between Nasikh and Atish parallels the contrast drawn between *Dihlavīyat* and *Lakhnavīyat* in the Two School literature. It might best be expressed as a difference between Nasikh's flamboyant, self-dramatising, exaggerated challenge to convention; and Atish's more generalised, often subdued, maintenance of the ghazal's aesthetic status quo. Atish tends to reiterate the rather melancholy, fatalistic stance of conventional *'āshiqī* which is occasionally tempered by gusts of bravado; while Nasikh loves to push the prescribed, familiar stock of themes and conventions to (and occasionally beyond) their limits, to create a somewhat different aesthetic. Nasikh's poetry comes closer, perhaps, to reflecting *an individual's* experience of *'āshiqī*, compared to the more *general* experience of *'ishq* which forms the core of Atish's poetic expression.

In the following pages samples of poetry by Nasikh and Atish are compared. The initial comparison made in light of various choices the two poets make in a structurally-controlled environment: as in Chapter X, *she'rs* from ghazals composed in the same *zamīn* are compared.

This approach will later be varied by comparing a number of verses by the two Lakhnavi masters which have been chosen on the basis of theme, or *maẓmūn*, without respect to *zamīn* or other purely generic structural constraints. Both approaches offer insight into the choices made by individuals in a heavily prescribed literary tradition such as the Urdu ghazal. As in the Delhi-Lucknow poetic comparison of Chapter X, these comparative experiments are offered as illustrations of potential methods of analysis rather than as rigorous "proofs."

Ensuing examples of verse highlight the contrast between Nasikh as more flamboyant, aggressive and innovative; and Atish as more passive and reiterative of the ghazal's status quo. While Atish's narrator alternates between a certain languor and the occasional blustery bravado of the conventional *'āshiq*, Nasikh's stretching of conventional limits can especially be seen in a certain resort not only to belligerence, but to braggery sometimes expressed in macabre images. Comparative statements regarding the poetry of these two *ustāds* are based on extensive study of both masters' poetry, though the *she'rs* included in the following discussion are relatively few. Of necessity, the verses are presented with extensive explicative notes, for they make clearer the degree of technical elements contributing to choices in theme, diction and mood.

Comparison of Two *Maṭla's* in the Same *Zamīn*

In traditional literary circles it was common, when planning a *mushā'ira*, to set a *zamīn* specifically for the occasion. Each poet was expected to compose a ghazal in that *zamīn* and bring it to the assembly. This practice set an arbitrary standard against which contemporaries and rivals could pit their literary prowess and demonstrate their poetic accomplishment (*ustādī*) to one another. In a fiercely competitive literary environment like the Lucknow *markaz*, the consensus of assembled experts at these *mushā'iras* played a significant role in the establishment and maintenance of poetic reputations. Because Nasikh and Atish were contemporaries, and we hear reports of their legendary rivalry, it seems plausible, even probable (in the case of the first *zamīn* examined here), that some of the ghazals we are about to examine were composed in just such situations as described above, perhaps even for the same *mushā'iras*. There are striking enough resonances between some of the sets of *she'rs* to justify the speculation. A pair of *maṭla's* (opening *she'rs*) begins this chapter's comparison:

زخمِ دل بھرتا ہے جلوہ چہرۂ پُرنور کا
چاندنی میں یاں اثر ہے مرہمِ کافور کا

{A: 58.1} Zakhm-i dil bhartā hai jalva chahra-i pur nūr kā
Chāndnī meñ yāñ asar hai marham-i kāfūr kā

The sight of that lustrous face
heals my wounded heart:
Glowing moonbeams soothe
like dressings soaked in camphor.

کیا اثر میری سیہ بختی کے آگے نور کا
ماہ ہے اک خالِ رخسارہ شبِ دیجور کا

{N:I .15.1} Kyā asar merī siyah-bakhtī ke āge nūr kā
Māh hai ik khāl-i rukhsāra shab-i daijūr kā

What use is radiance
in the face of my black fate?
The moon is but a mole on the cheek
of winter's longest, darkest night.

The task of each poet was to construct a *she'r* around the *qāfiyah* "*-ūr*" and the *radīf* "*kā*". In fact, it is quite possible that this *zamīn* was posed to both poets by the host setting the first *miṣra's* end as *nūr kā* (*nūr* meaning "light, splendour, lustre, brilliance").

The point of departure between Atish and Nasikh lay in their individual choices of the *qāfiyah* word for the second *miṣra*' which, in turn, determined what image (*maẓmūn*) would be central to the verse. The only real constraint—and it was shared by both poets—was that the syntactic subject of their sentence must be a masculine noun, so as to agree with the masculine *radīf* "*kā*;" and the word leading into the *radīf* must end in the sound "*-ūr*."

Both poets responded to the conventional connotations of the word *nūr*, and thus the face of the beloved, which is likened to the full moon. *Nūr* is a word of positive connotation in the ghazal. Atish chose to elaborate upon these positive connotations, equating *nūr* with the beloved's radiant face, and explaining its healing and restorative effect on the suffering *'āshiq*. His central image is, though conventional, nevertheless very pleasing.

In the first part of Atish's first line the *'āshiq* announces himself by referring to his heart's wound (*zakhm-i dil*), and then sets up a standard opposition in the second half with his announcement that a vision of the lustrous face (*chahra-i pur nūr*)—and we understand it to be the beloved's—closes up, or heals, the heart's wound. This notion reiterates the conventional situations of both characters: the beloved is beautiful and elusive to a point that wounds the hearts of her admirers; and the *'āshiq* is wounded and suffering, due to the beloved's beauty, cruelty and inaccessibility. But the merest glimmer or revelation of the beloved face is enough to strengthen the *'āshiq*, to restore him so that he can live on to continue his adoration of her, and thereby maintain the ghazal's status quo. Though the heart's wound opens the verse, we know right away that the central theme in this *she'r* is to be the healing power of the beloved's face, because the full opening line reads: "Revelation of that lustrous face heals, or closes, the wound in [my/one's] heart." In other words, so much does the *'āshiq* desire the sight of that face that even a momentary dropping of her veil, or some other passing glimpse, somehow assuages his pain and injury.

This verse conforms to the *tamṡīlī* model, where the first *miṣra'* contains a statement or claim, and the second either "proves" that statement, or elaborates upon it, or makes a parallel or counter-statement. Since the healing power of revelation of the beloved's face is declared in the first line, the second line must prove how that healing effect is brought about. The second line explains that the rays of light emanating from that lustrous face are like soothing moonbeams, each moonbeam acting as a bandage or dressing soaked in camphor ointment to heal the wound in the *'āshiq's* heart: *chāndnī meṅ yāṅ aṡar*—here the effect of a moonlit night—*hai marham-i kāfūr kā*—is that of a camphor dressing.

The word *chāndnī*, which has soft and soothing associations, is a good choice for Atish's equation with camphor dressings, because it can mean moonbeam, which is white and cool[11] (as is camphor, a common ingredient in ointments). The creation of this image[12] is therefore visually justified. Thus, while reiterating a conventional theme, the association between the beloved's face and moon-like radiance, Atish also makes a contribution to the standard image by equating soothing moonbeams with camphor-soaked dressings.

Nasikh's verse ("What use is radiance...") works on contrast, and departs from some of the ghazal's more standard connotations: already given *nūr* (light) in the first line, he chose to end the second with a word ending in the sound *-ūr* but signifying darkness, the antonym of *nūr*. The word he used was *daijūr*. The primary meaning of *daijūr* is "dark, pitch dark, black, obscure."[13] Secondarily it indicates a dark night without moonlight (offering contrast to the suggestion of moonlight in the first line's use of *nūr*), darkness and obscurity. Finally, the term *shab-i daijūr* is a term in astronomy, signifying the night of conjunction of sun and moon, the longest, darkest night of the year, or winter solstice.

Nasikh masterfully exploits the standard connotations of *nūr* by building the statement in the first *miṣra'* around its sense of light, radiance and warmth, in other words, *nūr*"*s* positive connotations. But he also sets the stage for contradiction by asking, "What effect can the presence of splendid light have *on my black fate*?" This rhetorical question—whose implicit claim is that *not even* splendid light can ameliorate the narrator's condition—additionally works to establish the tone of the *she'r*, and announces the *'āshiq*, in keeping with convention, as a person of misfortune and despair. We now expect that the *'āshiq's* black fate will be the central theme of the *she'r*, and that it will be contained in the verse's second line.

Since this is, as was Atish's verse, a *tamṡīlī she'r*, we expect the second *miṣra'* to prove why even the splendour of the moon has no ameliorating effect on the *'āshiq's* condition. Nasikh's choice of *shab-i daijūr* for the *qāfiyah* phrase accomplishes the task convincingly, since his claim is that the moon is nothing but a (white) speck on the enormous face of the longest, darkest night of the year. By metaphorical extension, we know that *shab-i daijūr* is, in fact, the *'āshiq's* desperate condition, his "black fate," containing all the enormity and uncertainty connoted by the inverted perspective of the moon as nothing but a small white speck on the enormous face of the black, long night—instead of the more familiar image, that the moon's radiance and lustre dominate the night and light it up. The exaggerated claim of the first line, that no known illumination is strong enough to affect the darkness of the *'āshiq's* lot, is thus corroborated by taking the exemplar of light and reducing it to the size and significance of just a facial beauty mark.

To summarise, Nasikh manipulated both technical and thematic conventions in composing this dramatically forceful *maṭla'*. Thematically, he drew upon the conventions of the suffering *'āshiq* (as did Atish), and on the *'āshiq's* standard claims about the extent and depth of his suffering; he also drew upon the equation of the beloved's face with the moon, and on the moon's positive connotations in the world of the ghazal (as did Atish). However, while Atish reiterated the standard connotations evoked by the word *nūr*, Nasikh demonstrated the reverse of what we would have expected from the exemplar of beauty and splendour: the unfriendliness of the universe toward the suffering *'āshiq*, a dark unfriendliness overwhelming even to the moon.

Nasikh's use of black-white imagery supported the *she'r's* central inversion. The moon's importance, and its exemplary symbolism, was diminished, even discarded, by implication. While this particular reversal is not really unique in the world of the ghazal, Nasikh demonstrated a pleasing ingenuity in unfolding the "surprise" as gradually as the *she'r* unfolded at a structural level. His love of the macabre, and of blackness as an intensifier[14] are reflected in this verse; as well as his employment of extreme exaggeration to produce a dramatic effect on his audience.

The contrast in poetic personalities between Nasikh and Atish lies here in Nasikh's self-dramatising, exaggerated challenge to convention; as opposed to Atish's more generalised, less flamboyant reiteration of the ghazal's established aesthetic. Not only can we see this contrast in the way each responded to the set word *nūr*, but we also see it manifest in subtler ways. For example, Atish uses a colloquial expression (*zakhm bharnā*—for a wound to close up or heal) to set up his image; while Nasikh punctuates his own with *shab-i daijūr*—an expression whose employment I have noticed far less in the ghazal.[15] In this way Nasikh also demonstrates his learning and intellectual bent, of which we are told he was inordinately proud.

The final point of contrast between these two *maṭla's* is as follows: the *'āshiq* in Atish's *maṭla'* bears an unexceptional identity, and is healed by the moonbeam dressings. These features reinforce his passive relation to the beloved, and to the universe in general. Nasikh will not rest content with the prescribed, confined universe of the ghazal, however: he must invert the image of the moonlit night and make the moon an insignificant speck on the vast face of his own cruel fate. In other words, his *'āshiq* claims exceptional qualities for himself, and supports his claim through the poet's image reversal.

Resignation and Assertion

In the first pair of verses we showed how Atish's and Nasikh's different choices of *qāfiyah* word in a *maṭla'* produced two very different *maẓāmīn*. In the next pair of *she'rs* from this "*-ūr kā*" *zamīn*, the essential topic is the same, but the two poets employ different images. Both take on a philosophical tone as they ruminate upon the labour of love:

where they differ is that Atish's rather abstract imagery reflects his tenrdency to speak in universal terms of *'āshiqī*; while Nasikh's image reflects again his bent toward particularisation of the *'āshiq* into a specific individual dramatically voicing his own, specific experience of *'ishq*. This pair of *she'rs* bears the *qāfiyah* word *mazdūr*, (wage labourer, servant, hired help, stonemason):

کچھ نہ حاصل ہووے کیسی ہی مشقت کیجئے
عشق بازی کام ہے بیگار کے مزدور کا

{A :58.3} Kuchh na ḥāṣil hove kaisī hī mashaqqat kījiye
'Ishq bāzī kām hai begār ke mazdūr kā

Strive however hard
there's nothing to be gained:
The labour of love
is indentured labour.

and

مجھ سے اوّل خانۂ زنداں میں تھا مجنوں تو کیا
ہر محل میں پہلے ہوتا ہے گذر مزدور کا

{N: 15.7} Mujh se avval khāna-i zindāñ meñ thā Majnūñ to kyā
Har maḥal meñ pahle hotā hai guẓar mazdur kā

So what if Majnun was here
in this prison before me?
The first to pass through any dwelling
must be the stonemason.

Atish uses *mazdūrī* to characterize the plight of the *'āshiq*, who struggles eternally for a hopeless cause (to win the love and recognition of the cruel, indifferent beloved). The rhetorical challenge in the first line is, "Since nothing is likely to come of it, why should one strive so hard, expend so much effort?"[16] In the omniscient reply of the second *miṣra'* we learn that one must struggle, even if it is to be of no avail, because that is the task of those fated to love, to be enslaved by *'ishq*.

This verse is among the most succinct and eloquent expressions in Atish' poetry of the Sisyphean nature of *'āshiqī*. Its tone captures the sense of the *'āshiq's* eternal bind, the hopeless situation he lives with: he finds no fulfillment of his desires, yet there is enough satisfaction in the mere striving after elusive fulfillment to keep him engaged.[17]

Not so with Nasikh. He presents his narrator/*'āshiq* as the most exemplary lover there ever was, by comparing him favourably with Majnun. As we have mentioned elsewhere, it is a common practice in the Urdu ghazal to claim recognition as an exemplary lover by finding legendary figures wanting in comparison with one's own feats or demonstrations of love and dedication. Here Nasikh focuses upon the theme of degradation and disgrace which are bound to come to any true *'āshiq*. The archetype for this theme is Majnun, who went mad, was imprisoned, then banished; and spent his life wandering deranged, in the desert, in search of Laila. Though a pathetic figure, Majnun has been a role model for lovers in Persian and Urdu literature for centuries, because the plight he accepts represents the triumph of devotion in love.

Nasikh's narrator speaks from prison, too (*k͟hāna-i zindān*), be it the metaphorical prison of love, or an actual prison. The first *miṣra'* queries: "So what if Majnun was here in this prison before me?" Rhetorically, this line alerts us to the fact that this is a *tamṡīlī* verse; and, by inference, that the narrator is going to somehow discount Majnun's suffering or disgrace and set up his own situation as archetypal. The second line explains that any building or dwelling is temporarily occupied by those who construct it, but that they are not the inhabitants for whom the structure is truly intended: "The first to pass through any dwelling/must be the stonemason," the implication being that Majnun's imprisonment was by way of paving the way for a true prisoner of love, i.e., this particular *'āshiq*. On a hierarchical level, too, to refer to Majnun as a *mazdūr* is to further distinguish between his mettle as an *'āshiq* and the superior mettle of this verse's narrator. After all, Majnun is the exemplary *'āshiq*, whose sacrifice is legendary, and who is, therefore, to be revered rather than denigrated. Day labourers in India are among the lowest of the low in terms of class, while according to the legend, Majnun was of *sharīf* (noble) stock.[18] To refer to him as a *mazdūr* is, thus, all the more outrageous.

The difference in uses and evocations of the *qāfiyah* word, *mazdūr*, partially reflects the character difference between Atish and Nasikh as poets. In Atish's verse we saw the narrator ally himself with the universal *'āshiq*, with the condition of any person caught in a dubious love. In Nasikh's *she'r* attention was drawn to the exceptional nature of the '*āshiq*'*s* situation. Because of each poet's particular stance, we reiterate, Nasikh often expresses himself in a witty, flamboyant, excessive, even perverse manner (this particular *she'r* is witty and employs what is seen as specious, yet telling, logic); while Atish strikes us a more passive, emotional, less cerebral poet.

In the last pair of verses from this *zamīn*, the *qāfiyah* word is *angūr*, or "grape." Here Atish's '*āshiq* gives voice to the bravado which he conventionally juxtaposes with languor. While Atish's *she'r* below contains a little *maẓmūn āfirīnī*, Nasikh's carries the same basic *maẓmūn* to an even further flight of fancy than his rival:

میں وہ میکش ہوں چمن میں جس کی صورت دیکھ کر
آب ہو جاتا ہے شیرہ دانۂ انگور کا

{A: 58.4} Maiñ voh mai-kash hūñ chaman meñ jis kī ṣūrat dekh kar
Āb ho jātā hai shīra dāna-i angūr kā

I'm the kind of wine-drinker
the sight of whose face in the garden
turns the grape's very juice to water.

and

ہجر میں ساغر سے آئی مجھ کو ساقی بوئے خوں
بادہ کھنچوایا ہے شاید زخم کے انگور کا

{N: 15.8} Hijr meñ sāghar se āʼī mujh ko sāqī bū-i khūñ
Bāda khinchvāyā hai shāyad zakhm ke angūr kā

In separation, Saqi
there wafted to me from the goblet
the smell of blood:
Have you drawn your wine
from the grape of my wound?

Atish's basic strategy here is to boast of his great drunkenness, since drunkenness is a telling symptom of '*āshiqī* (whether the '*āshiq* be drunk on real wine or divine spirits.) The first *miṣra*' declares: "This is what a drunkard I am," and then goes on to say that even the grapes still on the vine in the garden fear to be his prey. Be it an elusive ploy or merely out of fear itself, the *'āshiq* claims that, "When they see my face the seeds and juice within the grapes turn to water." The indirect claim of the *she'r* is, of course, that the narrator's thirst is so rapacious as to consume not only wine, but any substance related to it, such as the juice in the grapes still on the vine. And there is word-play here, since both *āb* and *shīra* can secondarily signify wine.

Atish often expresses love of wine, of the tavern, and of revelry. Since his reputation is that of a retiring man dedicated to living a spiritual life, his interest in *mai-kashī* (wine-bibbing) is considered by critics to exist on a purely metaphorical, mystical level. Stretched a bit, this *she'r* could lend itself to a *ḥaqīqī* interpretation as well as to a *majāzī* reading. The image of grapes turning to water is plausible and, therefore, rhetorically justified. Whether one reads this *she'r* as a statement of *'ishq-i ḥaqīqī* or *'ishq-i majāzī*, however, its stance of *'āshiqī* remains the same in its exuberant bravado.

Nasikh's *she'r* is much more complicated, and slightly macabre.[19] Instead of the scent of wine which we would expect to waft to the drinker from his wine-cup, he tells us it is the scent of blood (*bū-i k͟hūñ*). Up until that point, the end of the first line, there are no surprises, and the syntax of the line is reasonably clear: "In separation [there] wafts from the goblet the smell of ..." When we hear the word *k͟hūn* instead of a word for wine, such as *sharāb* or *mai*, we are caught off guard. The smell of blood in the beloved's lane might be expected, since it is the place of slaughter and execution, but it is not part of the ghazal scenario for carnage to occur in the tavern. How, then, is the poet to reconcile us to the smell of blood wafting from a cup full of wine? Certainly, there is some correlation between wine and other deep-red substances, such as the rose, or blood, but the drinking of blood seems quite out of place in the tavern.

The rhetorical tension created by Nasikh is heightened on a thematic as well as structural level because the riddle is not solved until the very end of the *she'r*, by the *qāfiyah* word *angūr*. Throughout the remainder of the second line, however, the tension is sustained, as the statement slowly unfolds: "Has wine perhaps been extracted (*bāda khinchvāyā hai shāyad*) from the wound's grape *zak͟hm ke angūr*?

Only now is the *tamṣīl* resolved and the relationship between blood and wine justified in terms of this verse. Nasikh has justified his claim by making a play on the word *angūr*, which generally signifies "grape." There is a less common meaning of *angūr*, however: "scab, or cicatrice." One reason for the success of this play on words by Nasikh is that he precedes the critical *angūr* with *zakhm ke*, (providing a context for the "scab") which justifies this particular use of *angūr*.

This is a bizarre image, what with the *sāqī* serving the *'āshiq* wine squeezed from the *'āshiq's* own wound. Yet the notion that a wounded *'āshiq's* scabs might generate the intoxication he seeks in the tavern can actually be justified, in terms of *aṣlīyat* (reality): it is, in fact, the lover's suffering which often feeds his love, since that suffering is the most tangible aspect he has of *'ishq*. Because of this justification, Nasikh "gets away with" the *she'r's* wild flight of fancy. Here Nasikh does what he loves best, and what any good Urdu poet will attempt: to exploit legitimate images and associations while challenging standard connotations in the ghazal's lexicon. And yet the lasting impression will be that peculiar image with which Nasikh makes this individualistic statement. He is a true master of *maẓmūn āfirīnī*.

We have just observed three pairs of verses by the two great Lakhnavis which demonstrated their different poetic tendencies. The four *qāfiyah* words in this same *zamīn* in Chapter X—with one exception—bore out this same dichotomy.[20]

In the following section the focus turns to treatment of specific *maẓāmīn*, particularly to the poets' different choices of tone and stance in their narrative.

Ṣayyād

Common epithets for the beloved in the Urdu ghazal are murderess, executioner, or huntress (*qātil, jallād, ṣayyād* respectively). The focus of discussion in the following pages will be upon a number of *she'rs* by Atish and Nasikh which employ the "beloved-as-slayer" motif; and that of the *kū-i yār*, or "the beloved's lane." These themes have been selected for the following reasons:

1) They occur relatively often in the poetic selections from which most of our discussion in this study draws:
2) They serve as useful showcases for two of the essential conditions the ghazal seeks to address, which are:
    a. the various facets of the relationship between the *'āshiq* and his beloved; and
    b. the abiding, Sisyphean circumstances into which the condition of *'āshiqī* locks the lover.

3) As showcases to display issues at the heart of the ghazal, they offer insight into the kinds of choices made individually by Atish and Nasikh, though both are masters of the same highly prescribed, heavily conventionalised, formulaic genre.

The first set of examples will feature the motif of the beloved as *qātil* (slayer); or as *ṣayyād* (hunter); or as *jallād* (executioner or punisher). We begin with a discussion of verses in which the beloved is depicted as a hunter:

فکر مرغانِ چمن کی ہے بہار آئی ہے
جھونپڑا ڈالا ہے صیاد نے گلزار کے پاس

{A: 188.6} Fikr murg͟hān-i chaman kī hai bahār ā'ī hai
Jhompaṛā ḍālā hai ṣayyād ne gulzār ke pās.

I worry about the nightingales
now that spring has come:
The hunter pitches camp
right outside the garden.

خیال اس صید افگن کا ہے یوں ہر صیدِ ہامون کو
تمنا آمدِ لیلیٰ کی تھی جس طرح مجنوں کو

{N: 194.3} K͟hayāl us ṣaid-afgan kā hai yūñ har ṣaid-i hāmūñ ko
Tamannā āmad-i Laila kī thī jis ṭaraḥ Majnūñ ko.

Every beast in the desert
thinks only of the hunter
Awaiting her arrival with
Majnun's eagerness for Laila.

The idea that the *āshiq's* life is willingly delivered into the hands of the beloved is not new to the Urdu ghazal: it is, rather, an understood facet of his devotion. It is also understood by the audience that the beloved's cruelty and indifference are such that she will kill, or not kill, as her fancy takes her. On the other hand, death has a very attractive feature within the realm of the ghazal, since the *'āshiq* sees it as the highest and most eloquent way of expressing his love. Yet to characterise the beloved as a murderess or huntress is to highlight the dimension of cruelty in her persona to the point where it supercedes her definitional indifference to the *'āshiq*.

Nasikh draws to its own logical extension the transmuted image of the beloved-slayer, demonstrating how his special poetic personality differs from that of Atish, even though both of the following verses employ the image.

In building this image, Atish calls upon the reader's assumed equation of nightingale with *'āshiq* (the phrase *murgh-i chaman* being generally synonymous with *bulbul*). It is generally assumed or expected that the beloved be represented by the symbol of the rose when the nightingale is evoked. Yet here the nightingales are being pursued, and are at risk. Normally the *bulbul* pursues the rose; but here, the birds of the garden are in danger of being hunted. Ultimately, as is conventional in the ghazal, the *'āshiq* is in a vulnerable position, and by being in the garden (the beloved's forum), he may be sacrificed for his love.

In Nasikh's "*khayāl us ṣaid-afgan kā hai...*" there is a reversal which may not dawn upon the audience immediately, since the verse is cloaked in the garb of the "Laila and Majnun" motif, and looks at first to be very conventional. In fact, Nasikh reverses the most standard of stock themes in the ghazal with this *she'r*. The first *miṣra'* states a maxim, that "every game animal in the desert is thinking about the hunter." This statement sets up the standard equations, that "prey-*'āshiq*" and "hunter-Beloved." The expectation thereby created is that their (the beasts') thoughts of the hunter are imbued with a certain dread or apprehension.

In the second *miṣra'*, however, Nasikh achieves a clever turn by then comparing the game animals with Majnun and their contemplation of the beloved with Majnun's frenzied, eager anticipation of Laila's arrival. Equating the hunted animals with Majnun is fully supported by the ghazal scenario which determines that both they and he roam the desert. In Majnun's case, as the ghazal audience well knows, the roaming is of a rather deranged nature, and is conducted in the hope that poor Majnun will somehow come upon the caravan of Laila's people. It would not be assumed, or necessarily expected, that the desert's beasts roam in search of the hunter. (Rather, it may be assumed that they would normally hope to avoid encountering the hunter in their peregrinations.) Even so, it is completely consistent with ghazal convention, once the beasts are imbued with qualities of an *'āshiq*, that they seek out their beloved.[21]

Atish will generally rest content to achieve an uncomplicated, uncontroversial, yet pleasing, fluid expression. To evoke the tried and true equation between the *'āshiq* and the nightingale, while offering the irony of the nightingale as the hunter's object of pursuit, suffices for him. He manipulates the stock themes and images, while ultimately maintaining the familiar melancholy mood in which an *'āshiq* often contemplates his beloved. But Nasikh must create a stir, give a twist to his lines, even if that twist is relatively mild and fully legitimate in the context of the ghazal. This he has done by offering a new insight into the manner of the desert beasts' agitated waiting.

Qātil

As we examine further *she'rs* depicting the beloved as slayer, we will see that a companion to this depiction is a certain shift in the *'āshiq's* persona as well. His characteristic passive self-sacrifice sometimes shifts to something more willful. He grows eager for death at the beloved's hands. Such is the background for the two following *she'rs*:

اجل آ ورنہ اب یہ رشک مجھ کو قتل کرتا ہے
عزیزاں پاؤں کو پھیلائے سوتے ہیں مزاروں میں

{A: 235.4} Ajal ā varna ab yih rashk mujh ko qatl kartā hai
'azīzāñ pā'oñ ko phailā'e sote haiñ mazāroñ meñ.

Come to me, O death !
this jealous yearning kills me:
My friends repose, feet splayed
out among the tombs.

and

اضطراب دوریِ محبوب میں معذور ہوں
کیوں نہ تڑپے اس قدر قاتل سے گھائل دور ہے

{N:2-438.6} Iẓṭirāb-i dūrī-i maḥbūb meñ ma'ẓūr hūñ
Kyoñ na taṛpe is qadar qātil se ghāyal dūr hai.

I can't but be restless with agitation
in separation from the beloved:
Why should not the wound writhe
when the executioner's blow
is distant yet?

In these two *she'rs*, rather than "worrying" about the proximity of the hunting lodge to the garden (as in the previous section) the *'āshiqs* are back again in their customary position of longing for the beloved. They are therefore doing pretty much what is expected of them; and the beloved is also doing pretty much what is expected of her, in that she is not delivering what is sought: the killing blow.

Atish's verse, characteristically, expresses a certain familiar wistfulness, as the *'āshiq* bemoans the fact that Fate has not yet caught up with him. He offers a vivid picture of the repose he expects it to afford him in his description of his "sleeping" friends, feet stretched out in their tombs.

Nasikh too expresses impatience for death, but his tone is more agitated than wistful. Similarly, his desire is focused less on the end of death than on the physical blow by which he expects to achieve it; and, of course, that blow is to be dealt him at the hands of the beloved executioner. The contrast between separation and union is underlined because of the physicality of the image: he expects a blow, decapitation; and he writhes in anticipation. His writing intensifies the lack of resolution in life, and the eagerness with which he seeks to achieve resolution in death.[22] Ironically, the serenity of union is to be brought about by violence, a forced resolution.

The jealous yearning to which Atish refers in his *she'r* is muted by the image of his dead friends' repose, thus suggesting that repose is actually his final goal. By contrast, Nasikh remains focused on his present agitation, and the primary image in his *she'r* is physical and charged.

Nasikh has written another verse which captures the image of the executioner's blow, lending to it a note of macabre triumph which also includes sexual overtones:

تہہِ شمشیرِ قاتل کس قدر بشّاش تھا ناسخ
کہ عالم ہر دہانِ زخم پر تھا روئے خنداں کا

{N:11.17} Tah-i shamshīr-i qātil kis qadar bashshāsh thā Nāsikh
Kih 'ālam har dahān-i zakhm par thā rū-i khandāñ kā.

What manner of joy was Nasikh's
beneath the executioner's sword?
The mouth of every wound revealed
a smiling face.

Nasikh seems to positively glory in the gory attainment of his desire for death by the beloved's sword. He takes a ghoulish delight in having gotten the beloved to kill him, since it is proof that his will has prevailed over hers (and her will is to ignore and deny him). He even savours the blood she has spilled, touting it as a token of his own compelling *'āshiqī*. Such macabre triumph is spelled out explicitly in the following *she'r*:

جوشِ سودا سے سیہ تھا کیا ہی ناسخ کا لہو
ہے سیہ تاب اس بتِ سفاک کی تلوار پر

{N: 96.16} Josh-i saudā se syah thā kyā hī Nāsikh kā lahū
Hai syah-tāb us but-i saffāk kī talvār par.

Was that Nasikh's blood
turned black with madness?
The idol-butcher's blade
gleamed a glossy pitch.

It is as though the blackness, the concentration of his blood on the executioner's sword, signals some power he has gained over her. In any case, one senses that Nasikh derives satisfaction from the pitch black glossiness overtaking the instrument of his slaughter. An *'āshiq* may not be able—may not even aspire—to vanquish the beloved, he seems to say, but at least he can make some tangible impression on her. She will have to either look at the black glossiness on her sword or she will have to remove it. In either case she will be forced to extend some implicit recognition or acknowledgement to the one who caused it to be there. This is a far cry from the *'āshiq* who takes whatever he can get from the beloved, even though it is usually nothing.

The previous *she'rs* have served to illustrate that Nasikh, in his *'āshiq* persona, often challenges the notion of the hopelessly futile, desperate man whom we generally expect to find in the ghazal. Let us again compare this special tone of Nasikh with that of Atish, as he employs the motif of the *qātil*, the beloved-as-executioner. Even with a common background the tone varies, depending upon what special shade the poet intends to lend his expression. In the following *she'r*, for example, Atish uses this background to achieve the sort of effect we had in Nasikh's last example, using the sword-blade as the focal point of the act of execution:

سینکڑوں تشنۂ دیدار ہیں معلوم نہیں
کس کی قسمت کا ہے پانی تری تلوار کے پاس

{A:188.4} Saikaṛoñ tishna-i dīdār haiñ ma'lūm nahīñ
Kis kī qismat kā hai pānī tirī talvār ke pās.

Untold thousands thirst
for your sight:
who knows whose destiny rests
on the cutting edge of your sword.

Here Atish employs *maẓmūn āfirīnī*, using a familiar background to achieve an unusual effect.[23]

The focal image in the present *she'r* is on the sword-blade of the executioner, but the vehicle by which that image is created is a description of the '*āshiq's* condition. The new image is gradually built in the course of the *she'r* unfolding.

The entire verse is cloaked in quasi-mystical garb. It begins with a conventional enough introductory idea: that "untold thousands thirst for your sight" wherein we understand that "your sight" is that of the beloved. This notion fits completely within the mainstream of ghazal thought, offering the possibility of both *majāzī* and *ḥaqīqī* interpretations. Regardless of whether the beloved is Divine or human, the '*āshiq* desperately wishes to have a glimpse of him/her; and withholding that vision from the '*āshiq* is the most crucial characteristic shared by mortal and immortal beloveds.

The next statement complements and substantiates the ostensible idea that '*āshiqs* seek a vision of the beloved; and that they would consider such a vision to be the fulfillment of all they desire from their destiny. The phrase *ma' lūm nahīñ* —no one knows—evokes the universality of the human experience as represented by separation from the beloved; and that universal condition is the core of the ghazal's expression.

The third semantic unit, *(kis kī qismat) kā hai pānī*, is the crucial clause in this *she'r*. Atish's play on the word *pānī* is brilliant here. *Pānī* is the essential element for quenching thirst. It can also mean "lustre, mettle, polish, gleam, cutting edge," all nuances complementary to the last semantic unit of the verse's reference to swords and daggers—*terī talvār ke pās*—"alongside, near, at the hand of your sword." When destiny is the "water" for quenching "thirst for the sight/vision" of the beloved, one can see how a *ḥaqīqī* reading might be taken.

The sword of even a human beloved/*qātil* can bring about the culmination of mortal destiny, propelling the '*āshiq* toward union with the Ultimate beloved, and his (hopefully) ultimate destiny. The sight (*dīdār*) can be taken to be a reflection in the gleam of the beloved's sword, and the image is revealed to be an equation of the beloved's sword with a mirror. The mirror, an image of central importance to Sufi doctrine, is a mystical metaphor for the relation between the temporal world and Divine Creation.

Thus, we see that Atish has used *maẕmūn āfirīnī* to ultimately reiterate the fundamentals of '*ishq*, which is the stated topic of the ghazal genre.

Both this verse and Nasikh's "Was that Nasikh's blood..." are unusual in their effect; are excellent examples of *maẕmūn āfirīnī*; and yet serve to illustrate fundamental differences between Atish and Nasikh as poets. In Atish's *she'r* the stance of his narrator/'*āshiq* ultimately remains one of passivity toward the beloved, and still carries a note of wistfulness about it. Nasikh's verse leaves a macabre taste in one's mouth—he gets to us in an eerie way. Atish manages to make an impact while remaining within the familiar boundaries and prescribed roles, while the force of Nasikh's impact is largely contained in pushing at the normal boundaries of convention, by emphasizing his clever unusualness: Nasikh's '*āshiq* calls attention to himself with the stain his blood makes on the executioner's sword; while Atish's narrator keeps the focus on the execution of '*āshiqs* in general, as the fulfillment of their destiny.

Atish's Bravado

While we have said that Nasikh is the more aggressive, assertive of the two Lakhnavis, Atish too can show himself to be a poet of great bravado. In this way he parallels the '*āshiq* who, though usually long-suffering, will also make great claims for himself, even for his extraordinary ability to endure suffering. In the following two *she'rs* his manner of address to the beloved is peremptory: he not only longs for execution, he even calls for it, demands it of her:

چن چن کے قتل کیجئے انصاف شرط ہے
حاضر ہیں بے گناہ و گنہگار دیکھئے

{A: 329.11} Chun chun ke qatl kījiye inṣāf sharṭ hai
Ḥāẓir haiñ begunāh-o gunahgār dekhiye.

The execution of justice
requires a discriminating eye:
Innocents stand attendance amongst sinners—
choose carefully whom you slay.

and

ایڑیاں شوقِ شہادت میں کہاں تک رگڑوں
اب تو جلاد کو بھجواؤ گنہگار کے پاس

{A: 188.10} Eṛiyān shauq-i shahādat meñ kahāñ tak ragṛūñ
Ab to jallād ko bhijvāo gunahgār ke pās.

How far down must I grind my heels
standing in wait for martyrdom?
Send the executioner out now
to face this sinner.

In the first *she'r* the '*āshiq's* observation carries a note of cautionary warning to the beloved. He is making claims about the superior quality of his '*āshiqī*, implying that he is a real sinner, rather than one of those "innocents" also standing by waiting for—though undserving of—the *jallād's*, or executioner-beloved's, particular attentions. But he still does not press his case beyond a certain strictly prescribed point: he does not cry out, "Kill me!" Instead he leaves her to exercise her choice of victims, thus paralleling the situation of a *bazm* where all her admirers cluster hopefully by, awaiting her attentions.

In the second verse the tone can either be weary, or wistful, or even peevish or fretful. The "send out the excutioner now" might be seen as a last-ditch attempt to move the powers that be. But it also strikes the reader that the narrator of this verse is pretty fed up, and therefore somewhat inclined to abandon the meekness which is characteristic of his persona, and which has caused him to "wear down his heels." In that case the more aggressive or belligerent tone of "I'm tired of waiting, send her out now!" would not only be plausible to the audience, it might even be assumed on the part of the *'āshiq* in hopes that it would provoke some—any—result or action on her part.[25] The uses of the phrase *eṛiyāñ ragaṛnā*—which means "to be in distress or agony" as well as the more literal "to wear or rub down one's heels"—would tend to support a less than formal tone of address. In fact, the request/order is indeed delivered in the imperative, second person singular form of the verb (*bhijvāo*). The first verse's commands "choose carefully whom you kill" and "look at the sinners and innocents standing in attendance" were delivered in the more formal "*āp*"—the second person plural form of the verb, which is commonly employed in colloquial language to distance the speaker from the person addressed, and so to gain the upper hand in a verbal exchange. But the occurrence in this second verse of such bluster enhances the interest, the emotional charge.

The verses in our selection from Atish's two *dīvāns* which address the theme of the beloved-as-killer tend to focus on the condition of the victim, the condition of his desire for death at her hands. His categorical depiction of the beloved rarely goes beyond informing us of her killing role, of setting up a background image of the *qātil*. Atish is more interested or concerned with exploring how the *maḥbūb*, in this particular valence, affects the condition of the *'āshiq*. His approach to *'āshiqī* is more general, or abstract, than the concrete images employed by Nasikh in his poetry. While Atish seems to identify with the general state of *'āshiqī*, Nasikh often seems more interested in identifying the *'āshiq* as himself, especially in glorifying the aspect of "*āshiq*-as-victim."

Kū-i-Yār

Another standard ghazal theme employed by both Nasikh and Atish in their *dīvāns* is that of the lane outside the beloved's house, known as the *kū-i yār*. Examination of several verses by each Lakhnavi which incorporate the *kū-i yār* motif will show some of the different ways it can be used in the ghazal.

To briefly recapitulate the stock image of the *kū-i yār*, it is here that the '*āshiq* and his rivals camp out, in the vain hope that time will grant them a glimpse of the object of their adoration. They sit there obsessively, knowing that her lane is likely to be as close to her as they ever get. This obsession causes the beloved's admirers to abandon all other concerns and responsibilities in favour of simply sitting in dubious attendance; and their casting off of even basic social responsibilities brings about their disgrace, even degradation, in the eyes of the rest of society. This is the situation depicted in the following *she'r* by Atish:

تیرے کوچے کا ہے اے خانہ خراب افسانہ آج
شیخ کعبہ چھوڑتا ہے برہمن بت خانہ آج

{A: 155.4} Tere kūche kā hai ai k͟hāna-k͟harāb afsāna āj
Shaik͟h ka'ba chhoṛtā hai barhaman butk͟hāna āj.

What stories they tell, you home-wrecker,
of the pull of your lane:
The shaikh abandons the Ka'ba today,
the Brahmin his idol-house.

In addressing the beloved, Atish's narrator invokes both the power she has over men and the desirability of courting even disgrace ot be in her lane, near her house. He alludes to at least one of the kinds of disgrace which an '*āshiq* can expect—broken homes (the word he uses to address her is *k͟hāna-k͟harāb*, or "home-wrecker"). He illustrates his point by citing examples of normally venerated members of society—religious leaders such as the Muslim shaikh and the Hindu Brahmin—who run from their houses of worship, risking everything just to be part of what goes on in that lane. This verse can be read as expressing either divine or human love, but its message is unaffected by either interpretation. The message still comes through loud and clear: genuine '*āshiqs* will pursue their beloved regardless of where it takes them and what the consequences. The worse the consequences, in fact, the more sacrifice is required, and the greater is therefore proved their commitment. A corollary to this message is that the sacrifices made in this fashion, being worldly and temporal, are ultimately of less value than their prospective, eternal reward—*viṣāl* (union) with the Divine beloved.

Atish's inclusion of the Brahmin into the realm of *'āshiqī* implies an equation between him and *shaikhs*, who hold a high position in Muslim society on account of their religious status. The apparent blasphemy of this equation is justified by the mystical interpretation of *'ishq*: the One God does not observe sectarian differences, even between *kāfirs* (idolators) and Muslims. This is, in fact, what he signifies with the phrase "Shaikh and Brahmin": he also means Hindus and Muslims, in a general way. Infidels have as much need of God as do Muslims, and their search is essentially the same. Furthermore, the holy men of both religions leave their "homes" (the *butkhāna* and Ka'ba) because God is not to be found there anyway. Viewed in this light, and in light of the fact that it only pretends to mildly rebuke the beloved (for being heartless enough to lure even the clergy to their own disgrace on her account) while actually using the alleged rebuke to praise her irresistibility; the *she'r* falls completely within the prescribed parameters of the Urdu ghazal, and reiterates the passive, self-deprecating quality of the conventional *'āshiq*, as well as his universal identity.

In the two *she'rs* below we see symbolic possibilities of the *kū-i yār* motif as a metaphor for aspects of *'ishq-i ḥaqīqī*—and, thus, for the human condition in general. In both verses the *'āshiq* is not actually in the lane of the beloved; rather, he longingly contemplates gaining access there. He speaks from isolation, from beyond her realm. His stage of *'āshiqī* is not of the most advanced—as it will be in the verses following this pair—so the tone of both *she'rs* in this pair, rather than being desperate or frenzied (which would reflect a more advanced state of *'āshiqī*), is wistful and languid. Their tone and imagery reflect the desire of the seeker of mystical union with the Divine, as well as that of a human being for an earthly beloved:

ہوائے کوئے قاتل کا کبھی عالم نہیں پایا
چمن کو بارہا دیکھا ہے جا جاکر بہاروں میں

{A: 235.5}

Havā-i kū-i qātil kā kabhī 'ālam nahīn̄ pāyā
Chaman ko bā-rahā dekhā hai jā jākar bahāron̄ men̄.

I never could find the lovely effect
of the lane of that murderess
though spring upon spring I went
and gazed into the garden.

Although Atish refers to the beloved as *qātil*, the narrator's locale (the lane outside the beloved's house) forms the *she'r's* central image. The *'āshiq* expresses a wistfulness for that most desirable of places (the *kū-i yār*), preferring it to the place in which he actually finds himself. He alludes, in passing, to the dangers of her lane when he refers to the beloved as *qātil*, a murderer, dangerous to be around. The primary statement in this *she'r* is that he wishes he were *there*, near her, instead of here, in separation. Furthermore, the "lovely effect" in the lane of the beloved is its intensity of color, created by all the blood from her murdered victims, which surpasses the colors in the garden full of flowers.[26]

راہ پائے تیرے کوچے میں جو وہ آنے کی
نہ رکھے بادِ صبا پاؤں گلستاں میں کبھی

{N: 242.8} Rāh pā'e tere kūche meñ jo voh āne kī
na rakhe bād-i ṣabā pā'oñ gulistāñ meñ kabhī.

Were it to find the path by which
to enter your lane
Never again would the morning breeze
set foot inside the garden.

In this *she'r* Nasikh uses the beloved's lane as a backdrop against which to contrast things as they are with the way we would have them be. Atish also drew this contrast in a clearly wistful and acquiescent tone. But Nasikh's verse is different in that its tone of wistfulness is rather ambiguous. On the one hand, he ostensibly adopts the tone of wistful acquiescence with which we would normally associate the *kū-i yār* motif, ruminating—as did Atish—on how desirable a place it is to be. Even the morning breeze, which has an entrée into the garden, would be willing to relinquish paradise in favor of the beloved's lane.

On the other hand, the subjunctive mood of the opening clause, "If it were to gain entry to your lane (*tere kūche meñ āne kī rāh pā'e*)" can be seen as a sort of complaint about her inaccessibility, cloaked in apparent praise of the beloved's chastity and modesty.

The explicit statement in this *she'r* is that "If it had the choice, even the morning breeze would cease its roaming through the delightful garden, opting for the less tangible pleasures of the lane outside her house." In other words, even the breeze would rather be confined by the beloved than free to roam, if it means being far from her. But, of course, she is so off-putting to potential admirers that even the breeze cannot find its way to her.

To fully appreciate this verse it will be useful to briefly state the symbolic importance of the garden, and the contrast it represents to the *kū-i yār*. The garden is a metaphor for paradise on earth, even for heavenly paradise. It is cool, pleasant, alive and bursting with beautiful flora and fauna. In the garden one's every wish and desire is fulfilled. In short, in Islamic culture it represents the just rewards for piety and righteousness, for struggling to maintain a moral being in this world. As Annemarie Schimmel writes:

> ...The Koran promises the faithful in many of its verses that they would dwell in 'gardens of delight,' in 'gardens under which flow rivers.' The garden and what is in it became a symbol of God's creative power, of His grace, and a prefiguration of the paradisical bliss which the faithful will experience at the end of times...[27]

What, in contrast, are the qualities we associate with the lane outside the beloved's house? It is a place which inevitably brings disgrace or death on those who remain there; in addition, it is infused with an air of wretched despair on account of all the immobilised '*āshiqs* who are its willing prisoners. The beloved herself only passes through upon occasion, always coming from or going to someplace else. In other words, it is only the pathetic '*āshiqs* who are its immobilised captives.

An example of the desirable pathos of the *kū-i yār* is implied, though not explicitly stated, in this verse by Nasikh—and it carries that characteristically macabre tinge to it. The breeze has been to the garden time after time, but the fragrance it finds there is the *bū-i gul*, that of the rose. The *bū* in the *kū-i yār* is the *bū-i khūn*, the smell of blood, because of all the poor '*āshiqs* who have been slaughtered there. The breeze would rather smell this latter *bū*, because it reminds it of the beloved more than does the fragrance of the rose, which is not nearly so striking.

The breeze in both verses serves as a contrast to the hardships of '*āshiqī*, presenting an all-around positive image: it is cool, it is pleasant, it brings refreshment to the world, it even carries messages of love upon occasion. Also it is mobile, independent, admired and desired by others, and can come and go freely in the garden. But all these admirable qualities, asserts the narrator of Nasikh's verse, would be as nothing to the wind if it could be an *'āshiq*. It would willingly forego its privileges in lieu of sitting in the lane outside the beloved's house, even though that lane be permeated with the smell of death.

شوق قاتل کی گلی کا ہو فرشتہ نقال
لاشہ اپنا نہ رہے گورِ غریباں میں کبھی

Shauq qātil kī galī kā ho farishta-naqqāl
Lāsha apnā na rahe gor-i g͟harībāñ meñ kabhī

My desire for the murderer's lane
would, like an angel, transport my body:
My corpse would never have to rest
in a stranger's grave.

In this *she'r* Nasikh combines the two images of the *kū-i yār* and the beloved as *qātil* to achieve a tone of classic *'āshiqī*. The *'āshiq* speaks of his desire for the lane outside the beloved's house, almost anticipating his death there (after all, she is a *qātil*). But even if he attained the death he desires there, he would not have to suffer a mass grave—which would be appropriate for any of the disgraced and disowned creatures who routinely inhabit that lane—for the force of his desire would bear him away, he claims, saving him from the ignominy that other slain *'āshiqs* suffer after their death. In other words, he is such an exemplary *'āshiq*, so driven by desire, that he would rise above the lot of the common lover.

Finally, in the *she'r* below, Nasikh addresses the ultimate risk—and aspiration—involved in sitting in the *kū-i yār*. Again, he seems to delight in the image of slaughter at the beloved's hands, and yet again, ultimately identifies the quintessential *'āshiq* as himself.

دوستو جلدی خبر لیں کہیں ناسخ نہ ہو
قتل آج اسکی گلی میں کوئی بیچارہ ہوا

{N: 11.21} Dosto jaldī k͟habar leñ kahīñ Nāsikh na ho
Qatl āj us kī galī meñ koī bechārā huā.

Quick, friends, run to her lane—
make sure it wasn't Nasikh:
Some poor soul was slaughtered there today.

Still staying the familiar bounds of the ghazal, and of the *kū-i yār* image, Nasikh injects a wistfulness as well as irony into this *maqṭa'*. The speaker is not actually in the lane. Rather, the goings on in that lane (*us kī galī meñ*) form the substance of gossip elsewhere in the town. In this case the narrator hears that there's been a death there, and dispatches a messenger to "make sure it was not Nasikh."

His alleged concern is, of course, insincere. The poet is actually suggesting that if someone has given up the ghost in the *kū-i yār* it positively must have been Nasikh. He, unlike these gossipers—the verse's narrator included—can be expected to be found in the lane of the beloved, because he is well-known and an exemplary '*āshiq*. In fact, we are meant to infer that Nasikh's '*āshiqī* is so great, and his pursuit of the beloved so dedicated, that it could hardly be any other whose destiny was fulfilled by dying in the *kū-i yār*. The use of the term *qatl honā* to signify death (evoking the *qātil* nature of the beloved), also suggests that the destiny of the victim has been fulfilled at the hands of the beloved herself, that she has actually killed him. In this way the abject position of the lover who sits in the *kū-i yār* is counterbalanced by an implicit praise in the narrator's voiced concern and his admiration at the rewards of Nasikh's devotion (his slaughter, or execution). Furthermore, the "concern" works against another implicit condition of sitting in that lane—disgrace and condemnation: it is implied that Nasikh is well-regarded, admired and respected amongst his peers, even considered a role model; and that his death, though a personal triumph, would represent a definite loss to others on the path of '*āshiqī*. Ultimately then, Nasikh puts himself forward as the disgraced victim, but flaunts his fate as proof of his exceptional '*āshiqī*.

By manipulating the convention of injecting the poet's *takhallus* into the final verse (*maqṭa'*) of a ghazal, combined with his characteristic tone of irony, Nasikh manages to sing his own praises while also claiming for himself the selfless devotion which characterises '*āshiqī*.

Chapter Summary

This study agrees with the critics—and has offered some illustration of the observation—that there exist discernible differences in style between the two Lakhnavi *ustāds* Nasikh and Atish. However, these differences are not unique to the two Lakhnavis; in fact they might well be seen as the reflection of a general point of distinction applicable to most Urdu poets. It is based not on geographical or group criteria but on a choice of one of two general verbal styles available to every Urdu poet. There is, on the one hand, a sparer, more lyrical diction (with which Urdu readers tend to associate Mir, Dard, Mushafi, Momin and Atish). On the other hand a more complex, witty diction, exists which often includes verbal pyrotechnics of the sort people associate with Sauda, Nasikh, Insha and Ghalib. Of course, good poets are masters of both voices, and this is the case with Mir, Ghalib and Nasikh, to some extent.[28]

I would suggest that the famous rivalries (*ma'rike*) which are observed between the top poets of nearly every generation might prove fertile ground for exploring these two basic styles. For example, T. Grahame Bailey reports that "every age of Urdu has had its pair of poets: one natural, the other artificial, writing more for effect ... the first in each of the following pairs being the natural poet: Mir and Sauda, Mushafi and Insha, Atish and Nasikh, Dagh and Amir ..."[29] And Annemarie Schimmel writes:

> Urdu literary history often shows two poets working simultaneously and representing two approaches to poetry, one more natural, the other more sophisticated ... in the long list of these syzygies of poets we find Mir and Sauda, Mushafi and Insha, Zauq and Ghalib, Dagh and Amir, and, in the field of marthiya-writing, Anis and Dabir. In Nasikh's time his poetical counterpart was Atish.[30]

Both Bailey's and Schimmel's remarks would seem to corroborate this view to some extent, and call out for some study that could address these pairings as possible points of departure for testing the hypothesis of two schools of poetry based on textually-specific features.[31]

It is a little surprising that the phenomenon of these literary *ma'rike* has not been drawn more into the Two School debate. Exploration of this phenomenon would, one expects, perhaps unravel some of the anomaly of labelling the great masters Dihlavi or Lakhnavi. It would certainly offer a welcome substitute to the uncomfortable labels such as "Lakhnavi-like Dihlavi" for Zauq and Shah Nasir; and "Dihlavi-like Lakhnavi" for Atish, which we have noted. By discussing Nasikh and Atish in light of a bifurcation which permeates Urdu poetry in general—and by suggesting that other poets might also be studied in a similar light—I hope I have taken one more step in the direction of unravelling the puzzle of the Two School debate, and suggested other possible bases for further study.

NOTES

1. Z.A. Siddiqi, ed. *Kulliyāt-i Atish*, Allahabad, Ram Narayan Lal Beni Madhav, 1972, p. Emphasis mine.
2. Ahmed Ali, *The Golden Tradition*, p. 214. Emphasis mine.
3. Cf. Rashid Hasan Khan, *Intikhāb-i Nāsikh*, p. 116.
4. Ibid., p. 177.
5. M. Sadiq, *A History of Urdu Literature*, p. 134. The question of what constitutes Indian elements in Urdu poetry is unsettled at best. Although Nasikh and many followers reportedly removed much Hindi vocabulary from literary Urdu, references to Indian customs and religion appear in verses of almost every major Urdu poet.
6. Cf. Schimmel, *Classical Urdu Literature from the Beginning to Iqbal*, p. 198; Z.A. Siddiqi, *Kulliyāt*, p. ل· Ahmed Ali, *The Golden Tradition*, pp. 212-214.
7. Sadiq, *A History of Urdu Literature*, p. 138.
8. Azad, *Āb-i-Ḥayāt*, pp. 355-6; Ahmed Ali, op. cit.; Safi Ahmad, *Two Kings of Awadh: Muhammad Ali Shah and Amjad Ali Shah (1837-1847)*, Aligarh: P.C. Dwasdesh Shreni and Company, 1971, p. 139.
9. Ironically, the only Urdu major poet who really was a Sufi was Dard. Nonetheless, Sufistic leanings tend to be highlighted in literary criticism and conventional wisdom. Not surprisingly, there were Sufis who wrote poetry, but not every Sufi poet is judged superior to other poets: Fritz Lehmann points out that the poetry of Ayatollah Jauhiri, a Sufi of Patna, is recognized to be inferior [personal correspondence, 18 April 1985]. Yet because of its Sufistic nature—despite its inferior quality—Jauhiri's poetry is known, at least in Patna.
10. Ahmed Ali, *The Golden Tradition*, p. 214.
11. Whiteness and coolness are attributes of camphor, as was suggested in Nasikh's *she'r* where the heart was such a flame-seeking moth that "*Dil hamāra is qadar sozish ṭalab parvāṇa hai...*" Ch. X.
12. *Maẓmūn āfirīnī*—the creation of novel images—was discussed in Chapter X. It is considered to be a trademark of Lakhnavi poets, though they are by no means the only Urdu poets to have employed this technique, as we saw in Chapter X's sample comaprison of Lakhnavi and Dihlavi poetry.
13. Platts, p. 556.

14. See discussions of blackness in the "motifs" section which concludes this chapter.
15. Frances Pritchett notes that *shab-i daijūr* is to be found in *dāstān* literature, however. *Dāstāns* are narrative prose romances.
16. The use of the word *mashaqqat* to refer to the struggle evokes the more common, verbal form *mashq karnā*,—to practice, do one's lessons, etc.—and intensifies the sense of distress and belaboured effort.
17. This is a *she'r* of *kaifīyat*, one in which a mood or response is evoked in the audience by indirect reference to the entire background of the ghazal, not necessarily through the actual employment of a concrete image, or a new *maẓmūn*. The simplicity of the verse's message appears to strike a profound chord in the audience, who can emphathise with the sentiment because it so succinctly addresses the human experience of *'ishq*, which it is the ghazal's primary concern to express.
18. The father of Qays [Majnun] was a Sayyid and chief of the Arabian Bedouin tribe, the Banu Amir. See R. Gelpke, ed. and trans. of *Nizami's Layla and Majnun*, Boulder: Shambhala Publications, Inc., 1978, p. 9.
19. This verse was also discussed in Chapter X.
20. Recall, for example, that in the *qāfiyah* which used *kāfūr* Atish's *'āshiqs* branded rosy scars on their breasts—which was not an original *maẓmūn*, though the *she'r* was colloquial and pleasing; while Nasikh's *maẓmūn āfirīnī* spoke of an *'āshiq's* heart that was "a flame-seeking moth" of such intensity as to run away from even dregs of cool camphor. Only in the "*ḥūr*" *qāfiyah* did Atish create a greater flight of fancy than Nasikh, employing a lighter, more flamboyant tone. See Chapter X.
21. Such an image will also call to mind the ghazal's most famous case of the victim/*'āshiq* seeking out its beloved nemesis (the moth and the flame).
22. Also, the *'āshiq* will not be able to see his beloved until she comes to kill him, so he writhes in the double anticipation of joy and death.
23. Nasikh's "Was that Nasikh's blood..." was also an example of *maẓmūn āfirīnī*.
24. Platts, p. 221.
25. It would certainly be better than the uncertainty of standing around indefinitely. From his point of view, even a punitive or enraged reaction from the *ma'shūq* is preferable to none at all.
26. Many thanks to C.M. Naim for his explication of this *she'r* to me.
27. *The Triumphal Ṣun*, p. xiv.
28. S.R. Faruqi's commentary brings out both elements of Mir's *ustādi* in his as yet unpublished commentary on the *Kulliyāt-i Mīr*; and Rashid Hasan Khan says, in *Intikhāb-i Nāsikh*, that "there is also a portion of Nasikh's writing which displays *sādagī* and in which there is an

agreeable deliciousness, or *kaifiyat*, which we have attempted to draw out in this *Intikhāb*..." p. 132.

29. T. Grahame Bailey, *A History of Urdu Literature*, London: Oxford University Press, 1932, p. 50.
30. Schimmel, *Urdu Literature from the Beginning to Iqbal*, p. 197.
31. These pairings were referred to as *ma'rike*, and highlighted one-upmanship between famous poetic rivals, but there is reason to look for more complicated foundations of *ma'rike* than just personality. For example, the competition for patronage might well have impelled certain poets to concentrate on a particular verbal style. For fuller discussions of the phenomenon of *ma'rike*, see Dr. Muhammad Ya'qub 'Amir, *Urdū ke Adabī Ma'rike: Inshā se Ghālib Tak*, New Delhi: Taraqqi-i Urdu Biyuro, 1982; and Amir Hasan Nurani, *Urdu ke Adabī Ma'rike: Saudā ke 'Ahd se Chakbast-o Sharār tak*, Delhi University: Department of Urdu Publication, 1967.

CHAPTER XII

Cultural Identification and Literary Principles

Chapters X and XI offered illustrations of how the terms in which the Two School theory is articulated do not reflect the literary reality of Dihlavi and Lakhnavi poetry. The special characteristics (*khuṣūṣīyāt*) of *Dihlavīyat* and *Lakhnavīyat* ("Delhi-ness" and "Lucknow-ness") failed to distinguish Lakhnavi from Dihlavi poetry to any degree that would justify the designation of separate *dabistāns* for those two bodies of poetry.[1] The prevalence of the Two School theory within the analytical framework of literary criticism has given rise to distorted perceptions on the part of even informed readers, especially distorted perceptions of Lakhnavi poets and of Dihlavi poets considered to manifest *Lakhnavīyat.* A regrettable result has been that a large and rich body of classical poetry (that composed by Dihlavis like Shah Nasir, as well as the poetry of Lakhnavi *ustāds*) has remained almost unknown to Urdu readers.

This final chapter offers an initial and speculative discussion of why, in a cultural context, the concept of Delhi and Lucknow schools continues to hold such sway in Urdu critical literature. What motivated the school-designating critics to pin literary distinctions on extra-textual factors (such as the perceived influences of various *marākiz*) rather than on structural factors in the poetry itself? That the underlying causes of the Two School designation lie elsewhere than in the poetry itself has been openly argued throughout this study; that suggestion is now argued even further. Discussion, which has been drawn largely from secondary sources, will touch upon phenomena in Indo-Muslim cultural identification which support this study's interpretation of the Two School theory as, ultimately an expression of cultural rather than literary values.

The following discussion is not predicated on the notion that Urdu critics have deliberately perpetrated a hoax with their Delhi-Lucknow "school" distinction. It proceeds rather from the conviction that there were perhaps unexamined or unrecognized elements in the critics' own cultural identification which caused them to misidentify as the elements of separate schools genuinely perceived differences between the poetry of Lucknow and that of Delhi. The following discussion may be seen as an attempt to reconstruct the particular socio-political and historical circumstances in which critics like Azad and Hali were working to negotiate a relationship with the authorities of their time. It is hoped that this discussion might provide a plausible point of departure for further study of these issues.

With the important role of Urdu poetry in Indo-Muslim cultural identification, the role of poets and critics is also tremendously important: poets and critics are the creators and guardians of poetry as a cultural signifier. Attention must be paid, therefore, to the relationship between early critics and poets in their culturally symbolic roles.

This study's review of literary criticism, for instance, presented examples of the ways in which *Āb-i-Ḥayāt's* critical comments appeared to reflect certain personal biases of Maulana Azad. Particular attention was paid to how his cultural prejudices as a Dihlavi intellectual were expressed in his discussion of Lucknow and Lakhnavi poets.[2]

Azad and Urdu's other early literary critic, Altaf Husain Hali, were both men who came from the class of Indian Islam's intellectual and ruling élite. This class of people had been demoralised by the unequivocal and final failure of Muslim rule in India in the face of the expanding British Raj. Given the proselytic framework of Muslim political expansion from the Middle East right through Asia, with justification read in political success, there were numbers among the Muslim élite in India after 1857 who were inclined to attribute their final loss of political power to a cultural and religious failure in Indian Islam.[3] In other words, political success was seen as guaranteed for, and reflective of, a righteous cause; while political failure was seen to reflect loss of righteousness or worthiness.

Political failure in the face of the British ascendancy was contrasted with the earlier political success of the Mughal empire during the preceding several centuries. Inextricably tied to the Mughal political puissance of that period was an overwhelming success in the realm of culture. During the great period of Mughal success[4] India had attracted and maintained exponents of art and culture from all over the Islamic world. Jan Marek refers to this period as the "Golden Age of Indo-Persian Literature."[5]

As earlier chapters mentioned, central to the Delhi-Lucknow rivalry was a competition for cultural authority. This competition was, in turn, an outgrowth of the struggle for political legitimacy. The ultimate political legitimacy in Muslim India had been that of the Mughal empire. That Mughal achievement was held very dear by Indian Muslims is reflected in the following remarks, which were first written around the middle of the nineteenth century:

> Muslims in general identify with the Mughal dynasty, long for its restoration, and conceive of themselves as the former ruling class. 'Whether they really were so matters not; they persuade themselves or their children that they were.[6]

During the seventeenth century, at the height of its cultural and political ascendancy, the Mughal empire had been centred at Delhi.[7] Lucknow, as has been described, was the capital of a successor state which maintained political autonomy from the Mughal empire through most of the eighteenth and half of the nineteenth-century.[8] While the Red Fort in Delhi during Bahadur Shah's rule and heir apparency was indeed the scene of a thriving court culture, there is no question that the scale of cultural activity in the contemporaneous Lucknow *markaz* was far greater.

It has already been noted that the artistic style which came to be thought of as characteristically Lakhnavi—flash, flamboyance, fleshliness, superficiality—can be applied to Dihlavi artists as well. Ali Javad Zaidi based his refutation of the two schools in large part on this very argument. A conclusion drawn from the poetic comparison in Chapter X of this study was that these characteristics perhaps illustrate the general taste in nineteenth-century Urdu poetry rather than just the popular taste of Lucknow. Without detracting in any way from Ghalib's unique genius, one can legitimately observe that verbal dexterity and intricacy, playfulness and sensuality, even obscurity, mark his Urdu poetry. The same has been said of Zauq and Shah Nasir, all leading Dihlavi *ustāds*.[9] Whereas the tradition has been more willing to discount the achievements of these latter two poets as being "not different from the Lakhnavi style," it has been quite reluctant to say the same of Ghalib, because Ghalib was the greatest Urdu poet of all. He must, therefore, remain unadulteratedly Dihlavi in character. Associations with the Delhi *markaz* are necessarily positive.[10] In other words, the Lucknow *markaz* can be seen to characterise Indo-Muslim culture during the relatively late period of political and societal decline—while the Delhi *markaz* continues to symbolise Indo-Muslim glory.

These facts lie at the heart of the rivalry, which was born with the inception of Lucknow's court culture: both Delhi and Lucknow were seats of culture, one ascendant and one descendant; both sought recognition as the *markaz* of a single, Mughal-identified, Indo-Muslim élite. The competition between them ran unabated through the nineteenth century and the birth of a critical literature in Urdu.

Behind the designation of the Two School theory lies this Delhi-Lucknow rivalry.[11] That designation, spurious though it be in literary terms, reflects crucial elements of cultural identification among the élite who were Urdu's literary critics. And this cultural identification is, by and large, a reflection of how Mughal culture has been perceived.

Among the most important elements in what Mughal culture signifies to Indian Muslims is the concept of *sharāfat*, or nobility. In Chapters I and II of *Aligarh's First Generation* David Lelyveld describes the *ashrāf* (plural of *sharīf*), or noble gentlemen.[12] His picture of the nobility's own concept of *sharāfat* does much to illuminate the writings of someone like Azad, whose perception of himself as a Dihlavi and *sharīf ādmī* (noble gentleman) informed the literary criticism of *Āb-i-Ḥayāt*. Similarly, a picture of the role played by the reformist Aligarh movement in the late nineteenth century—with which Altaf Husain Hali was closely involved[13]—provides special illumination to the values expressed in Hali's written works. Both men's beliefs about Lakhnavi culture and society, inherited from the well-established Delhi-Lucknow rivalry, combined with the kind of reformist values espoused by the Aligarh Movement, provided the moral values and aesthetic principles upon which their literary criticism was based.

Since poetry was a central focus of identification for this cultural élite, and since literary critics were this élite's spokespeople, these critics sought explanations for Indo-Muslim cultural failure in the poetry of the nineteenth century, which they saw exemplified in the work of Lucknow's poets.[14]

It is clear from reading *Āb-i Ḥayāt* and *Muqaddma-i She'r-o Shā'irī* that both Azad and Hali were at pains to have Urdu literature express their ideal of Indian Islam. Central to this ideal was *sharāfat*, the practice of which was no doubt seen as consistent with the role of ruler.[15] The following section will summarise, and relate to the present context, Lelyveld's discussion of who was, and what it meant to be, *sharīf*, in Muslim India during the nineteenth century.

Sharāfat

Lelyveld describes Mughal culture as a "variant of the international Islamic culture," which was "centered on the Persian language and [took] inspiration from courtly styles of Saffavid Iran."[16] He writes:

> The class of people who moved in this cultural mileu were sometimes called *sharīf* (literally 'exalted')...in Mughal India indicating respectabiliy in terms of cosmopolitan Mughal criteria...[17]

What, in fact, were the elements of *sharāfat*? Lelyveld offers the following summary:

> A *sharīf* man was one of dignified temperament, self-confident but not overly aggressive, appreciative of good literature, music and art, but not flamboyant, familiar with mystical experience but hardly immersed in it. *Sharīf* social relations involved a pose of deference, but were above all a matter of virtuosity within the highly restricted bounds of etiquette.[18]

The elements described above directly echo many of the terms in which the ghazal is discussed in literary criticism. A good poet, certainly, is one who displays virtuosity within highly restricted boundaries; and a good *she'r* reiterates the ghazal's well-known sensibilities while expressing them in some unique or novel fashion. It may be said, then, that the ghazal itself is an expression of *sharāfat*; and that poets too, by extension, should be *sharīf*.[19]

A *sharīf ādmī* is primarily a man of noble character and dignified temperament, one who manipulates "a pose of deference" in order to display his own virtuosity. There could be no better words to describe the style of Maulana Azad, as discriminating critic and literary historian, in *Āb-i Ḥayāt*. Although Lelyveld's discussion does not state it explicitly, one function of *sharāfat*—as a signifier of the cultural élite—is to distinguish the ruling class, or the nobility, from the ruled.[20] This particular function is abundantly applied, as we have seen, in Azad's discussion of certain poets.

It has already been noted that in his descriptions of Nasikh's style, and throughout *Āb-i Ḥayāt's* anecdotes about "Shaikh Sahib," Azad seems to imply that Nasikh was not *sharīf* while simultaneously demonstrating that he, Azad, is. The disqualifying characteristics were Nasikh's depicted excesses—in his physical bearing, in his dietary habits,[21] in his obscure birth, and in his relationships with other people. And on page 347 of *Āb-i Ḥayāt*, Nasikh's inordinate pride in his own physical strength is commented upon, where the Maulana observes that "Shaikh Sahib" made uncalled-for displays of his prowess. None of these incidents reflects any *sharāfat* in Nasikh's character.

The unarticulated, but not understated, contrast to Nasikh's overbearing and garrulous style is offered in the Maulana's own elegant diction, in his "pose of deference". An example of this *sharīf* pose of deference can be seen in Azad's copious expression of ostensible praise for Nasikh's command of poetic principles. Such praise is often followed, as was noted earlier, by other comments which serve to reverse or diminish the force of the initial praise:

> In his ghazals there is much grandeur of language, loftiness of speech and delicacy of conception but little genuine effect [*tāṣīr*] on the heart of the reader or listener...[22]

These rhetorical devices certainly undermine the notion that Nasikh fits the description of Lelyveld's characteristic *sharīf ādmī*, who is a person "appreciative of good literature, music and art, *but not flamboyant...*[23] The effect is that Nasikh's manner of expression, bearing, and, ultimately, his poetry exclude him from the realm of *sharāfat.*

Sharāfat in the Polarisation of Naṣikh and Atish

Attitudes concerning *sharāfat* also colour critical comparisons between Nasikh and his more favoured rival, Atish. Recall that Nasikh's parentage was questionable, and that he had been raised, allegedly, by a Lahori tentmaker in the eastern provincial town of Faizabad; while Atish had been born into an old established Dihlavi family descended from a long line of dervishes.

While it was not exclusively true, "one usually acquired *sharāfat* by birth."[24] Though it has since come to bear mostly on connotations of social and cultural "nobility" the *ashrāf* were originally people of "special religious prestige along genealogical lines"[25] although, in

Islam, hereditary sanctity is ultimately "less important than religious knowledge."[26] Dervishes, by definition, have religious knowledge and experience. Despite Islam's ideal of equality and brotherhood among all the faithful,[27] to be born into the nobility and into a family of dervishes, as Atish was, was to manifest *sharāfat* in two essential ways. Those two qualities have consistently figured in Urdu critics' perceptions of Atish's poetry.

In contrast to Nasikh's poetic and physical flamboyance, so richly illustrated in *Āb-i Ḥayāt's* anecdotes, Atish is celebrated as a person of retiring demeanour, unaffected by the attraction of Lucknow's luxurious court life. In just the ways that Atish is *sharīf*, in other words, Nasikh is not. The two poets are consistently discussed in light of these contrasts, from *Āb-i Ḥayāt* (written in Urdu in 1880) through *The Golden Tradition* (written in English in 1973). Recall, for example, Ahmed Ali's remarks:

> He [Atish] escaped many pitfalls [common to Lakhnavi poets] by virtue of his aesthetic nature and religious background. In fact, he founded a rival school to Nasikh; and his works are characterized by a simplicity of style, in spite of an occasional vulgarized use of Persian idiom and of Urdu. He is less flamboyant, and even achieves nobility of thought in a period of effeteness. His imagery is more sensuous than sensual; and he displays a naturalness in his descriptions of the fashionable paraphernalia of a woman's toilet [that were] popular in his day...while Nasikh employed them with exuberance and erotic pleasure.[28]

Ahmed Ali's characterisation of Atish is telling. It reflects that polarisation which criticism has created between him and Nasikh. It even takes that polarisation to the extreme of designating separate poetic schools, or *dabistāns*, for the two *ustāds*. Furthermore, it baldly states that Atish is more "noble"—at least in thought—than his rival; and that he is less "flamboyant by virtue of his aesthetic nature and religious background." Setting aside Atish's "aesthetic nature," a term which carries no concrete meaning here at all, Ahmed Ali has essentially argued that Atish is favoured as a poet because he exhibits *sharāfat*; and that his poetry is fundamentally different from Nasikh's because of this. Combined with his perception of Atish as *sharīf*, Ahmed Ali attributes a "naturalness" and simplicity of style to his poetry which renders it very much the sort of poetry of which Hali and the Indo-Anglian literary reformers would have approved.

Given the crucial position of Urdu poetry in Indo-Muslim cultural identification—which is mirrored in a venerated scholar's assertion that "the cultural expression of Islamic India is best reflected in its literature"[29]—one can appreciate why poets who satisfy cultural conceptions of *sharāfat*, as does Atish, tend to be valued more than their colleagues who are considered to be less *sharīf* even if more accomplished. A muted acknowledgement of this phenomenon can be seen in critical attempts to realign "*sharīf*" Lakhnavis like Atish and Mushafi with "the Delhi school;" and, as has been noted, to simultaneously group obscure-born or flamboyant Dihlavis like Zauq and Shah Nasir with "the Lucknow school."

Sharāfat in the Delhi-Lucknow Rivalry

Just as notions of *sharāfat* have served to distinguish between more-favoured and less-favoured individual poets in literary criticism, so too have they coloured Indian Muslims' perceptions of Dihlavi and Lakhnavi poetry. In *Āb-i Ḥayāt*, again, Azad praises the refinement of language instituted in Lucknow, but reverses the thrust of his accolades with observations like "though in Lucknow they[30] did full justice by poetry, tell me, what is gained by turning the linguistic parrot into a mynah?"[31] The Maulana thus contradicts his initial praise, and, referring to Lucknow's supposedly characteristic excesses, reminds us that Lakhnavis are not *sharīf* and are therefore unworthy of recongition as the standard-bearers of Urdu language and culture. Whereas he evokes the following with respect to Dihlavi poets' language:

> In the metropolis of Delhi, which was the mint-town of Urdu composition and poetry, first of all Mirza Rafi' Sauda, then Shaikh Ibrahim Zauq brought forth the purity of language, the chasteness of words and the nimbleness of composition. Mir Taqi Mir and Khvaja Mird Dard presented superb themes of lamentation, dejection and despair of the world. Ghalib mostly kept the highest standards though he was a lover of *ma'nī āfirīnī*. And because he concentrated on his Persian poetry he brought forth no more than one or two hundred pure verses in Urdu...[32]

It is interesting to note here that the poets praised are, except for Azad's own *ustād* Zauq, the three most-cited of Urdu's "Four Pillars" and they are all from the eighteenth century. The tacit argument is that these ancient Dihlavis appreciate and create art without resorting to flamboyance, and are thus *sharīf*, suitable symbols of Mughal culture. Ghalib must be honoured in this company because of his tremendous stature in the culture, but even then the praise is muted, and the quantity of his achievement is downplayed to "only a hundred or two hundred" really good Urdu verses. But we reiterate that the highest words of praise are used for eighteenth century poets, and nineteenth century poets are carried along in their wake. Without denying that changes may have come in the ensuing century, esteemed poets of Azad's time are also dusted with ancient glory when presented in this fashion.[33]

Overstated differences between Delhi and Lucknow, such as those expressed in the following *she'rs* by Mir and Mushafi, evidence the pride Dihlavis took in their place of birth; and the importance with which the uniqueness of Delhi was imbued:

یارب شہر اپنا یوں چھڑایا تو نے
ویرانے میں مجھ کو لا بٹھایا تو نے
میں اور کہاں یہ لکھنؤ کی خلقت
اے وائے کیا کیا خدایا تو نے

Yārab shahr apnā yūñ chhuṛāyā tū ne
Vīrāne meñ mujh ko lā biṭhāyā tū ne
Maiñ aur kahāñ yih lakhna'u kī khilqat
Ae vā'e kyā kiyā khudāyā tū ne (Mushafi)

You've robbed me of my own city
and led me into this wilderness:
What can there be between me and these Lakhnavis?
Dear God, what have you done to me?

and

خرابہ دلّی کا وہ چند بہتر لکھنؤ سے تھا
وہیں اے کاش مر جاتا سراسیمہ نہ آتا یاں

Kharāba dillī kā dah-chand bahtar lakhna'u se thā
Vahīñ ae kāsh mar jātā sarāsīma na ātā yāñ (Mir)[34]

Far better than Lucknow
were the ruins of Delhi:
Would that I had died back there
than that my madness lead me here!

This chauvinism, expressed particularly by Dihlavis who emigrated to Lucknow, was also illustrated in the earlier passage from Insha's *Daryā-i Laṭāfat* (1807).[35] in which the Delhi-born Lucknow resident Insha acknowledged Lucknow's cultural eminence but attributed it to Lucknow's high concentration of displaced Dihlavis (i.e., "genuine," *sharīf* Mughals). A final passage from Azad reiterates this theme of mourning for Delhi's demise while lambasting Lakhnavi achievement:

> Now these gentlemen [Lakhnavi men of letters] laid claim to mastery of language, and adorned it. But it must be said at this juncture that the early men of talent and achievement in Lucknow, or their descendants, were the expatriates of Delhi...[36]

All the associations of Delhi with the centre of Mughal culture, and of the Mughal empire with *sharāfat*, may be seen as having prejudiced Mughal-identified Muslims toward Dihlavi, and against Lakhnavi, cultural endeavours. The synonymity, in their minds, between Dihlavi demise and Mughal demise will be seen to have great bearing on the literary reforms of the Aligarh movement.

As has been said, not only should rulers be *sharīf*, but the *ashrāf* should rule. The literary criticism directed toward the *ashrāf*—as Urdu's literati—must also be understood as informal prescriptions and proscriptions for a social group upon whom it was incumbent to become absorbed into a new rubric of rulership, that which had replaced the Mughal rubric. It is appropriate, at this juncture, to briefly review Mughal political and cultural history as a means of explaining the strength of Indian Muslims' identification with the Mughal empire.

Mughal Identification

The Mughals' achievement had indeed been extraordinary. In the sixteenth and seventeenth centuries Akbar and his heirs had solidified and legitimated the Muslim presence throughout India. They had managed to draw together, and sustain, an enormous amount of territory under one system of centralised administration. Only once since the Gupta dynasty in the fourth century A.D. had this been accomplished.[37] Mughal success is attributed by most historians to a relaxation of patterns which had previously kept the foreign ruling élite separate and alienated from the indigenous ruled.[38] While, as Lelyveld mentions, noble birth (and, preferably, direct descent from the Prophet) was originally the primary means of assigning *sharāfat*, birth was by no means the exclusive criterion for determining *sharāfat*. Extraordinary merit in the service of the emperor or the empire could suffice to render a person of common birth, or a Hindu, *sharīf*.

Among Akbar's new policies, for instance, was that of making marital alliances between the Mughal rulers and daughters of Hindu princes, thus expanding the ranks of the nobility to include men of Hindu, or partially Hindu, blood. While the Mughal *mansabdārī* system did originally rely upon the Muslim nobility, M. Athar Ali has shown that the Rajputs and other Hindus accounted for a large minority of the Mughal nobility by the middle of the seventeenth century.[39]

Mughal success was Islamic success, but it was also genuinely Indian because of the rulers' eclecticism. As well as drawing non-Muslims into the Muslim system, the Mughals themselves sought to learn about Indian arts, philosophies, sciences, etc. and to integrate them into their (essentially) Islamic systems. The balance of power in favour of Persianate culture and Muslim marriage remained, but integrating elements of Hindu civilisation into that Islamic supra culture was a significant breakthrough for Muslim rule in India.[40] Perhaps surprisingly, there is no evidence to indicate that these rather logical, and certainly pragmatic, innovations had been implemented on this scale during the four previous centuries of Muslim rule (that is, during the Delhi Sultanate).

The kind of eclecticism just mentioned is what Lelyveld refers to in his characterisation of Mughal culture as an "increasingly distinct variant of the international Islamic culture." The Rajputs, especially, flourished under Mughal rule,[41] because they were able to respond to the new regime in modes that were both familiar to them and compatible with the Mughal system.[42] That that system was successful—at least in northern and eastern India— and that the Mughals' culture as well as their government was accepted, is evidenced in the integration of certain architectural and artistic styles into traditionally Hindu aesthetic realms.[43] In addition to its ventures into traditionally Indian cultural realms, the Mughal court remained legitimate in Muslim eyes, perhaps by virtue of its continued allegiance to Persian culture. That allegiance motivated the Mughals to sponsor a cultural efflorescence of Persian arts on Indian soil which the Safavid courts themselves were unable to match.

One can appreciate, then, why later Indian Muslims were not only eager for, but jealous of, their Mughal affiliation. It represented a combination of their cultural heritage from Persia and their own nativity to India. But most of all it served to legitimise their claim to power. Later on, especially in eighteenth and nineteenth century India,

> Lower levels of the regime...included an increasing number of Hindus who identified with Mughal styles of dress, manners, architecture, painting, literature, athletic skills, and amusements—the whole complex of cultural forms that established the dominant patterns of communication and ambition.[44]

Increasing inclusion of Hindus throughout the Mughal cultural hierarchy was a logical result of the integration which Akbar and his heirs had begun. There were those Mulsims, after 1857, who believed that exactly this manner of "excessive" Indianisation had contributed to Mughal decline: too many Indian elements, they perhaps believed, had undermined the essentially Islamic character necessary to sustain a Muslim state.

The court and culture of Lucknow presented a case in point. Its official court language was Urdu, an Indian language; and many of the art forms developed there (especially Kathak dance and the *ṭhumrī* style of vocal music) were unabashedly Indian—in fact Hindu—in theme.[45] It may have been the case that, in the eyes of nineteenth century Dihlavis, Mughal culture was *sharīf*, in the "dignified and restrained" sense of the word, and Indian culture was its opposite—excessive, flamboyant, etc. Lucknow's integration of Indian culture therefore compromised the *sharīf* character of Indo-Islamic culture in general, and rendered both its citizens and Lakhnavi artistic endeavours suspicious in nature. Integration might thus represent a compromise to what some conservatives perceived as "traditional" (i.e. Mughal) identification with Persian culture. That it was well within the Mughal tradition to integrate Persianate culture with Indian, as had been the case in Akbar's court[46] long before the establishment of a court at Lucknow, was apparently not taken into account.[47]

The apparent inconsistency in the outlook of conservatives and reformers reflects, perhaps, a somewhat compartmentalised view on the part of Urdu critics and scholars as to the blend of models their own culture represented. The two most significant elements in this blend were the Persian and the Victorian.[48]

Indo-Persian Cultural Elements

Lelyveld's description of Mughal culture as a "variant of the international Islamic culture," focused on Persian language and Safavid culture as central elements in the Mughal nobility's own identification. Indeed, command of Persian plays a large part in Urdu critics' assessment of poets' credentials. Even as recently as 1973 the critic Ahmed Ali praised Atish's poetic diction "in spite of an occasional vulgarized use of Persian idiom..."[49] and it was also noted earlier that Azad[50] indulgently overlooked Atish's imperfect understanding of Persian in favour of his colloquial diction.[51] Even though Nasikh was known for his erudition in Persian and Arabic, Azad had cast aspersions on his knowledge of the two languages by writing that, of course since "Shaikh Sahib" had attended the Firangi Mahal he must have benefited somewhat from proximity to his revered and learned teachers.[52]

The significance of Urdu literature's connection to other literary traditions must not be underestimated. The ghazal's aesthetics are direct descendants from those of Persian poetry; and modern Urdu criticism was founded upon a combination of the inheritance from Persian and principles borrowed from English literature.[53] These connections greatly influenced Hali and Azad, inducing a two-fold cultural conflation. The first kind was Indo-Persian and the second was Indo-Anglian.[54] This section addresses the first, Indo-Persian cultural conflation.

Indo-Persian Cultural Conflation

While Urdu literature is considered as an essentially Indian cultural product, it does reflect the profound impact of Persian culture on Indo-Muslim society.[55] It eventually came to pass, in the context of cultural authority, that Persian served as a convenient evocative term for Urdu critics and social historians, and the term "Mughal" another. These two streams of authority can be seen in the struggles to which the Delhi-Lucknow rivalry gave rise.

By the 1800s, Muslim culture in India had experienced about a century's development in the sole hands of a group of artists bred on Indian soil.[56] The waves of Persian migration which had rolled into Mughal India since the fifteenth century had now begun to subside. Most of the cultural and ruling élite, though descended from Iranians, Afghans and Turks, were purely Indian in experience. Values received in literature and religious culture as "Persian" to these Indians would probably have been shunned unequivocally by Persians in Shiraz or Isfahan as "hopelessly Indian."

That they do not appear to have acknowledged differences between how Iranians and Indian Muslims viewed Persian (or Persianate) culture in India suggests that Urdu critics of the nineteenth century were indeed the products of a cultural conflation. If fact, it suggests that they may not have been aware of differences between Persian culture in Iran and Persianate culture elsewhere. Certainly, an integrated view of these distinctions could not have been as accessible to Urdu critics of the last century as it is to us in the late twentieth century.

The above observation might well have been hotly denied by many Indian Muslims of the last century. Yet Iranian disdain of Indo-Persian poetry is well documented. Shamsur Rahman Faruqi writes that the Urdu ghazal's innate "Indianness"

> can be judged from the fact that its immediate predecessor and model (which also continued to exist contemporaneously with it), the Persian poetry written in the Indian style (*sabk-i Hindī*) has never been acknowledged by Iranians. Its greatest exponent, Mirza Bedil, is even today practically unknown in Iran; exponents of Iranian origin who lived and worked in India (Sa'ib, Urfi, Naziri, Abu Talib Kalim, etc.) still do not form part of the classical canon of Persian poetry.[57]

Muhammad Umar Memon, too, has written that "although *sabk-i Hindī* originated in Iran it soon came to be disowned by the Iranians. Indian poets who perfected this style were never granted recognition in Iranian literary circles.[58]

But even without an official Iranian stamp of approval the Mughals could take great pride in their literary and cultural accomplishments: they could see how drawn were Iranians to Mughal India throughout the period in which Persian poetry was dominated by the *sabk-i Hindī*.[59] The continued connection between Iranians and India must have belied, to Indian Muslims, the abovementioned disdain in which Iranians are reported to have held Indo-Persian culture.

Lucknow's ruling family represents a case of Persian descendants who were completely Indian in experience. When they broke away from the nominal control of the Mughal empire in 1818 to take on the title of "Kings" in Avadh, they may have been anxious to establish some alternative source of legitimacy. Until then their continued claim of allegiance to the Mughal throne had carried with it a vicarious cultural legitimacy. Now, in the new absence of the legitimacy and authority which had come hand in hand with position at the Mughal court, they began to draw upon Persian connections. It seems reasonable to speculate that the rulers of Avadh looked to Iran not only because of familial links but also to legitimise the Lucknow court; and that they did so much because the Mughals themselves had acknowledged and employed Persian as a source of authority.

The state of Avadh had been founded by Saadat Khan Burhan ul-Mulk, an immigrant from Iran. To be of Iranian origin in seventeenth and eighteenth century Mughal India had generally afforded access to the kinds of privilege and opportunity enjoyed by immigrants like Saadat Khan. It was, in turn, those opportunities which had helped him to build his own autonomous state in Mughal India. In other words, the historically special status of Persians in Mughal India paralleled the special status enjoyed by Dihlavis in late—and post-Mughal India. Viewed in this light it was logical that the rulers of Lucknow reassert their Persian identity and reestablish a cultural preference for what were perceived as Iranian modes. Avadh's rulers' pursuit of the kind of legitimacy they sought—which was not available to them once they broke with Delhi—eventually forced Lakhnavis, by conscious choice or otherwise, to attempt an eclipse of Mughal authority altogether.

The court and culture of Lucknow moved, then, toward a re-institution of Persian customs and values in the nineteenth century. Religion was a primary aspect of shared identity, since the ruling family were Shi'as, and Shi'ism was the religion of Safavid Iran. Related to this was the increased patronage of the *marṣiya* as a primary literary genre in nineteenth century Lucknow. And one scholar reports that there was a conscious attempt on the part of Lakhnavis to look, dress and act as much like Safavid Persians as possible.[60] While this cannot be documented, we would suggest that, in the realm of literature, this identification with Safavid Iran is illustrated in a poetic style which is strongly reminiscent of the verbal style that had earlier characterised the Indo-Perisan poetry known as *sabk-i Hindī*. Nasikh can be seen as the foremost exponent of that style, and it is almost certainly that style to which Mushafi referred in the *taẓkira* of new Urdu poets which prefaced his sixth *dīvān*.[61]

Even so, the art forms from that period reveal how irrevocably Indian had élite Muslim culture become.[62] Descriptions of some of these Lakhnavi religious festivals—especially that of Mohurram—remind the reader of a Hindu *melā*, perhaps even of Holi celebrations. The official period of mourning was extended from ten to forty days, and much pomp and circumstance were added. King Nasirud Din Haidar (r. 1827-1837) is even reported to have tried to institute a rite which involved *achhūt kanyās* (virgins who were "untouchable" because of their purity).[63] So, while its celebration of Shi'ism certainly reflected the ruling family's Iranian origins, the Lakhnavi manner of certain religious celebrations ultimately relfects the fact that the Lucknow court was, above all, Indian.

Urdu was the paramount language in Lucknow, especially the literary language of the new *markaz*; while the official court language in Mughal Delhi had remained Persian throughout the 1700s. Although it became all the rage to compose poetry in the vernacular during this time, there were few poets of Delhi who wrote exclusively in Urdu: they still saw their main avocation as Persian composition. The late Mughals, taking great pride in their achievements in Persian literature while fondly nurturing the new vernacular, were torn between two linguistic streams. Although emotionally attached to Urdu as their mother tongue; and although proud of Urdu poetry as a triumph of Mughal culture; the official status of Persian—and the concomitant availability of patronage for Persian composition—seems to have maintained a stronger pull on eighteenth century poets than did Urdu. Similarly and ironically, in Lucknow, where the court was comprised of Persian-identified Indians, refinement of the Urdu language was and still is considered to have been the primary cultural achievement. Persian language, enjoying lesser currency, always connoted the esoteric.

By 1800 the Lakhnavi *markaz* was a quarter-century old, and the need for "refinement" of Urdu as a literary language began to be expressed by poets like Insha[64] and, later, Nasikh. In striving toward that "refinement," the masters worked to apply the principles of Persian, since Persian provided their literary models. Here again the Indo-Persian cultural blend was acted out: the role of Persian culture in Indo-Muslim society may have become more esoteric, but Persian language itself had never lost its cultural authority.

What resulted from this process of "refinement" was Urdu literature and language with a heavy Persian flavour, and it represented a unique development in Muslim culture. Though the flavour may have been Persian, the stock was unarguably Indian. Dazzled, perhaps, by the glamour of Lakhnavi Urdu's Persian vocabulary, the attention of theoreticians toward the end of the last century did not focus much on this literary language's distinctly Indian nature. As a result the principles of an Indo-Persian aesthetic blend were not integrated into a critical framework specifically appropriate for Urdu poetry (rather than one appropriate for Persian poetry or for English peotry), although Hali especially strove to create such a framework.

When literary criticism began to be written in Urdu, the critics' analysis did not separate Urdu literature's identity from that of Persian, probably because Urdu's Persian origins were still such a source of pride. Yet Urdu literature had developed dramatically during its nearly two centuries of evolution in northern India, and was now very different from its contemporary literature in Iran.[65] Critical analysis suffered in part because it did not focus upon or discuss Urdu poetry as a "modern" literature.[66] Struggling to come to terms with what was "wrong" with it, critics suggested sometimes that it was not "traditional" enough (i.e., not "Persian" enough); and at other times, contradicting themselves, that it was too modern, too "artificial" and stilted in comparison with the generally less-complicated colloquial diction of earlier Urdu. There was also, of course, the additional problem of trying to apply foreign literary and aesthetic criteria to an indigenous literature.

Because this refined, literary Urdu was neither Persian nor colloquial to early-eighteenth centry Delhi, it could not fulfill the critical expectations or requirements of either of the two streams which had been blended to create it. The "defect" in Urdu poetry which critics struggled to identify might be better understood as an illustration of their own critical apparatus, still in the developmental stage. This is not to say that they had no grounds for discontent with the literature of their times, just that they settled upon explanations for their discontent which strike us as unsatisfactory in retrospect, a number of decades later.

Particularly unsatisfactory was the Urdu critics' seizure of "tradition"—or lack thereof—as the proper explanation for what was "wrong" with Lakhnavi poetry. Stated simply, the reasoning of early critics seems to have proceeded as follows: 1) The literary tradition which we inherit from Persian is unimpeachable. 2) Lakhnavi poetry is objectionable. 3) Therefore Lakhnavi poetry is objectionable because it fails to uphold the principles of Persian literature.

At this point the critics ran aground. One reason they did so was probably because they did not specify what constituted "traditional," or Persian, literary principles. They did agree, however, that the era when Lucknow was the centre for Urdu arts and culture was the same period during which a definite change began to be perceived in Urdu poetry. Since there appeared to be few tangible explanations for this change in literary terms, the critics directed their attention to the more tangible area of cultural differences. They tried to identify what were the essential differences between the culture of Delhi (whose poetry, they all agreed, was indeed traditional and of the highest quality) and the culture of Lucknow. It would seem that they thought they had thereby found satisfactory explanations for what was "wrong" with Lakhnavi poetry; and for how, literarily, to articulate its difference from Dihlavi poetry. A reminder of this logic is offered by the following passage from Abul Lais Siddiqi's *Lakhna'u kā Dabistān-i Shā'irī*:

> Just as the Navab Vazir obtained freedom from the Delhi court, Lakhnavis freed themselves in every respect; new standards arose in culture, society and civilisation, including new fashions in apparel, new adornments and dressing. There arose differences in polite discourse. In keeping with all this, writers and poets also began to rebel against the literary conventions which had been in vogue [in Delhi]...[67]

That the critics' logic strikes one as inconsistent, and that they failed to distinguish Lakhnavi poetry from Dihlavi *in literary terms* has been demonstrated. Caught in their particular moment of cultural identification, these critics appear to have overlooked the fact that the Urdu ghazal itself represented a departure from the Iranian Persian ghazal of the seventeenth and eighteenth centuries.

In fact, I would suggest, the verbal styles identified by Two School critics as *Dihlavīyat* and *Lakhnavīyat* can be seen as two different—but equally valid—kinds of inheritance from Persian literature. While *Dihlavīyat*—as the critics identify it—featured the "charming similes" of *fārsī tarākīb*—*Lakhnavīyat* can be seen as an approximation or attempted reconstruction into Urdu of the more complicated Indo-Persian poetic style called *sabk-i Hindī*.[68] Given this dual inheritance, it is ironic that the critics did not incorporate as acceptable or desirable the concept of innovation within traditional literature.

Compounding this difficulty concerning the relative virtues of a strict observance of tradition in literature, the early Urdu critics were under considerable constraints from another source of authority quite outside the realm of either Persian or Indian culture. This other authority was English. Literary principles of Victorian England were adopted by Indian Muslims of the Aligarh Movement, largely under the patronage and supervision of the British Raj's English educators.

Indo-Anglian Cultural Elements

Discussion up to this point has been concerned with a hypothesised conflation of Indian and Persian cultural elements in the self-identification of Indian Muslims generally, and in Urdu's early literary critics specifically. The role of Iranians in Mughal India, and of Persian language and culture, were discussed in connection with the concept of *sharāfat*. *Sharāfat* has been a point of focus in this exploration of Mughal cultural values, which have, in turn, informed Urdu literary criticism. It has been noted how *sharīf* identification among Indian Muslims, "which was centered on Persian language,"[69] influenced the critics' assessment of Urdu poets. Certain poets' command of Persian, as well as family heritage and general demeanour, figured particularly prominently in Maulana Azad's ostensibly literary evaluations. Throughout this study we have seen how cultural values can be expressed, and accepted, as criteria for literary analysis even when those criteria do not seem to be comfortably or accurately applied to the poetry itself.

In the following pages our discussion of Indo-Muslim cultural conflation continues, this time in its "Indo-Anglian" guise. Much as Indo-Persian (Mughal) cultural conflation is represented for us in the voice of Maulana Azad, the manifestation of Indo-Anglian cultural conflation can be heard in the voice of Hali, whose *Muqaddma* might well be called the literary exemplar of the Aligarh Movement.

Others have amply documented the phenomenon of the reformist Indo-Anglian (Aligarh) movement and its influence on the careers of Maulana Azad, Altaf Husain Hali, and other Urdu writers of the late-nineteenth century.[70] Their work will be drawn upon in the following discussion.

In 1835 Lord William Bentinck passed legislation to propagate English education in India. Referring to the latter part of the nineteenth century, Sadiq writes that "there was at this time a keen desire on the part of Indians to acquire the knowledge which was considered to be the secret of the progress and efficiency of Western nations."[71] Certainly this desire was shared by Sayyid Ahmad Khan, the leader of the Aligarh movement. Indian Muslims, it is widely agreed, were demoralised by the crushing defeat of the Mughal empire's last stand in 1857. Many saw its failure as the inevitable outcome of a moral and spiritual turpitude into which Indian Islam had fallen. The key to survival in a country where they were neither the indigenous people, nor any longer the ruling élite, was, in Sayyid Ahmad's eyes, to emulate the new rulers as closely as possible. He was firmly convinced, in the words of Sadiq, that the salvation of his community lay in the assimilation of Western culture;[72] and that the best chance for securing a favourable place for Indian Muslims in British India was to forge as close a relationship as possible with the Raj. A graphic, and disturbing, illustration of Sir Sayyid's admiration for the British and his own condemnation of his countrymen can be seen in the following pronouncement:

> Without flattering the English, I can truly say that they are not far wrong their opinion of us. . .the natives of India, high and low . . .when contrasted with the English in education, manners and uprightness, are as like them as a dirty animal is to an able and handsome man. . .[73]

Hali, who was one of the most zealous Aligarh writers, took to heart the notion that Western cultural models were to be emulated, and that Urdu poetry had grown contemptible. Laurel Steele, in her study of Hali's *Muqaddma*, reiterates the notion that the English, because of their political supremacy in India, had become the new arbiters of cultural legitimacy for Indian Muslims:

> Using English critics to substantiate his opinions is Hali's attempt to seek confirmation for certain aspects of Urdu and Persian poetry by heeding a new group of thinkers. These new thinkers were part of the conquering group. . .It followed, for Hali and many others, that the Europeans had something to say that would benefit Urdu poetry, and their ideas were used to support or reject whatever was under examination. This need to use European critical ideas to lend legitimacy to any analysis of Urdu poetry is now a tradition...[74]

On the one hand, Hali asserts the paramountcy of Europeans in literature, science, the arts and industry,[75] and on the other he fervently touts the glories of Islamic literature. In fact, his best known and most popular piece of creative writing, a long poem in *musaddas* form,[76] is a monument to the past glories of Islam and an injunction for Muslims to rise out of the decay into which they have since fallen. Attempting to integrate both his commitment to the present superiority of the West and the former glory of his own tradition, he argues that in at least one key respect the foundations of Islamic literature are based on the earliest Western literature: he writes that "In Hebrew and Arabic poetry there has been the greatest passion—'*Ibrānī aur 'Arabī shā'irī meñ sab se zyāda josh thā*; and that, in fact, the *josh* in Arabic poetry was derived from the Hebrew poetry "upon which it was based."[77] In the *Muqaddma's* survey of poetry in other societies Hali hails the "natural" virtues of the old Persian poets Rudaki, Omar Khayyam, and Firdausi[78] as well as those of the English poets Milton and Oliver Goldsmith.[79] His message is that Urdu writers should follow the example of the English in revivifying their own decaying literature by making it "natural" as Goldsmith, Coleridge and Wordsworth had done.[80]

Surprisingly, Hali denied that his own poetry was influenced by English poetic principles, or that there was anything in his poetry "that could be ascribed to a pursuit of English ways or could be castigated as an abandoning of traditional ways."[81] This apparent contradiction offers a striking indication of the constraints under which Hali was working, and the understandable ambivalence he must have felt as to where, exactly, his loyalties lay. His piety and devotion to Islam were sincere and fundamental: they impelled him in the direction of whatever action he was able to take toward the betterment of his fellow Indian Muslims' condition. Although the Aligarh reformers openly admired British culture they drew a definite distinction between the virtues of Western civilisation and the objectionable treatment of Indians at British hands. Hali was very concerned lest his desire for the advancement of Indian Islam through assimilation of Western models be construed as a betrayal of his own culture. Both he and Sayyid Ahmad Khan were torn between genuine conviction that British ways were superior to those of contemporary Indian Islam, and (in Hali's case) a deep and abiding faith in Islamic tradition.

Moral authority has played a significant part in literary criticism. In didactic religions, analysis often proceeds from a moral basis, whether the subject at hand be lyric poetry or theological jurisprudence.

In Chapter VI of this study it was mentioned that much of Hali's literary analysis was apparently inspired by moral principles. Similarly, his *Musaddas*, "The Ebb and Flow of Islam," has been aptly described by one scholar as having established a "homiletic tradition" for modern Urdu literature.[82] The poem is a moral discourse on the wages of sin. In this case sin is Indian Islam's moral decay, and its wages are the vanquishing of Muslim rule in India by the British Raj.

Critical writings on the subject of Urdu poetry should be viewed in the context of this "homiletic tradition." Such a context would offer some explanation for why literary criticism which is allegedly concerned with Urdu poetry has given greater voice to the notoriety or the moral rectitude of the poetry's different social milieus than it has to specific literary issues. Urdu critics' treatment of Lakhnavi and Dihlavi poetry certainly represents an enormous case in point.

The following passage recapitulates the importance of moral values on Urdu literary criticism right from its inception. It was written by Hali to a colleague during the process of writing the *Muqaddma*:

> I am writing an extensive essay on the poetry of Muslims, in which I will write about the true situation of Urdu poetry from the earliest times to the present. The goal of this work is to point out ways of reforming Urdu poetry, which has become very bad and noxious, and to make apparent the extent to which poetry can be useful to the nation and to art, if it be based on high principles.[83]

The poetry "based on high principles," to which Hali refers means poetry based on moral themes (*akhlāqī maẓāmīn*). He acknowledges that to incorporate and popularise such themes into a genre which has been essentially "erotic" (*'ishqīyā*) in nature would be extremely difficult, and though it might engender a great deal of resistance from both poets and their audience, it is essential. Moreover, writes Hali, the ways in which the world is presently being turned upside down should provide ample grist for the new mill.[84]

Although Azad better exemplifies the Mughal, *sharīf*, aesthetic orientation than the reformist outlook which dominates Hali's literary perspective, both men called for reform in the ghazal's thematic content. Azad, too, deplored what Hali referred to as the "outdated and morally unsuitable themes"[85] in the ghazal of their days:

> It is unfortunate that our poetry has become trapped in the net of base themes such as eroticism, drunkenness, and the manufacture of fantastic fragrance in the absence of the flowers or a flower garden...[86]

Like Hali, he called for poets to "fully express our every goal and every kind of desire in our hearts."[87]

But overall, suggested reforms for the ghazal do not form *Āb-i Ḥayāt's* core. Rather, as Sadiq has said, it is a monument to the past glories of *sharīf* Mughal culture. While Azad was as devastated as other members of the Muslim élite by the ignominious termination of Mughal aspirations in 1857, he did not stay closely allied with the Aligarh movement during the final decades of the nineteenth century. His identification as a Muslim was strong, but it may be seen as primarily cultural, rather than religious or moral.[88] His aesthetic preference remained Mughal, or Indo-Persian, rather than Indo-Anglian.[89] This conclusion is supported by the following words of Sadiq:

> The most important feature of Azad's mind...and the foremost characteristic of him as a critic is his romantic, passionate love for the past. Its greatness and goodness is an article of faith with him...The genesis of this romanticism is not hard to seek. Azad was too much steeped in the Mughal civilisation to be able to adapt himself to the new order.[90]

It was somewhat different for a pious, but not overly orthodox, Muslim. The moral order of India's new Victorian rulers was compatible with his own in key respects. Both outlooks shared an emphasis on chasteness, austerity and authority. Both Victorian Englishmen and pious Muslims deplored sensuality and licentiousness; and both groups saw those deplorable elements in nineteenth century Urdu poetry, especially that of Lucknow. Just as the British considered many Indian rulers unfit on account of their moral laxness and sensual self-indulgence,[91] so too did they find Urdu poetry distasteful and objectionable for the eroticism and sensuality which they saw in it.

Those same moral attitudes have been carried over into Anglicized Indian literary tastes in this century as well. Ahmed Ali's earlier characterisation of Atish's poetry, for example,[92] reflects a total integration of the distinction introduced by Romantic poets between "sensuous" and "sensual," though he does not cite them.[93] Ahmed Ali's use of these terms surely reflects an awareness of Milton's call for "natural poetry," which would be "less subtle and fine, but more simple, sensuous and passionate" than the poetry of his predecessors.

Nor could there be a more eloquent illustration of the inculcation of Victorian literary and moral standards than Muhammad Sadiq's denunciation of the entire ghazal form, when he says that "The ghazal stands very low in the hierarchy of literary forms;"[94] and the "ghazal is the least poetic of all forms, because it least admits of inspiration..."[95]

While Sadiq's sentiments are the logical result of British-oriented English education in India during a century of increasing alienation between India's British rulers and Indian ruled, they are far stronger than Azad's and Hali's decrying of "worn-out themes" in the ghazal and call for modernistic reform.

Azad's literary criticism can be seen as reflective of the Mughal ruling élite's values; reformist literary criticism of the time—such as Hali's *Muqaddma*—reflects, in turn, a changing definition of who constituted the ruling group in India a hundred years ago. The ruling group was beginning to expand, and it was no longer necessarily the *ashrāf* in whom power would be invested. The former rulers of India—*sharīf* Mughals and their retinue—were, on the contrary, perceived by the British Raj as its primary political rivals. Thus, the essentially middle-class British administrators were more favourably inclined toward the emerging, English-educated, Indian middle class. With English education increasingly available to all those who would make use of it, the numbers of Indians who would be able to participate in government in British India would far outstrip the numbers of the *ashrāf* who had ruled before. It was to these new numbers that the Aligarh reformist literature was addressed, and that literature fell very much within the homiletic tradition referred to earlier.

One cannot say whether the Muslims who called for thematic reforms in the ghazal found a convenient ally in Victorian morals or whether they were responding to the cries of "Shame!" emanating from British mouths. In either case Indian Muslims who ascribed the cause for final Mughal defeat to the same morally suspect conditions that were enumerated by champions of British rule in India were content, even eager, to back their own opinions with the authority carried by British opinion as well.

The characterisation of Dihlavi and Lakhnavi literature within this particular framework met certain needs of the critics, whether conscious or otherwise. If the deplored state of the Urdu ghazal could be pinned on the morally-suspect influences of the Lucknow court—a court which the British had overthrown for alleged moral laxness and administrative inadequacy, in other words for its oriental despotism—then the literature of Urdu's other *markaz*, Delhi, could be promoted with relative impunity. The only recently-bygone Indo-Muslim tradition could then be stored and honoured with a reverence available solely to the past. The new ruling group of middle-class Indians could hark back to that one-generation-removed (Dihlavi) glory and identify themselves with it, while making peace with the advent of a modern, British dominated era, where different values pertained, but did not compete.

NOTES

1. Those illustrations were offered as ancillary to Ali Javad Zaidi's full scale, point-by-point refutation of Abdus Salam Nadvi's and Andalib Shaḍani's designated *k͟huṣūṣīyāt* for the two so-called literary schools.
2. His extravagant praise of his own *ustād*, Zauq, was noted, for instance, in contrast to the relatively short shrift Azad gave not only Lakhnavis, but also Zauq's Dihlavi contemporaries, Ghalib and Momin.
3. Hali's famous *Musaddas* will be discussed later in this context.
4. The reign of Shah Jahan [1628-1658] is generally considered to have marked the zenith of Mughal cultural efflorescence, although Jan Marek mentions cultural patronage by the Sultans of Delhi as a source of attraction for Persian poets even as early as the eleventh and twelfth centuries. See Jan Rypka, *History of Iranian Literature*, Dordrecht, Holland: D. Reidel Publishing Company, 1968, pp. 713-717., passim.
5. In "Persian Literature in India," p. 721 of Rypka's *History of Iranian Literature*.
6. David Lelyveld, *Aligarh's First Generation: Muslim Solidarity in British India*, Princeton University Press, 1978; together with W.H. Sleeman, *Rambles and Reflections of an Indian Official*, London: J. Hatchard and Son, 1884. I, p. 284.
7. Although it was referred to, in Shah Jahan's days, as Shahjahanabad.
8. See Barnett, *North India Between Empires: Awadh, the Mughals, and the British, 1720-1801*, University of California Press, 1980, for an excellent study of Avadh's political history during the eighteenth century; and John Pemble, *The Raj, the Indian Mutiny, and the Kingdom of Oudh, 1801-1859*, Harvester Press Limited, 1977, for an account of Avadh during the nineteenth century.

9. Sadiq says that "Zauq ... reproduced in his verse the peculiarities of the Lucknow School" which "was then the arbiter of taste and fashion." *A History of Urdu Literature*, 2nd edition, p. 230.
10. This is not to say that, in comparative discussions of the two *marākiz* by literary critics, it has not been acknowledged that Delhi showed signs of decline inasmuch as the society in general was in decline. However, I do not recall reading any critique that considers the degree of societal decline in Delhi to have exceeded that of Lucknow. In comparison, Delhi tends to come out ahead.
11. The most recent reference to this rivalry, perhaps, is to be seen in Frances W. Pritchett's survey, *Marvelous Encounters: Folk Romance in Urdu and Hindī*, New Delhi: Manohar Publications, 1985, p. 22: "[Abdul Halim] Sharar's disdain for Mir Amman Dihlavi ... is no doubt partly a function of the Delhi-Lucknow rivalry so prominent in the history of Urdu literature."
12. By extension, the term also signifies the Indian Muslim aristocracy.
13. We refer here to the circle of men around Sir Sayyid Ahmad Khan. See Lelyveld.
14. This study does not necessarily corroborate the view that Indian Islam was in cultural crisis, or that there was, in fact, a cultural failure. Rather, it seeks to understand the actions and writings of those reformers who did.
15. Other features were, of course, the sheer military and political puissance of the Mughal empire and divine sanction for righteous causes.
16. *Aligarh's First Generation*, p. 29.
17. Lelyveld, pp. 29-30.
18. Ibid.
19. According to S.R. Faruqi, the Urdu scholar Rashid Ahmad Siddiqi of Aligarh seriously believed that a morally deficient person could not be a good poet. Personal interview, 25 December 1985 (New Delhi).
20. By implication, then, not only should a ruler or a leader be *sharīf*, but the *ashrāf*—the plural of *sharīf*—or noble class or people, should rule.
21. Nasikh's appetite and great interest in food is widely discussed, at one point in the context of his having been so impatient for a meal that he ate a servant's food instead of his own. *op. cit.*, p. 349.
22. *Āb-i Ḥayāt*, p. 354. Azad goes on to say that "fashioning well-aimed similes and *tams̤ils* from his own creative genius, he created images and painted such gems as often fall into the furrows of Bedil and Nasir Ali, and in Urdu this has brought him the distinction of a master..."
23. Lelyveld, p. 30. Emphasis mine.
24. Ibid., p. 30.
25. Lelyveld, p. 28.
26. Ibid.

27. Needless to say, women did not figure in the articulation of such ideals.
28. Ahmed Ali, *The Golden Tradition*, New York: Columbia University Press, 1973, p. 214.
29. Aziz Ahmad, *Islamic Surveys 7: An Intellectual History of Islam in India*, Edinburgh University Press, 1969, p. 66.
30. Nasikh, Atish, Rind, Saba, Wazir, etc. are the specific poets named by Azad in this context.
31. *Āb-i Ḥayāt*, p. 81: "*...shā'irī kā ḥaq adā kiyā. Magar phir yih khayāl karo kih faqaṭ zubāni ṭoṭa maine banāne se ḥāṣil kyā?*" It is unclear to this writer exactly what the expression "to turn the linguistic parrot into a mynah" means.
32. *Āb-i Ḥayāt*, p. 82.
33. Again, there is an implicit indication that flamboyance marks nineteenth century poetry more than that of the previous century. Such a notion calls for examination by a literary historian of the classical ghazal.
34. Fourth Divan, *Kullīyāt-i Mīr*, volume I, p. 597.
35. Previously cited in Chapter IV: "The reason Lucknow stands above other cities is that poets who were born and beloved of Delhi have come to this city..."
36. *Āb-i Ḥayāt*, p. 340.
37. That, too, had been by Alladudin Khilji, another Muslim.
38. Cf. J.F. Richards' *Kingship and Authority in South Asia*, Madison: South Asian Studies, University of Wisconsin Publication Series—Publication No. 3, 1978, pp. 252-285.
39. *The Mughal Nobility Under Aurangzeb*, List of Nobles, pp. 175-271.
40. It also occasionally met with vigorous opposition from the Muslim orthodoxy.
41. For example Akbar's heir, Jahangir, was half-Hindu, born of a Rajput wife, as was Jahangir's son and successor, Shah Jahan.
42. See Ziegler, "Some Notes on Rajput Loyalties During the Mughal Period," in Richards, *op. cit.*, pp. 230-231.
43. A partial exception to this acceptance was that of the Marathas, who were one Hindu group notable for their eventual refusal to succumb to the Mughals. But it should also be remembered that Shivaji and his heirs, under whom Maratha resistance was most vigorous, were the adversaries of Aurangzeb, and he is not to be grouped, in this case, with Akbar *et al.* Some scholars hold the opinion that far from pursuing eclecticism, Aurangzeb earned a reputation as an orthodox, reactionary Muslim ruler. Ironically, too, his reign began the slow disintegration of the empire.
44. Lelyveld, p. 30.
45. Both art forms featured narratives of the loves of Krishna as well as other Hindu legends.

46. Especially in the architectual styles of Fatephur Sikri.
47. A possible exception would be Maulana Azad's *Darbār-i Akbarī*, Lucknow: Maktaba-i Kalyan, n.d. which, in dramatic contrast to his *Āb-i Ḥayāt*, is generally ignored by the critics under discussion.
48. It has been necessary here to state rather boldly views that are admittedly speculative. Nonetheless, the risk of so doing seems justified inasmuch as such speculations provide new avenues of exploration into the complicated realm of cultural interpretation.
49. *The Golden Tradition*, p. 214.
50. *Āb-i Ḥayāt*, p. 339.
51. Ibid.
52. *Āb-i Ḥayāt*, p. 345. Even if one takes Azad's remark at face value, viz. that he was offering genuine recognition of Nasikh's academic credentials, the point still remains that a poet's preparation in these two languages is a standard criterion of discussion in literary criticism.
53. In addition to Milton and Macaulay, whom Hali quotes freely in the *Muqaddma*, there are passages which paraphrase the Romantic *Manifesto* of 1798, with which William Wordsworth and Samuel Taylor Coleridge introduced Wordsworth's *Lyrical Ballads* to the world. Cf. Stephen Gill, ed., *William Wordsworth*, New York: Oxford University Press, 1984, pp. 591-619.
54. The term "Indo-Anglian" is distinguished from "Anglo-Indian," which generally refers to the manifestation of English culture or society, by the English, in the Indian environment. The most convenient illustration of this distinction would be Anglo-Indian literature as opposed to Indo-Anglian literature: the former is written by English authors and its themes are generally Indian; the latter is literature written by Indians in English. In contrast to the term "Anglo-Indian literature," "Indo-Anglian" suggests nothing at all about the literature's thematic content.
55. Persian's impact on Indo-Muslim culture is also a reflection of the impact of Persian culture on Muslim courts throughout central and southern Asia during the fifteenth through eighteenth centuries.
56. This is not to suggest that there had not been earlier artists of purely Indian experience, like Amir Khusrau, Muhammad Quli Qutb Shah, Abul Fazl, Faizi, etc. rather that the fairly constant influx of artists from Persia which had occurred during the previous several centuries had significantly subsided by this time.
57. "Expression of the Indo-Muslim Mind in Urdu Ghazal," p. 13 of *The Secret Mirror: Essays on Urdu Poetry*, Delhi: Academic Literature, 1981.
58. See the Preface, p. xvii of *Studies in the Urdu Ghazal and Prose Fiction*, South Asian Studies, University of Wisconsin-Madison Publication Series, Publication No. 5, 1979.

59. Cf. E.G. Browne on *sabk-i Hindī*, also Bausani and Rypka. Admittedly, it was patronage rather than purely aesthetic motivation which brought artists to Mughal India. Nonetheless there was a remarkable proliferation of the "Indian style" among both Iranian and Indo-Persian poets during this time.
60. Dr. Naiyaṛ Masud, in an interview at his home in Lucknow, 5 February, 1982.
61. Mushafi had written about the new poet, Nasikh, his particular kind of diction which, he, Mushafi, had also decided to adopt. See Rashid Hasan Khan, ed. *Intikhāb-i Nāsikh*, Delhi: Maktaba Jami'a Limited, 1972, pp. 64-65.
62. We refer again to such artistic genres as *ṭhumrī* and *kathak* dance.
63. The origin of this proposed rite is uncertain. It may have been inspired by Hindu goddess worship, embodied in virgin girls. Regardless, the more orthodox forces in Nasir's court are reported to have vigorously, and successfully, resisted it. Accounts of Nasirud Din's reign are taken from Abdul Ahad's *Tārikh-i Bādshāh Begam*, translated into Urdu by Muhammad Taqi Ahmad, reprinted Delhi: Idarah-i Adabīyat, 1977.
64. See his *Daryā-i Latāfat*, Urdu translation by Brij Mohan Datatariya Kaifi, Aurangabad: Anjuman-i Taraqqi-i Adab [Deccan], 1935, pp. 110-125 passim.
65. See E.G. Browne, *A Literary History of Persia*, vol. 5, Cambridge: Cambridge University Press, 1964; for a picture of nineteenth century Persian literature, especially the *Bāz-gasht* movement. This discussion does not take into account the evolution of Urdu literature in Dakani, which began even earlier and blended more indigenous elements than in the north.
66. On the other hand, critics had a vested interest in maintaining an unchanged status quo, and so were not disposed to recognise Urdu as a "modern" literature. Hali did discuss it as a new or "unfinished" [*nāmukammal*] language, whose poetry was still in infancy. *Muqaddma*, p. 65 —"*Ek aisī nāmukammal zabān jaisī kih Urdū hai, jis ki shā'irī abhī tak maḥz ṭufūlīyat ki ḥālat meñ hai . . .*"
67. L.D.S., p. 55; cited fully in this study, Chapter IV, pp. 28-29.
68. Once again, this hypothesis can be nor more than speculation, as there is no known documentation for it. It is merely hypothesis, but one which it is hoped qualified scholars of Urdu and Persian might discuss further.
69. David Lelyveld, quoted, p. 277.
70. In addition to Lelyveld, *op. cit.*, see also P. Hardy, *The Muslims of British India*, Cambridge University Press, 1972; M. Sadiq, *Muhammad Husain Āzad: His Life and Works*, Lahore: West-Pak Publishing Co. Ltd., 1965, Chs. III, IV, and V; M. Sadiq, *A History of Urdu Literature*, London: Oxford University Press, 1964, Chs. XII,

XIII and XIV; and Laurel Steele, "Hali and his *Muqaddamah*: The Creation of a Literary Attitude in Nineteenth Century India," in *Annual of Urdu Studies*, No. 1, 1981, pp. 1-45.

71. *A History of Urdu Literature*, p. 214.
72. *Op. cit.*, p. 252.
73. Quoted from Sadiq, *op. cit.*, p. 251.
74. Steele, *op. cit.*, p. 16.
75. *Muqaddma*, p. 155.
76. The *musaddas* is a six-line stanza with the rhyme-scheme [aaaa, bb, cccc, dd]. Hali's poem, in this form became so famous that it is presently known as "Hali's *Musaddas*," although its full title was *Musaddas Madd-o Jazr-i Islām*, the Ebb and Flow of Islam, published in 1879. Translated by Gail Minault in *Annual of urdu Studies*, No. 1, 1981.
77. *Muqaddma*, p. 78. Arabic poetry's natural expression of emotion is invoked on pp. 33-34 and 43.
78. *Muqaddma*, pp. 23-26.
79. Goldsmith, according to Hali, reformed and made natural the English poetry of his forebears, "which had been based on lies, exaggeration, and the desires and lusts of the flesh." *Muqaddma*, p. 41.
80. As was stated earlier in these pages, the prescriptions for *necaral shā'irī* were directly inspired by John Milton's formula for great poetry: that it be simple, sensuous and passionate. The translation into Hali's terms rendered that prescription as "Great poetry is that which is simple, full of emotion, and based on truth." *Muqaddma*, p. 68.
81. This excerpt translated by Steele from Wahid Quraishi's edition of the *Muqaddma*, p. 69.
82. Gail Minault, "Homage to the Silent," p. 47 in *Annual of Urdu Studies*, vol. 1, 1981.
83. Hali, Altaf Husain, *Muqaddma-i She'r-o Shā'irī*, ed. Wahid Quraishi, Aligarh, 1975. This excerpt is from p. 72 of the Introduction. Translated by Laurel Steele in *op. cit.*, p. 16.
84. This is a paraphrase, rather than a translation, of Hali's discussion on page 140 of the *Muqaddma*.
85. *Muqaddma*, p. 130.
86. *Āb-i Ḥayāt*, p. 81.
87. Ibid.
88. Lelyveld, too, has remarked upon the fact that Mughal culture "could harldy be called 'Islamic' with reference to God's revelations or Muhammad's exemplary life." p. 29.
89. For a *sharīf ādmī* to fully embrace English patronage—i.e., government institutions—was considered degrading, since it would necessitate mixing with "vulgar people," those with whom there

would not have been lateral social relations in the Mughal social paradigm. Lelyveld, p. 92.

90. *Muhammad Husain Azad: His Life and Works*, pp. 84-85.
91. This was how they characterised "Oriental Despotism," which they abhorred.
92. This chapter, p. 187.
93. Coleridge wrote: "I have adopted from our elder classics the word *sensuous* because *sensual* is not at present used, except in a bad sense..." See the manifesto, or the Preface to Wordsworth's *Lyrical Ballads*.
94. Sadiq, *A History of Urdu Literature*, London: Oxford University Press, 1964, p. 19.
95. *Op. cit.*, p. 20.

Bibliography

Published Sources

Abdullah, Dr. Sayyid, *Mubāhis*, Lahore: Nazim Majlis-i Taraqqi-i Adab, 1965.

————, *Valī se Iqbāl tak*, 3rd ed. Lahore: Maktaba khayaban-i Adab, 1966.

Ahad, Abdul, *Tārīkh-i Bādshāh Begam*, Muhammad Taqi Ahmad, trans., reprint, Delhi: Idara-i Adabiyat-i Dilli, 1977.

Ahmad, Aziz, *An Intellectual History of Islam in India*, Islamic Surveys 7, Edinburgh: Edinburgh University Press, 1969.

————, *Studies in Islamic Culture in the Indian Environment*, Oxford: Clarendon Press, 1964.

Ahmad, Kalimud Din, *Urdū Tanqīd par ek Nazar*, 5th ed. Lucknow: Idara-i Farogh-i Urdu, 1981.

Ahmad, Muhammad Taqi, *Vājid Ali Shāh*, Luckow: Markaz-i Adab-i Urdu, 1975.

Ahmad, Safi, *Two Kings of Awadh: Muhammad Ali Shah and Amjad Ali Shah*, Allahabad: P.C. Dvasdesh, Shreni and Co., 1971.

————, *British Aggression in Awadh*, Meerut: Meenakshi Prakashan, 1969.

Ali Ahmed, ed. and trans., *The Golden Tradition: An Anthology of Urdu Poetry*, New York: Columbia University Press, 1973.

Amir, Dr. Muhammad Yaqub, *Urdū ke Adabī Ma'rike*, New Delhi: Taraqqi-i Urdu Bureau, 1982.

Ansari, Musharraf, ed., *Intikhāb-i Saudā*, Lahore: Sang-i Mel Publications, n.d.

————, *Aspects of Islamic Civilization*, London: George Allen and Unwin, Ltd., 1964.

Asar, *Kāshiful Haqā'iq*, Lahore: Maktaba Ma' niul Adab, 2nd edition, 1956.

Askari, Mirza Muhammad and Fazil, Muhammad Rafi, eds. *Kalām-i Inshā*, Allahabad: Hindustani Akedmi, Uttar Pradesh, 1952.

Atish, Khvaja Haidar Ali, *Dīvān-i Ātish*, Delhi: Pocket Book edition, 1972.

———, *Kulliyāt-i Ātish*, Lucknow: Naval Kishore, 1888.

———, *Kulliyāt-i Ātish*, 2 vols. Sayyid Murtaza Husain Fazil Lakhnavi, ed., Lahore: Majlis-i Taraqqi-i Adab, 1973.

———, *Kulliyāt-i Ātish*, Dr. Zahir Ahmad Siddiqi, ed., Allahabad: Ram Narayan Lal Beni Madhav, 1972.

Athar Ali, M., *The Mughal Nobility under Aurangzeb*, Bombay: Asia Publishing House, 1968, 1970.

Azad, Muhammad Husain, *Āb-i Ḥayāt*, Allahabad: Ram Narayan Lal Beni Madhav, 1980.

———, *Darbār-i Akbarī*, Luckow: Maktaba-i Kaliyan, n.d.

Azami, Khaliqur Rahman, *Muqaddma-i Kalām-i Ātish*, Aligarh: Anjuman-i Taraqqi-i Urdu, 1959.

———, *Navā-i Ẓafar*, Delhi: Anjuman-i Taraqqi-i Urdu (Hind), 1975.

Bailey, T. Grahame, *A History of Urdu Literature*, reprint, Calcutta: Association Press, 1932.

Barker, Muhammad Abd-al Rahman, *Classical Urdu Poetry* (*Naqsh-i Dilpaẓīr*), 3 vols. Ithaca: Spoken Languages Services, Inc., 1977.

———, *A Reader of Modern Urdu Poetry*, Montreal: McGill University, Institute of Islamic Studies, 1968.

Barnett, Richard B., *North India Between Empires: Awadh, the Mughals, and the British, 1720-1801*, Berkeley: University of California Press, 1980.

Bausani, Alessandro, "Altaf Husain Hali's Ideas on Ghazal," in Tauer, Felix, Kubickova, Vera and Hrbek, Ivan, eds., *Charisteria Orientalia*, Prague: Ceskoslovenske Akademie Ved, pp. 38-55.

Bhatnagar, G.D., *Awadh Under Wajid Ali Shah*, Varanasi: Bharatiya Vidya Prakashan, 1968.

Browne, E.G., *A Literary History of Persia*, 4 vols. Cambridge: Cambridge University Press, 1964.

Chandra, Satish, *Parties and Politics at the Mughal Court, 1707-1740*, New Delhi: People's Publishing House, 1972.

Chughtai, Muhammad Ikram, *Shāhān-i Avadh ke Kutbkhāne*, Karachi: Anjuman-i Taraqqi-i Urdu, 1973.

Dagh Dihlavi, Mirza Khan, *Dīvān-i Dāgh*, Dr. Muhammad Ali Zaidi, ed., Allahabad: Ram Narayan Lal Beni Madhav, 1976.

Dard, Khvaja Mir, *Dīvān-i Dard*, Rashid Hasan Khan, ed. Lahore: Khayyam Publishers, 1981.

Faiz Bakhsh, Muhammad, *Tārīkh-i Farah Bakhsh*, translated as *Memoirs of Delhi and Faizabad* by William Hoey, Allahabad: North-western Provinces and Oudh, Government Press, 1889.

Faruqi, Khvaja Ahmad, *Delhī Urdū Akhbār*, Delhi: Delhi University Urdu Department, 1972.

Faruqi, Shamsur Rahman, "*Do Adabī Iskūl*" a review in *Shab Khūn*, no.81, Allahabad: February, 1973, pp.74-75.

————, *The Secret Mirror: Essays on Urdu Poetry*, Delhi: Academic Literature, 1981

Fazil Lakhnavi, Murtaza Husain, *Intikhāb-i Nāsikh*, Lahore: Kitab Manzil, Educational Publishers, n.d.

Fisher, Michael H., *A Clash of Cultures; The Awadh, the British, and the Mughal*, New Delhi, Manohar Publications, 1987.

Gardezi, Sayyid Fateh Ali Husaini, *Tazkire-i Rekhta Goīyāñ*, Abdul Haq, ed. Aurangabad: Matbu'a-i Matba' Anjuman-i Taraqqi-i Urdu, 1933.

Ghalib, Mirza Asadullah Khan, *Dīvān-e Ghālib*, Imtiaz Ali Arshi, ed. 2nd edition, New Delhi: Anjuman-i Taraqqi-i Urdu (Hind), 1982.

Goetz, Hermann, "The Crisis of Indian Civilisation in the Eighteenth and Early Nineteeth Centuries," a Calcutta University Readership Lecture, Calcutta: University of Calcutta Press, 1938.

Gorakhpuri, Firaq, *Urdū kī 'Ishqīya Shā' irī*, Karachi: Maktaba-i 'Azm-o 'Amal, 1966.

Gordon, Stewart, "Legitimacy and Loyalty in some Successor States of the Eighteenth Century," *Kingship and Authority in South Asia*, J.F. Richards, ed., Madison: South Asian Studies, University of Wisconsin-Madison Publication Series, Publication no. 3, 1978, pp. 286-303.

Gubbins, M.R., *The Mutinies in Oudh*, 1st reprint, Patna: Janaki Prakashan, 1978.

Haidari, Dr. Akbar, *Intikhāb-i Mirāsī-i Mirzā Dabīr*, Lucknow: Uttar Pradesh Urdu Akedmi, 1977.

Hali, Altaf Husain, *Muqaddma-i She'r-o Shā'irī*, Delhi: Maktaba Jami'a Limited, 1981.

Haq, Maulvi Abdul, *Marhum Dihlī Kālij*, Delhi: Anjuman-i Taraqqi-i Urdu (Hind), 1945.

————, *Qadīm Urdū*, Karachi, 1961.

Harcourt, E.S. and Husain Fakhr, ed. and trans., *Lucknow: The Last Phase of an Oriental Culture*, Boulder: Westview Press, 1976.

Hardy, P., *The Muslims of British India*, Cambridge: Cambridge University Press, 1972.

Hasan, Amir, *Palace Culture of Lucknow*, Delhi: B.R. Publishing Corporation, 1983.

Hasan, Iqtida, ed.; *Kulliyāt-i Jur'at*, 3 Vols. Naples: Istituto Universitario Orientales, 1970-75.

Hasan, Mir Ghulam, *Taẕkira-i Sho'arā-i Urdū*, reprint, Muhammad Habibur Rahman Khan, ed. Delhi: 1940.

Hasan, Dr. Shabih, *Nāsikh: Tajzīya-o Taqdīr*, Lucknow: Uttar Pradesh Urdu Akedmi, 1974.

Hashmi, Nurul Hasan, *Dillī kā Dabistān-i Shā'irī* Lucknow: Uttar Pradesh Urdu Akedmi, 1971, 1980.

————, [*Firogh-i Urdu*], *Adabī Ma' rike Nambar*, Lucknow: Idara-i Firogh-i Urdu, January-February 1956.

Husain, Aijaz, *Intikhāb-i Kalām-i Ātish*, Allahabad: Hindustani Akedmi, Uttar Pradesh, 1972.

Husain, Mirza Jafar, *Qadīm Lakhna'u kī Ākhirī Bahār*, New Delhi: Taraqqi-i Urdu Bureau, 1981.

Husain, Dr. Sayyid Sulaiman, *Lakhna'u ke Chand Nāmvar Sho'arā*, Ist vol., Lucknow: Uttar Pradesh Urdu Akedmi, 1973.

Ikram, S.M., *Muslim Civilization in India*, New York: Columbia University Press, 1964.

Insha, Mir Insha'allah Khan, *Daryā-i Laṯāfat*, translated into Urdu by Abdul Haq, Aurangabad: Anjuman-i Taraqqi-i Urdu, n.d.

Irwin, H.C., *The Garden of India; or Chapters on Oudh History and Affairs*, London: W.H. Allen and Co., 1880.

Ishrat, Khvaja Muhammad Abdul Ra'uf Sahib, *Āb-i Baqā*, Mirza Ja' far Ali Sahib Nashtar, ed. Lucknow, 1918.

Islam, Khurshidul, *Kalām-i Saudā*, Aligarh: Anjuman-i Taraqqi-i Urdu (Hind), 1964.

Ivory, James, compiler, *Autobiography of a Princess*, also being the adventures of an American film director in the land of the Maharajas, San Francisco: Harper and Row Publishers, 1975.

Jouher, *Teẕkereh al Vakīat or Private Memoirs of the Moghul Emperor Humayun*, Major Charles Stewart, trans. reprint, Delhi: Idara-i Adabiyat-i Delhi, 1972.

Kakorvi, Dr. Zaki, *Ghazal Encyclopedia*, Lucknow: Markaz-i Adab-i Urdu, 1982.

Khan, Abdul Ghafar, *Tanqīdī Maẓāmīn*, Delhi: Khvaja Publishing House, 1969.

Khan, Amjad Ali, *Tārīkh-i Avadh kā Mukhtaṣir Jā'iza* Lucknow: Uttar Pradesh Urdu Akedmi, 1978.

Khan, Muhammed Najmul Ghani, *Tārīkh-i Avadh*, 2nd vol. Dr. Zaki Kakorvi, ed., Lucknow: Nizami Press, 1979.

Khan, Kazim Ali, *Tanqīdī Tajzīye*, Lucknow: Idara-I Farogh-i Urdu, 1972.

Khan, Rashid Hasan, *Intikhāb-i Nāsikh*, Delhi: Maktaba Jami'a Limited, 1972.

Khan, Dr. Yusuf Husain, *Urdū Ghazal*, 4th printing, Azimgarh: Matbu'a Ma'arif Press, n.d.

Knighton, William, *The Private Life of an Eastern King Together with Elihu Jan's Story, or The Private Life of an Eastern Queen*, reprint, London: Oxford University Press, 1921.

Lelyveld, David, *Aligarh's First Generation: Muslim Solidarity in British India*, Princeton: Princeton University Press, 1978.

Lewin, Malcolm, *Has Oude been Worse Governed by its Native Princes than Our Indian Territories by Leadenhall Street?* London: James Ridgeway, 1875.

Matthews, D.J. and Shackle, C., *An Antholgy of Classical Urdu Love Lyrics, Text and Translations*, London: Oxford University Press, 1972.

Muzahhab Lakhnavi, Azam Hazrat, *Daur-i Shā' irī*, 2nd vol. Lucknow: Muhafiz Urdu Book Depot, n.d.

Meisami, Julie Scott, "Allegorical Gardens in the Persian Poetic Tradition: Nezami, Rumi, Hafez," *International Journal of Middle East Studies*, no.17, 1985, pp. 229-260.

———, "Allegorical Techniques in the Ghazals of Hafez," *Edebiyat*, no. 4, 1979, pp. 1-40.

———, "Unity and Structure in a Ghazal of Hafiz: A Comparative Study," *Jadavpur Journal of Comparative Literature*, vols. 14-15, 1976 and 1977, pp.116-134.

———, "The world's pleasance: Hafiz's allegorical gardens," *Comparative Criticism*, no.5, 1983, pp.153-185.

Memon, Muhammad Umar, ed., *Studies in the Urdu Ghazal and Prose Fiction*, Madison: South Asian Studies, University of Wisconsin-Madison Publication Series, Publication No.5, 1979.

Metcalf, Barabara Daly, *Islamic Revival in British India: Deoband, 1860-1900*, Princeton: Princeton University Press, 1982.

Mir, Mir Taqi, *Kulliyāt-i Mīr*, 2 vols. Allahabad: Ram Narayan Lal Beni Madhav, 1972.

Momin, Momin Khan, *Kulliyāt-i Momin*, Dr. Masihuz Ẓaman, ed., Allahabad: Ram Narayan Lal Beni Madhav, 1971.

Mujeeb, Muhammad, *The Indian Muslims*, Montreal: McGill University Press, 1967.

Nadvi, Abdus Salam, *She'rul Hind*, 2 vols. Azimgarh: Matba'-i Ma'arif, 1926.

Nadvi, Dr. Hamidullah, *Lakhna'u kī Lisānī K͟hidmat*, Delhi: Maktaba Jami'a Limited, 1975.

Naim, C.M., "Ghazal and *Taghazzul*: The Lyric, Personal and Social," in *The Literatures of India: An Introducation*, Edward c. Dimock, Jr., ed. Chicago: University Press, 1974, pp.181-197.

————, " The Theme of Homosexual, (Pederastic) Love in Pre-Modern Urdu Poetry," in *Studies in the Urdu Ghazal and Prose Fiction*, M.U. Memon, ed., Madison South Asian Studies, University of Wisconsin-Madison Publication Series, Publication no. 5, 1979, pp.120-142.

Naqvi, Dr. Hanif, *Sho'arā-i Urdū ke Taẓkire*, Lucknow: Nasim Book Depot, 1976.

Narang, Gopi Chand, ed., *Anīs Shanāsī*, Delhi: Educational Publishing House, 1981.

————, " Ghalib and the Rebellion of 1857," Leslie Abel, trans., *Mahfil*, vol. 5, no. 4, pp. 45-58.

————,"The Tradition and Conventions of Classical Urdu Poetry," *New Orient*, no. 5, pp.50-53.

Nasikh, Shaikh Imam Bakhsh, *Kulliyāt-i Shaik͟h Imām Bak͟hsh Nāsik͟h*, Lucknow: Naval Kishore, n.d.

————, *Kulliyāt-i Nāsik͟h*, 2 vols. Lucknow: Naval Kishore, 1904-1905.

Nevill, H.R., *District Gazetteers of the United Provinces*, vols. 37, 43, Allahabad: Government Press, 1922, 1928.

Nizami, *Layla and Majnun*, R. Gelpke. Ed. and trans., Boulder: Shambhala Publications, Inc., 1978.

Nurani, Amir Hasan, *Urdū ke Adabī Ma'rike*, Lucknow: Nasim Book Depot, 1967.

Pemble, John, *The Raj, the Indian Mutiny, and the Kingdom of Oudh, 1801-1859*, Ist Indian edition, Delhi: Oxford University Press, 1979.

Platts, John T., *A Dictionary of Urdu, Classical Hindi and English*, reprint of 5th impression, London: Oxford University Press, 1974.

Pritchett, Frances W., "Convention in the Classical Urdu Ghazal: The case of Mir," *Journal of South Asian and Middle Eastern Studies*, vol.3, no.1, Fall, 1979, pp.60-77.

————, *Urdu Literature: A bibliography of English Language sources*, New Delhi: Manohar Publications, 1979.

Pybus, Captain G.D., *A Textbook of Urdu Prosody and Rhetoric*, Calcutta: Baptist Mission Press, 1924.

Qadir, Sir Abdul, *Famous Urdu Poets and Writers*, Lahore: New Book Society, 1947.

Qamber, Akhter, *The Last Musha'ira of Delhi*, a translation into English of Farhatullah Baig's modern Urdu Classic, *Dillī kī Ākhirī Shama'*, New Delhi: Orient Longman, 1979.

Raza, Dr. Jafar, *Mīr kī Chand Masnavīyāñ*, Allahabad: Ram Narayan Lal Beni Madhav, 1986.

Richards, John F. ed., *Kingship and Authority in South Asian Studies*, University of Wisconsin-Madison Publication series, Publication no. 3, 1978.

Rizvi, Sayyid Masud Hasan Adib, *Hamārī Shā'irī*, 14th ed., Lucknow: Kitab Nagar, 1979.

Russell, Ralph, "The Pursuit of the Urdu Ghazal," *Journal of Asian Studies*, Vol.29, no.1, Nov.1969, pp.107-124.

————, "Some Problems of the Treatment of Urdu Metre," *Journal of the Royal Asiatic Society*, April, 1960, pp.48-58.

———— and Khurshidul Islam, *Ghalib: Life and Letters*, Cambridge: Harvard University Press, 1969.

————, *Three Mughal Poets: Mir, Sauda, Mir Hasan*, Cambridge: Harvard University Press, 1968.

Ruswa, Mirza Muhammad Hadi, *Umrāo Jān Adā*, Delhi: Maktaba Jami'a Limited, 1981.

Sabiri, Imdad, *Dihlī ki Yādgār Hastīyāñ*, Delhi: Jamal Publishing Press, 1972.

Sadiq, Muhammad, *A History of Urdu Literature*, London: Oxford University Press, 1964.

————, *Muhammad Husain Azad: His life and works*, Lahore: West-Pak Publishing Co. Ltd., 1965.

Salam, Shah Abdus, *Dabistān-i Ātish*, Delhi: Maktaba Jami'a Limited, 1977.

————, ed. *Kulliyāt-i Navāb Mirzā Shauq Lakhnavī*, Lucknow: Uttar Pradesh Urdu Akedmi, 1978.

Santha, K. Srinivasa, *Begums of Awadh*, Varanasi: Bharati Prakashan, 1980.

Sauda, Mirza Rafi, *Kulliyāt-i Saudā*, 2 vols. Allahabad: Ram Narayan Lal Beni Madhav, 1971.

Schimmel, Annemarie, *Classical Urdu Literature from the Beginning to Iqbal*, Wiesbaden: Otto Harrassowitz, 1975.

————, *A Dance of Sparks*, New Delhi: Ghalib Academy, 1979.

————, *Mystical Dimensions of Islam*, Chapel Hill: University of North Carolina Press, 1975.

————, *The Triumphal Sun*, A study of the poetry of Jalalud Din Rumi, revised ed. London: East-West Publications, 1980.

Shadani, Andalib, *Taḥqīq kī Roshnī meñ*, Lahore: Shaikh Ghulam Ali and Sons, 1963.

Shah Nasir, *Kulliyāt-i Shāh Naṣīr*, Tanvir Ahmad Alvi, ed., 2 vols. Lahore: Majlis-i Taraqqi-i Adab, 1971, 1977.

Sharar, Abdul Halim, *Guẓishta Lakhna'u*, Lucknow: Nasim Book Depot, 1974.

Shibli Numani, Muhammad, *Shabāb-i Lakhna'u*, Lucknow, n.d.

————, *She'rul 'Ajam*, 3rd vol., Sayyid Muhammed Taqi Fakhr Da'i Gilani, Urdu trans., Tehran, 1955.

Siddiqi, Abul Lais, *Tanqīd-o Tabṣire*, Hyderabad: Urdu Book Centre, 1971.

————, *Lakhna'u kā Dabistān-i Shā'irī*, Lahore: Urdu Markaz, 1955.

Siddiqi, Dr. Khalil Ahmad Mushir, *Rekhtī kā Tanqīdī Muṭāla'a*, Lucknow: Nasim Book Depot, 1974.

Silver, Brian Q., "Nuclear Structure and Poetic Connotation in the Urdu *Dīvān* of Mirza Ghalib," Ph.D. Dissertation, University of Chicago, 1980.

Singh Khushwant and M.A. Husaini, trans., *The Courtesan of Lucknow: Umrao Jan Ada*, Delhi: Hind Pocket Books, n.d.

Spear Percival, *The Nabobs*, new impression, London: Curzon Press Ltd., 1980.

————, *Twilight of the Mughals*, reprint, New Delhi: Oriental Books Reprint Corporation, 1969.

Suroor, Al-i Ahmad, "*Lakhna'u aur Urdū Adab*," in *Masarrat se Baṣīrat Tak*, Delhi: Maktaba Jam'iah Limited, 1974.

————, *Tanqīdī Maẓāmīn*, Lucknow: Sarfiraz Press, 1954.

————, *Tanqīdī Ishāre*, Lucknow: Farogh-i Urdu, 1964.

Suroor, Rajab Ali Beg, *Fasāna-i Ajā' ib*, Sayyid Sulaiman Husain, ed., Lucknow: Uttar Pradesh Urdu Akedmi, 1981.

Tabataba'i, Sayyid Haidar Ali Nazm, *Maqālāt-i Ṭabāṭabā'ī* edited and reprinted by Dr. Ashraf Rafi, Hyderabad, 1984.

Tafil, Muhammad, *Naqosh*, Urdu Ma' rike number, Lahore: Idara-i Firogh-ī Urdu, 1981.

Thiesen, Finn, *A Manual of Classical Persian Prosody*, Wiesbaden: Otto Harrassowitz, 1982, pp. 182-209.

Wordsworth, William, Prefaces to *Lyrical Ballads*, (1798) and (1802), in Stephen Gill, ed. William Wordsworth, in the Oxford Authors series, New York: Oxford University Press, 1984, pp. 591-675.

Yar- Shater, Ehsan, "Safavid Literature: Progress or Decline," *Iranian Studies*, no.7, 1974, pp.217-265.

Zafar, Bahadur Shah, *Intikhāb-i Ẓafar*, Professor Adbul Qadir Saruri, ed., Hyderabad: Aijaz Machine Press, n.d.

__________, *Kulliyāt-i Ẓafar*, 2 vols. Delhi: Mashura Book Depoort, n.d.

Zaidi, Ali Javad, *Do Adabī Iskūl*, Lucknow: Uttar Pradesh Urdu Akedmi, 1971, 1980.

__________, *Fikr-o Riyāẓ*, Delhi: Maktaba Jami'a Limited, 1975, pp.41-101.

Zauq, Shaikh Muhammad Ibrahim, *Kulliyāt-i Ẓauq*, Dr. Tanvir Ahmad Alvi, ed., New Delhi: Taraqqi-i Urdu Bureau, 1981.

Ziegler, Norman P., "Some Notes on Rajput Loyalties During the Mughal Period," *Kingship and Authority in South Asia*, J.F. Richards, ed., Madison: South Asian Studies, University of Wisconsin-Madison Publication Series, Publication no.3, 1978, pp. 215-251.

Manuscripts

Nasikh, Shaikh Imam Bakhsh, *Dīvān-i Nāsikh*, mimeographed. Minneapolis: Library of M.A.R Barker, ms. no.159, n.d. (mid- nineteenth century), scribe unknown.

__________, *Dīvān-i Nāsikh*, mimeographed. Minnneapolis: Library of M.A.R. Barker, dated March, 1823. Said to be Nasikh's own copy, in which be wrote later ghazals.

__________, *Muntakhab-i Dīvān-i Nāsikh*, mimeographed. Library of M.A.R. Barker, dated 20 August, 1850. Scribe: Sayyid Kazim Raza Haydari, at Mohan, near Lucknow.

INDEX